On the Move for Love

PENNSYLVANIA STUDIES IN HUMAN RIGHTS

Bert B. Lockwood, Jr., Series Editor

A complete list of books in the series
is available from the publisher.

On the Move for Love

Migrant Entertainers and the U.S. Military in South Korea

Sealing Cheng

PENN

University of Pennsylvania Press

Philadelphia

Published by
University of Pennsylvania Press
Philadelphia, Pennsylvania 19104-4112

Printed in the United States of America on acid-free paper

10   9   8   7   6   5   4   3   2   1

A Cataloging-in-Publication record is available from the Library of Congress
ISBN 978-0-8122-4217-1

Contents

The Korean Peninsula and the three main U.S. military camp towns (*gijichon*).

Introduction
The Angel Club

One August morning in 1999 Winnie and six other Filipina entertainers ran away from the Angel Club in Dongducheon (known by GIs and Filipinas as "TDC"),[1] the largest U.S. military camp town (*gijichon*) in South Korea, with about thirty clubs and approximately two hundred foreign entertainers. They made a two-hour southward journey by train and subway into Seoul to seek refuge with a Filipino priest, Father Glenn. Their plan was to stay with the priest for a transition period. Five of them would return to Dongducheon to find jobs at other clubs, and the other two would find jobs in one of the small factories that had been hiring a large number of migrant workers over the previous decade. As it turned out, Father Glenn not only provided shelter for them but also persuaded them to file reports at a Seoul police station against the owner of the club. They spent an entire night, until early morning, giving testimonies at the police station with an interpreter. Armed with charges of forced prostitution, the withholding of salaries, physical assault, and other abuses, the Seoul police went up north to Dongducheon. They raided the club and arrested the fifty-six-year-old club owner, whom I will call Ajumma (Aunt) Lee, and her thirty-year-old son, Mr. Lee. They also took possession of the women's passports, which had been kept by the club owner.

Ten days after the Filipinas had taken refuge with Father Glenn, I met them in the capacity of interpreter-cum-mediator, at the behest of the Filipino priest. Mr. Lee, the son of the club owner, who had been released by the police, and his sister wanted to get their mother out of detention. They had called one of the Filipinas, who was staying at Father Glenn's shelter, to suggest meeting for a settlement. Father Glenn had called me at about 1:00 P.M. and said that he needed my help to meet with the women and the "club owners" at 3:00 P.M. in downtown Seoul. He wanted me to be the interpreter and to negotiate for compensation for the women in his place, as he would be busy holding a Saturday mass. I was concerned about my safety and the possible impact such involvement might have on my research in *gijichon*. However, failing to find a replacement, and unwilling to turn down Father Glenn's request, I went to the meeting with a male Korean Ph.D. student.

We met with the seven Filipinas and Mr. and Miss Lee in front of a convenience store in Jong-no, downtown Seoul. I introduced myself and went aside with the Filipinas to assure them that I had been sent by Father Glenn to help them negotiate for compensation. Some of them recognized me from a brief encounter in the fried chicken restaurant in Dongducheon, a favorite of the Filipinas when they wanted respite from the very different flavors of Korean cuisine. They liked the idea of compensation, but when I told them that Father Glenn had suggested a sum of ten thousand U.S. dollars per person, they all exclaimed that that was too much. I calmed them down to say that it was just a way to begin the negotiations. All of us then found a quiet meeting place in the backyard of a small church nearby. Over the ensuing seven hours the Filipinas, the Lees, the priest (who communicated with me by cell phone), as well as some Korean women activists who came midway through the meeting to assist with the negotiations, all had different opinions on how the dispute should be settled. Occasionally taking breaks to rest or for small group discussions, we sat on the four concrete benches placed in a square in the middle of the courtyard—the Lees on the bench across from my Korean friend and me, and the Filipinas on the other two benches.

The Lees began by proposing an agreement that they had already written out, which offered payment of salaries and the return of personal belongings in exchange for the Filipinas' dropping of charges against their mother. However, a clause stating that the Filipinas' employment was being terminated as a result of their own fault brought unanimous objection. The Korean women activists wanted to take the case over and get lawyers involved, but the Filipinas resolutely refused, saying that that would take too long. They just wanted the settlement and "peace of mind."

The multiple conversations were a mixture of hostility, ambivalence, and mistrust—but also of sympathy. Miss Lee, the daughter of the club owner, was screaming in tears at one point, pained by the thought of her mother sitting in the cold cell—yet she still refused to pay the compensation of ten thousand dollars[2] per person demanded by the priest. The Filipinas did not want Ajumma Lee to be jailed even though she was a mean employer and had not treated them right. Some put their arms around Miss Lee when she broke down. Some joked with Mr. Lee when we took breaks.

When it turned dark, we moved to a nearby Kentucky Fried Chicken, where the women signed and put their fingerprints on a second, handwritten agreement that promised them damages according to the length of time they had worked in the club, tickets back to the Philippines, and the return of their belongings.

It was then 10[:00 P.M. The Filipinas] [...], rather than return to the shelter, they w[...] to Dongducheon with Mr. and Miss Lee [...]d to retrieve their personal belongings fr[om ...] y fatigue, but I found it hard to understa[nd ...] with the Lees immediately after the exh[...] the club from which they had run away [...]ed to me that the tears shed, the voices ra[...] ith the levels of emotion and anxiety [...] ere being erased too quickly, too soon. [I was baffled but could only say g]oodbye for the night as they left with the L[ees for Dongducheon. Only whe]n we met a week later did I find out that they had all been eager to meet their GI boyfriends that night. In fact, for most of the rest of their stays in South Korea for the next two weeks they were put up in motel rooms by their boyfriends. Two of them, over the next two years, married their GI boyfriends.

Ajumma Lee was released three days after the conclusion of the negotiations. Before her release, the Filipinas received their promised compensation. Yet the drama developed exponentially. The day after the negotiation, on August 21, 1999, the police from Yongsan District in Seoul arrested Kim Kyung-su, the president of the Korea Special Tourism Association (a nationwide organization of *gijichon* club owners and the chief agent in bringing foreign women into *gijichon*). The arrest of Kim, a city council member in Dongducheon, for suspected crimes of forced prostitution made national news the next day.

Kim was held in detention for three days while investigations continued. All *gijichon* clubs went into emergency mode, fearing that the arrests would continue. Most businesses either closed or forbade entertainers from approaching customers in the clubs. The dominant sentiment among the club owners was a fuming bitterness against both the seven runaways and their club owner, who had failed to manage the foreigners. Petitions for Kim to resign as councilman appeared in local newspapers, on the grounds that he had undone the hard work of over seventy thousand Dongducheon residents to clean up the city's *gijichon* image.

With the arrest of the local councilman—a powerful local figure—and the emergency state of the *gijichon* clubs, the Lees expressed their concern for the Filipinas' safety and suggested that they return to the Philippines rather than continue to roam around in Dongducheon and its vicinity. I agreed with the Lees—I was concerned about my own safety as well, in spite of my only indirect involvement in the incident.

The Filipinas were, however, unaware of the severity of the wrath they had incited. In fact, Winnie even went bar-hopping in TDC with her staff-sergeant fiancé, Johnny, not realizing that one of the club owners recognized her as one of the Filipinas who had caused the havoc. The club owner called Miss Lee and threatened that if Winnie did not leave immediately, she would spend one hundred thousand won (approximately one hundred dollars) to have her killed by a Filipino. Miss Lee immediately called Winnie and asked her to leave and then called me the next day and asked me to convince the Filipinas that they should not return to the club area.

Judging from the hostility of other club owners, I agreed with the Lees that it was not safe for the Filipinas to stay. I told them my perspective, and the Filipinas came to agree with me—some reluctantly, as they were looking forward to hanging out with their boyfriends and finding jobs in other clubs.

However, their passports were being held by the Seoul police. I met with the seven Filipinas in Dongducheon, and we took a two-hour train journey to the Seoul police station to retrieve their passports. The police ignored us and also turned down the Philippine Embassy officials who personally visited the police station, on the grounds that the police needed the passports for their investigation. It was not until a week later that the police station called the embassy to say that officials could pick up the passports. Phone calls were made between the Lees and the club owners' association, the Korea Special Tourism Association, which immediately purchased air tickets for the women.

On their day of departure, I met the women at the airport. A Philippine Embassy official delivered the passports, which had just been picked up from the Seoul police station. At Immigration their passports were stamped, showing that the women were being deported and so would not be allowed back in South Korea for three years. I was perplexed when I saw the stamp—were not the police documents attached to their passports supposed to state that they had been victims of what might have been crime

and not criminals themselves?] Neither the Filipino priest nor his interpreter, who accompanied the women into the Immigration Office, understood why the women were being deported. Strangely enough, none of the
Filipinas, as they walked chirpily toward the gate, seemed to care.

*   *   *

The above chain of events will be revisited throughout the following pages,
as it contains all of the themes that this book sets out to explore. At the
center of the story are the migrant Filipinas who, like millions of mobile
people in this age of globalization, are in search of better lives through overseas employment. As migrants in a host country with limited protection of
their rights, they are vulnerable to employers' abuses. Just when seven of
them thought they were taking things into their own hands by running
away from the abusive owner of the club where they worked, a cascading
series of interventions effectively undermined not only their plans but also
their legitimacy. While most can sympathize with the injustice of their unexpected ejection from the country, many will probably find the women's
actions puzzling if not self-defeating—their trust in the club owner's family;
their intimacy with the GIs, whose very presence was the reason they had
gotten into the abusive situation in the first place; and their spurning of the
generosity of the Filipino priest and the safety of the shelter. [The Filipinas'
actions thus defy the binaries conventionally used to understand an inci- *American GIs*
dent like this: the binaries of innocent Third World women vs. powerful
First World men; well-intentioned nongovernmental organizations (NGOs)
vs. evil-intentioned employers; the protection and shelter of rescuers vs. the
danger of the clubs; and risks of migration vs. safety at home.]

These are the riddles that this ethnography tries to solve, first and foremost by understanding how the Filipinas make sense of their lives as migrant women in *gijichon*, where they are marginalized and stigmatized, yet
hopeful and agentive. The title, *On the Move for Love*, is a metaphor for
their visions and aspirations as transnational migrants.

These women's migration project is understood here as an expression
of their "capacity to aspire"—which, as suggested by Arjun Appadurai, is
"a navigational capacity," meaning "knowledge of pathways to achieve the
good life."[3] "Love"—for oneself, one's family, and one's romantic part-
ner(s)—is both a motivation and a pathway for these migrant entertainers
to pursue their dreams for the future. In other words, "love" embodies the

self-making project of these migrant women as cultural and social actors. In pursuit of and in the name of "love," they creatively act against their constraints and negotiate disciplinary regimes of different scales in the transnational field—those of gender, sexuality, ethnicity, nation-state, and global capital, to name a few.

The Angel Club Filipinas showed that their prime concern, and preferable source of support, was their GI boyfriends. This strange intimacy between the Filipinas and the GIs in the context of *gijichon* is a main theme this book will explore—"strange" because of the dominant/subordinate political, economic, and historical relationship between them, a structural relationship that has predominated in discourses about the U.S. military and women in rest and recreation (R & R) facilities. The ethnography in the following chapters shows that while these migrant entertainers' movement into *gijichon* makes the operation of power visible, it also opens up avenues for transgression and subversion and makes the women's aspirations, including the pursuit of desires and pleasure, possible. This ethnography takes an "experience-near approach"[4] to elucidate the logic of these migrant women's actions, desires, and dreams and their articulation with the changing political economy of the Asia-Pacific region. It examines how "romance" operates as a mode of agency for these women to develop their sense of self, pleasure, and work, and for the pursuit of an existential mobility toward a better future through migration.[5]

The ethnography privileges the voices of the women in order to understand their experiences of migration, with a keen awareness of the women's structural vulnerabilities but without any a priori understanding of them as victims whose sexuality has been violated. One of my arguments is that their romantic pursuits are rendered all the more comprehensible in relation to their vulnerabilities vis-à-vis the global system of material and symbolic inequality; the state apparatus of border control; and cultural constructions of racial, gender, and sexual hierarchies—in other words, the very structures that brought them into *gijichon*.

Since the late 1990s foreign migrant women have been working in the clubs in *gijichon,* the U.S. military camp towns in South Korea (*gijichon* literally means "military base villages"), as "entertainers"—the term stated on the E-6 visas stamped on most of their passports. U.S. military camp towns have been fixtures in South Korea since the Korean War (1950–53). Korean women working in *gijichon* clubs have earned such derogatory terms as "Western whore" and "Western Princess," which refer to the selling of their bodies, as well as their nation, to "the West"—specifically, to the United States. In the 1990s South Korea's rapid economic advancement, combined with the stigma and low pay attached to this work, led to a shortage of Korean women to serve these American soldiers. Club owners then sought to bring in cheap labor from developing countries, much as employers in the small and medium-size manufacturing industry did in the late 1980s.

The entry of foreign wage laborers is part of a restructuring of the South Korean labor market, which in turn is part of the country's globalization project within the changing political economy of the Asia-Pacific region. The entry of Filipinas marks the changing power relationships among the United States, South Korea, and the Philippines. While U.S. military domination continues in the Asia-Pacific region, it is no longer paralleled by exclusive U.S. economic might. South Korea's economic advancement has prevented many Korean women from following their predecessors in serving the U.S. military forces, and yet it has done so through the introduction of women from the "Third World" to fill the vacancies.[6] The increasingly conspicuous presence of foreign workers, including migrant entertainers, has precipitated new conversations about modernity, nationalism, ethnicity, and human rights in South Korea.

For the Koreans who work in *gijichon*, Filipinas have always been a "problem" (*munjae*): they are said to be lazy and difficult to control and have a reputation for selling themselves cheaply in *gijichon* and having sex with GIs for free. Such biased perceptions lay behind the death threat to Winnie. On the one hand, the threat suggests that a small sum (one hundred dollars) could make a Filipino not only give up his duty to protect a female compatriot but also lead him to inflict harm on her—implying that the nation as a whole is amoral and easily corrupted. On the other hand, it indicates the Koreans' sense of superiority in being able to manipulate Filipinos for their own ends. The threat thus embodies both a derision of Filipino people as a whole and a flexing of power by the Koreans.

From the perspective of border control, administrative regulation ensures that migrant entertainers remain as itinerants in the country. The E-6 visa is issued for six months and can normally be renewed only once. Most of the entertainers are on one-year contracts. The institutional marginalization of these migrant Filipinas is further exemplified in their encounters with the police and Immigration. The refusal of a local police station to accede to a diplomatic mission's request for the passports of its nationals—

who were plaintiffs and not suspects—indicates the power relationship between the host country and the visitors' country. I could not but wonder if the same thing would happen if the plaintiffs had been U.S. nationals and not Filipinas. The ultimate deportation of the Filipinas by the Korean Immigration Office further illuminates the institutional presumption that these foreign women are "bad women" and disposable workers.

In contrast, NGO activists such as Father Glenn and the Korean women activists have identified such women as victims in need of protection, on whose behalf they appealed to the legal system to penalize the club owners and to require them to compensate the women. It is from this perspective in particular that the women's affinity for the club owners and GIs becomes especially incomprehensible. This drive to identify such women as victims intensified with the burgeoning discourse of "trafficking in persons" at the turn of the twenty-first century. From 1999 onward various Korean and international NGOs, feminists, and media reports have identified the migrant entertainers studied here as "victims of sex trafficking," insisting that their plight is one of forced prostitution and that the deployment of these women reproduces the sexual objectification of Asian women for the reproduction of First World masculinity and military manhood. The emphasis on female passivity, innocence, and powerlessness that runs through this narrative of sexual victimhood can be found in a range of media, NGO, and academic representations. This ethnography, however, asks, To what extent do these representations reflect the experiences of women such as the Angel Club Filipinas? Echoing the upsurge of discourses about white slavery at the turn of the twentieth century, these discourses have a tendency to turn women into signifiers of victimhood and to overlook the complexity of contexts, identities, and agency involved. A critical lens may help us evaluate whether antitrafficking measures, peppered with claims to the protection of "women's human rights" and yet focused on crime and border control, are effective for alleviating the conditions of these migrant women, or whether they merely reproduce migrant women's marginality and vulnerability.

As women out of place—foreign women who have left home to work as "entertainers" (often understood to be a euphemism for "prostitutes")—these Filipinas draw the regulatory impulse of their interlocutors, who turn the Filipinas' story into their own; project anxieties about gender, sexuality, and the nation-state onto these women's transgressive bodies; and impose specific disciplinary rationality. This is vividly—yet only partially—illustrated by the chain of events following the Angel Club Filipinas' attempt to escape. The Filipino priest sought justice for his female compatriots from the Korean police; the Korean women activists wanted the legal system to penalize the club owners; the capitol police force went after the "bad guys" in the provincial *gijichon*; the vindictive club owner threatened mortal harm against the troublesome migrant entertainer; and the Immigration Office actively excluded unwanted aliens from South Korean territory. Because of their transgressive sexuality, whether understood as that of "prostitutes," "sex slaves," or "victims of trafficking," these migrant entertainers became valuable and malleable symbols for the expression of discontent about social disorder, colonialism, global inequalities, foreign threats, changing gender roles, and sexual mores.

My goal is to reveal some of the human stories entrenched in this phenomenon—stories that have been covered under the blanket definition of "sex trafficking." The complexity of these women's lives and their creative responses suggest that looking at them only through the lens of sexual victimhood would continue the practice of defining women exclusively by their sexuality and of erasing the multiplicity of their identities, as well as their drive, motivation, and determination to struggle against their subordination. This ethnography thus takes a bifocal analytical approach, situating personalized accounts of Filipina entertainers' lives within a multilevel, macroanalytical framework. Instead of flattening the experiences of the women as victims of an unbridled male sex drive and of transnational organized crime, we may understand better the context of their struggles—what they are struggling *for* and what they are struggling *against*—by recognizing them as migrant subjects and as desiring subjects.

A key task is to examine the women entertainers as *both* laboring *and* erotic subjects in migration, an intersection that has yet to be developed in migration and sexuality studies. The gendering of labor migration has brought women from developing countries into developed economies mainly as care workers—for example, domestic workers or nurses—and as "entertainers," while their male counterparts predominantly work in construction, in factories, and as seafarers. The migration projects of these women laborers are projects not just of need but also of aspiration, fed by desires for the commodities, lifestyle, and identities that overseas employment seems to promise. However, migration and laboring as foreigners come with intersecting sets of vulnerabilities and uncertainties, particularly for women who work in the R & R facilities and suffer from the "prostitute" stigma. From the diverse experiences of the women presented here, we may complicate the relationship between female victimhood and agency and develop an understanding of their vulnerability, not with reference to evil individuals or crime syndicates alone but also with reference to policies on labor migration, border control, and sexuality, as well as to larger structures of inequality engendered and maintained by neoliberalism.

Although they are deployed as disposable labor, marginalized as migrants, and employed to perform as objects of desire to inspire male heterosexual fantasies, these do not erase the fact that entertainers in *gijichon* are also themselves subjects of desire (erotic subjects). The women bring into their workplaces and their migrations their own romantic and erotic imaginings, continuously blurring the boundary not only between labor and love, but also between the public and private, and between performance and authenticity. Nicole Constable has shown how romantic and erotic desires between Filipina or Chinese women and U.S. American men have been shaped by gendered imaginings in the history of U.S. imperialism in the Asia-Pacific region. Individuals' erotic imaginings and yearnings, therefore, are shaped by what I call the "political economy of desires." Through such an optic we may also come to understand how intimate longing and relationships with the Other can also be critical commentaries on gender and regional hierarchies within the larger political economy.

In order to understand these women as migrant subjects, this ethnography draws on the literature of transnationalism and identity. Traveling on the lower rungs of transnational migration, these migrant entertainers devise their own "flexible citizenship"[7] through informal networks, forged documents, and recruiters—to attain their goals of cross-border travel and overseas employment. A case in point is provided by the story of the Angel Club Filipinas: even though all of them were deported with stamps on their passports prohibiting entry for three years, one of them soon returned to South Korea as an entertainer with another passport. In fact, using such forged documents is a commonplace strategy for transnationals "from below" in negotiating state regulation of population flows and borders.[8]

Thus, migrant Filipina entertainers are global actors who pursue desires and dreams shaped by the globalization of modernity and struggle for redistribution and recognition along their own paths, simultaneously reconstituting meanings and flows in the transnational field. As Marshall Berman suggests of modernization, "[t]hese world-historical processes have nourished an amazing variety of visions and ideas that aim to make men and women the subjects as well as the objects of modernization, to give them the power to change the world that is changing them, to make their way through the maelstrom and make it their own."[9] The main goal of this ethnography is to show how migrant Filipinas make their deployment to South Korea "their own," as migrant women do not merely obey the call of global capital and leave home as commodified labor or sex objects but are also moved by their capacity to aspire, their will to change, and their dreams of flight.

PART I

Setting the Stage

Chapter 1
Sexing the Globe

To understand the experiences of Filipina entertainers serving a U.S. clientele around U.S. military bases in South Korea, one necessarily has to grapple with the global forces that brought these disparate groups together. Equally, if not more important, how are women's sexuality and labor both premises for their deployment and sites of agency to negotiate within globalized hierarchies of race, class, and gender? In very broad terms, *gijichon* is what Denise Brennan, following Appadurai's idea of "ethnoscapes," calls an individual "sexscape." Drawing on her study of sex tourism in a Dominican town, Brennan suggests that "sexscapes link the practices of sex work to the forces of a globalized economy"[1] and are characterized by travel from developed to developing countries, consumption of paid sex, and inequalities. *Gijichon* as a sexscape has been subjected to a distinct set of forces from sex tourism—most prominently cold-war geopolitics, post-cold-war economic liberalization, and intraregional labor migration in the 1990s. How do these processes of globalization shape individual experiences in *gijichon*? How may these experiences generate new insights into women's mobility, sexuality, and labor in the transnational field? This chapter discusses the framework this ethnography uses to explore these questions.

Global Forces in *Gijichon*: A Brief History

U.S. military camp towns in the Asia-Pacific region, in countries such as South Korea, Japan, Vietnam, and the Philippines, are a legacy of cold-war politics. GI clubs in the Asia-Pacific region are the progeny of a global network of U.S. military bases[2] established as part of U.S. policy to contain communism and preserve U.S. geopolitical interests. Military stationed both onshore and offshore have access to the R & R facilities around the bases. Prostitution has been a key component of these R & R sites.[3]

The Korean Peninsula is still technically a war zone, as there was only a truce but no peace treaty to conclude the Korean War (1950–53). U.S. military forces landed in southern Korea as an occupation force in 1945 at the end of World War II, ending Japanese colonial rule. The number of U.S. forces accelerated with the Korean War, and the Mutual Defense Treaty (effective 1954) formalized the stationing of U.S. troops in South Korea. This led, during the poverty and homelessness of the postwar years, to the rise of boomtowns around U.S. military bases, settlements that catered to the needs of U.S. military personnel for livelihood and included shopkeepers, club owners, and prostitutes.

The number of U.S. military personnel in Korea has been heavily tied to foreign policy agendas in Washington, D.C., and to concerns of a North Korean attack in Seoul. In 1971 the number of U.S. military personnel in South Korea decreased from 64,000 to 43,000 in conformity with the Nixon Doctrine, which aimed to reduce U.S. military involvement in Asia. In 2000 there were 37,000 U.S. military personnel at 120 military installations in Korea. This number was reduced by 9,154 as of May 2006, as part of the restructuring of U.S. forces in the Pacific. The 2004 agreement between the U.S. and South Korean governments laid down plans to drastically reduce the Yongsan Garrison in central Seoul as part of the long-term goal to downsize U.S. troop presence in South Korea.[4] When President Lee Myung-bak took office in 2008, he confirmed that U.S.-Korea relations would be placed at the center of his foreign policy. The U.S. and South Korean governments agreed to keep the number of American troops at 28,500.[5] Thus, the continual presence of U.S. forces in Korea was assured, despite civilian groups' calls for their withdrawal.[6] Obviously, these governmental decisions regarding the presence, reduction, and redeployment of U.S. military forces in South Korea are central to the lives of those in *gijichon* and figure importantly in nationalist discourses in Korea.

In her study of *gijichon* women in the early 1990s, Katharine Moon makes an observation that forebodes the changing ethnoscape of *gijichon*. The Korean women Moon talked with in 1992 noted that the average GI could not afford to keep up with the high prices in the Korean economy and was no match for a Korean man in this respect, as the latter would "drop hundreds of dollars" in a bar. The U.S. dollars GIs had at their disposal had become "measly" and "ridiculous"[7] at a time when the Korean Peninsula had become home to the tenth-largest economy in the

world[8]—an astounding economic advance from the war-torn country of
the 1950s. For Korean women, the desirability of GIs as clients for a depend-
able income or a comfortable future began to decline with the rise of South
Korean economic power.

Since the mid-1990s foreign women, predominantly from the Philippines and the former Soviet Union, have entered the clubs to fill vacancies
left by Korean women. Mr. Shin was a *gijichon* club owner who had been
in Songtan, the *gijichon* right in front of Osan Air Base of the U.S. forces in
Korea, for fifteen years when I interviewed him in 2000. He was also chairman of the Songtan branch of the club owners' organization, the Korea
Special Tourism Association (KSTA). He claimed to have come up with the
idea of bringing Filipinas to work in the clubs to make up for the crippling
shortage of Korean women. In 1990 he brought in some Filipinas on a trial
basis, and the results were satisfactory to the KSTA, which then obtained
permission from the Ministry of Culture and Tourism to bring in foreign
women on E-6 (entertainer) visas in 1996. Diversification at a time of increased economic liberalism was, in Mr. Shin's view, favorable: "The American soldiers get fed up with women from only one country. We are thinking of getting women from other countries to come."[9] During my
fieldwork, women from mostly the Philippines but also Kazakhstan, Nepal,
and Sri Lanka were working in both Dongducheon and Songtan. In 1999
club owners had to pay $1,300 for each entertainer recruited through the
KSTA, followed by around $300 per month as salary for each woman in
their employ. By August 1999 the KSTA alone had brought in 1,093 women,
mainly from the Philippines and Russia, and had pocketed a total of $1.6
billion in agency fees.[10] From my visits to most of the clubs in Dongducheon and Songtan, my estimate of the number of Filipino entertainers in
Korean *gijichon* in 1999–2000 was 600.

Migrant entertainers enter into particular niches in the structure of the
entertainment industry in *gijichon*, which has four broad levels. At the high-
est echelon are clubs and bars, usually with female entertainers who accompany customers for the price of a "ladies' drink" (some women may provide sexual services for an additional payment). Second in importance and
price is street-level prostitution that usually relies on older women to solicit
clients. The third level consists of "contract marriages," in which women
play the role of wives for GIs during their stay in South Korea and receive
monthly allowances in return. Independent streetwalkers, who are very few
in number, make up the fourth level.

Foreign women work only in the clubs, which most GIs visit for drinks, music, dance, shows, and/or female company. Club owners need young women to work in the clubs to attract GIs. Other jobs in *gijichon* are less profitable and are usually taken by older Korean women. Some of the Korean women who enter into "contract marriages" may also be working in the clubs as madams. Waitresses and cleaners are usually but not always Korean women who used to work in the clubs in their youthful days but could not make it as madams or club owners. Other older Korean women work as vendors, going from club to club selling GIs stuffed toys, flowers, and little souvenirs, which the GIs then give to the Filipinas.

Clubs attract GIs with their duty-free alcohol (around two dollars for an imported beer), music, shows, and women entertainers. Since 1998 Filipinas have been present in most of the clubs. Only the larger clubs have shows and are usually available on Fridays and Saturdays. The divide between clubs that served only blacks and those that served only whites, which created serious problems in the 1960s and 1970s, has been much eroded, though segregation still existed in Dongducheon in 2000. There is still a club that white GIs tend to avoid—the Black Rose, owned by an African American and his Korean wife. Some clubs specialize in Latino music and attract a more Hispanic following.

For those who are interested in female company, a "drink" for a woman costs ten dollars and usually entitles the customer to around twenty minutes of the woman's time—for conversation, dance, or lap dancing. VIP rooms are found in some clubs, and a customer may bring a woman into the room (with her consent) for around half an hour if he buys the woman four drinks. A customer may pay a "bar fine" to take a woman out of the club. Depending on the time of the month (more expensive on paydays) and the length of time desired, bar fines range from one hundred to three hundred dollars. "Bar fine"—a term that has been used in the sex trade in the Philippines—was introduced into *gijichon* with the arrival of the Filipinas. "Short time" and "long time" were terms commonly used by the Koreans before that. The women usually get 20 percent of the money. Whatever happens in the VIP room or on a bar-fine outing is subject to negotiation between the woman and the customer.

In the 1990s the profile of customers extended from U.S. military personnel to include foreigners on business trips or working in nearby factories, as well as Koreans. Korean men often visit these clubs because of the exoticism of foreign women. With greater spending power than GIs, and usually extravagant spending habits (drinking bottles of brandy rather than beers and giving tips more eagerly than GIs), these Korean men are often a more important source of revenue for *gijichon* clubs. This is particularly true in Songtan, where Koreans are basically free to enter all the clubs, while clubs in Dongducheon—particularly those with strip shows and sexual services available—follow more stringently the "foreigners-only" rule.

The labor shortage in *gijichon* that led to the introduction of migrant workers echoed the much larger-scale problem in the manufacturing sector, especially in what were commonly known as "3D" (dirty, dangerous, and difficult) jobs. Since 1991 an estimated 222,000 production jobs of all skill levels could not attract domestic workers. The problem was particularly serious for low-skilled jobs in plastics, electrical machinery, and commercial fishing. This need for cheap labor has thus been partly filled with the introduction of "industrial trainees"—not "workers"—from developing countries under restrictive terms. The globalization initiative (*segyehwa*) under President Kim Young-sam in 1993 came in on the heels of the burgeoning economic growth, market liberalization, and, finally, democratization that characterized the period of rapid industrial and financial development over the previous three decades. As Korean capital also found its way into many developing countries, foreign laborers entered South Korea as flexible workers.

The introduction of these foreign workers took place within the development of intraregional migration in Asia starting in the late 1980s. A shrinking labor force and robust economic growth in industrial economies such as South Korea and Japan have been drawing migrant workers from developing countries in the Asian region.[11] The first significant influx of Filipino factory workers to South Korea took place after the signing of the Republic of the Philippines–Korea Economic and Technical Cooperation Agreement and the Korean Scientific and Technological Cooperation Agreement in 1986. Following the introduction of the "industrial trainee" system, the Agreement for the Promotion of Investment was signed in 1995, boosting overseas investment and exchanges of technology and labor. These measures by the Philippine and South Korean governments opened the official door for Filipinos' entry into Korea for work. In 2004 the Philippine government estimated that a total of 47,150 Filipino citizens were in South Korea, 9,015 of whom were irregular migrants.[12]

Forged out of cold-war geopolitics, *gijichon* came to participate in global capital's search for flexible labor in the late 1990s. Not only do *gijichon* clubs participate in the transnational network of labor recruitment, but they also adopt new ways to manage these ethnic others and increasingly serve an ethnically diverse clientele. Even though *gijichon* is largely a marginal site in the larger Korean body politic, the globalization of its sexual economy provides important insights into South Korea's regional integration and global engagements.

Sexing Power in the Globe

> In Okinawa, Korea, the Philippines, and Thailand, on the "morning after" the cold war, local people have "woken up" to the consequences of economies dependent on military prostitution·and the international tourist industry. Activists have overcome spatial displacement by attempting to forge links between communities in Thailand, the Philippines, South Korea, and Okinawa, where local women have suffered from the displacement of military sexualities onto the exoticised figures of Asian women. . . .
>   The time has come to start thinking about what is at stake in "sexing the globe."[13]

With a focus on the construction of female bodies and the male gaze, the feminist scholar Vera Mackie builds her examination of sex tourism and its linkage to military prostitution in the Asia-Pacific region to highlight the need for a "systematic analysis of 'sexuality and international relations.'" She analyzes the feminization, orientalization, and subordination of Asian women in the "scopophilic metropolitan gaze" (in regional centers such as the United States, Australia, and Japan) through a close reading of textual material: advertising, films, and books about Western men's travels to the region that naturalize racial, ethnic, and gender hierarchies. These are important insights. To be aware of the pervasiveness of these representations is important for grasping the cultural construction of sexuality and desire that pervades our everyday lives. The phenomenon that Mackie is addressing has much resonance for this study. In 1992 U.S. troops withdrew from the Philippines, meaning the end of the R & R facilities in the former U.S. colony. A few years later Filipinas began to migrate to South Korea to work as entertainers in GI clubs. The commodification of Asian women's sexuality has persisted. History seems to be repeating itself. However, for the Filipinas who migrate to South Korea, this ethnography suggests, everything is new.

I cite Vera Mackie here for what I see as the productive tension embedded in this brief excerpt from her conclusion. On the one hand, its critique of the "metropolitan gaze" echoes with much academic and nonacademic work that emphasizes masculinist instrumentalization of women's bodies. Katharine Moon (*Sex among Allies*) has shown in careful detail that *gijichon* women have been deployed as diplomatic instruments in the U.S.–South Korea relationship, maintaining a "release" channel in the overall engineering of masculine desires in the military, which include male bonding, fraternity, and the objectification of sex and women as masculine "needs." Other scholars as well as nongovernmental organizations have identified the migrant entertainers who are the subjects of this study as "victims of sex trafficking" for which the U.S. military constitutes a demand.[14] In this light, Mackie's suggestion to think about the stakes in "sexing the globe" refers more or less to how much women have "suffered" in the globalization of the sexual economy that reproduces the metropolitan gaze.

On the other hand, Mackie's concluding statement invokes Gayle Rubin's seminal article "Thinking Sex," a core text in radical sex and queer theory: "The time has come to start thinking about sex."[15] Rubin made this statement after critically analyzing the limits of feminism in understanding sexual injustices in the 1980s, and she called for a departure from a preoccupation with patriarchy and male dominance to examine how sexuality operates as a vector of oppression. Premised on an understanding of sexuality and its evaluation as a human construction, she warns that the attribution of women's oppression to nonmarital, nonreproductive, nonheteronormative sexuality such as prostitution and pornography reproduces a conservative sexual morality. This tendency perpetuates a sexual stratification that privileges some and persecutes others and that makes feminist rhetoric liable to appear in reactionary contexts, giving legitimacy to state and legal interventions that undermine sexual autonomy and erotic justice. A pluralistic sexual ethics that does not presume female victimhood is in order.

These two strands in Mackie's passage provoke for me three key questions in understanding migrant entertainers' presence, sexuality, and labor in U.S. military camp towns. First, if we take Rubin's critique of sex hierarchy to heart and do not presume women's victimization in sexual-economic exchanges or sexual objectification as the defining essence of women's experiences in these processes, what alternative perspective could we take to understand the sexuality of migrant women who labor in the sexual economy of *gijichon*? Second, whose stakes should we consider in thinking about this manner of "sexing the globe"? I draw on insights from transnational feminist theories to highlight the politics of location and difference in questioning the parameters of such a project. Third, if we start our investigation not with these preconceived notions of oppressors and sufferers, but with the consideration of *gijichon* as a site of transnational labor migration and examine the individuals therein as social and cultural actors, paying keen attention to both macroprocesses and micropolitics, what new perspective on these women's experiences could we gain? In other words, what insights could a transnational migration perspective offer these migrant entertainers' experiences?

Thinking about Migrant Entertainers in *Gijichon*

How could we understand women's sexuality beyond a sexual objectification framework? The very asymmetrical organization of male and female sexualities in prostitution for the military does make "patriarchy" and "male dominance" the most obvious analytics at first glance. The prevalence of the U.S. military in the Asia-Pacific region has inspired much research and activism and many regional coalitions to combat its effects on local populations. We have learned, not only from feminist scholars but also from the media, of the sexual victimization of women by U.S. military men. Reports of U.S. servicemen's sexual violence against Japanese and Korean women reach the international press at regular intervals and have fed a great deal of anti-American activity in the two host countries. Since the 1980s studies by political scientists and concerned critics of U.S. military prostitution have exposed how masculinist state projects rely on the mobilization of women's bodies.[16] The deployment of female sexual services for military men is, in a nutshell, an effect of military hypermasculinity.[17]

However, if we allow meta-analysis and individualized acts of violence to sum up the experiences of all women involved in military prostitution, we may unwittingly reproduce reactionary ideas about female sexuality and sex work. From an anthropological perspective, these analyses fall short of exploring the complexity of identity, motivation, and subjectivity in everyday interactions that do not fit with the binary understanding of the powerful and the powerless. In her discussion of state regulation of military prostitution, Cynthia Enloe asks, "Without myths of Asian or Latina women's compliant sexuality, would many American men be able to sustain their own identities, their visions of themselves as manly enough to act as soldiers?"[18] Although Enloe's question ushers consideration of sex work out of the realm of primordial male sex drive and brings in the social constructedness of sexuality and gender, it also portrays the encounter as one with women who are passive, exoticized pawns in men's (and the state's) project of masculinity. Part of this ethnography shows that the myths of women's compliant sexuality are not necessarily corroborated by actual encounters with the women, and that American men's visions of themselves as masculine and soldierly are often undermined by these very women. Even if encounters do happen the way Enloe predicts, we may also benefit from an analysis of the women's identities and of their visions of the encounters. Is it possible, for example, that the women enter into the interactions with their own myths of American men? Or that they play the role of the compliant Third World woman as a means to an end? If this is at all conceivable, then we must allow ourselves the space to consider Asian or Latina women's agency in a context of mutual though asymmetrical encounters.

Since the 1980s sex work, or prostitution, has been the subject of a key debate among feminists. Although some debates have included the involvement of men and transgender participation in commercial sex, the core concern has focused on women's agency or lack thereof in sex work. The radical feminist argument championed by Kathleen Barry and Catharine MacKinnon purports that sexual objectification is foundational to women's subordination and that prostitution is inherently a form of violence against women.[19] This line of argument sees the commodification of sex as a selling of a woman's sense of "self," violating the sanctity of the individual and of sexuality as beyond the sphere of economic exchange.[20] This position asserts that all women involved in prostitution are coerced. Since the late 1990s, under the rubric of trafficking, a changing terminology reflects the emphasis on women's powerlessness and victimhood—women in prostitution are "prostituted women," prostitute recruitment is "sex trafficking," and "sex trafficking" is "modern day slavery."[21]

In the same period, radical sex feminists and sex workers' rights scholars and activists have called for recognition of sex work as a form of labor. Confronting the argument that sex work is inherently degrading and violent, supporters of this argument contend that it is stigmatization and criminalization that engender and perpetuate violence against sex workers. Sex work from this perspective is the performance of a service (emotional and sexual labor) rather than the selling of the "self."[22] Sex workers are therefore entitled to the same kinds of rights protection as other workers have. For some, women's performance of sex work is articulated as a radical assertion of female sexual autonomy and subversion of patriarchy, and it opens the way to a "sex-positive culture."[23] "Sex trafficking" concerns since the late 1990s are, from this perspective, largely a revival of the white-slavery panic at the turn of the twentieth century—a matter of constructing fears of sexual danger at a time of increasing social mobility for women, and thereby reproducing middle-class respectability rather than addressing socioeconomic injustices that generate vulnerability.[24]

These are very distinct sets of ideas. Recognizing the diversity of women's experiences allows us to engage critically with these feminist debates about sex work and sex trafficking. Ethnographic works have been, in my view, most effective in dealing with the complexity of women's participation in sex work. They provide a contextual understanding of global and local structures of inequalities that engender marginalization and violence, but they also facilitate an understanding of women's creative responses to their subordination, as well as the blurring of an overly simplistic binary understanding of power relationships between men and women. Denise Brennan shows in *What's Love Got to Do with It?* how Dominican sex workers' performance of love with foreign male tourists is a strategy of advancement to pursue opportunities in the transnational social field, often with mixed results but nonetheless highlighting the women's agency in contesting local and global inequalities. Katherine Frank's autobiographical ethnography of working as an exotic dancer in gentlemen's clubs in the United States suggests how men's visits to these clubs could be considered touristic experiences[25] and as a distinct sphere of intimacy embedded in a complex web of commodification, performance, and search for authenticity. There is no final verdict—except that women's victimhood in sex work is not a universal truth.

Fundamentally, we need to ask ourselves seriously if there can be one and only one way of understanding commercial sexual exchanges—especially given the myriad forms that commercial sex has assumed in postindustrial societies. Feminists, historians, and anthropologists have argued extensively that bodies and sexualities are socially constructed.[26] If the definition of sex and the subjective experiences of it are shaped by larger sociohistorical forces, then any understanding of the meanings of sexuality should logically situate subjective experience within specific political, social, cultural, and economic environments. Just as state regimes, racial relations, family and kinship structure, discourses and technologies of bodies, and the reach and articulation of capital in this contemporary globalizing world undergo transformations, subjective meanings of desires and sexual expression find new configurations and forms of communication.[27] One excellent example is Elizabeth Bernstein's elegant and penetrating study of how sexual subjectivities and sexual expression are reconfigured by transformations in economic and cultural life in postindustrial society.[28] She unveils new forms of intimacy in the shifting geographies of sexual commerce and its regulation, paying careful attention to structural factors and social locations of the men and women who participate in these new labor and consumptive practices.[29] Concepts of self and sexuality are intimately embedded in each other and are entwined with larger social structures.

At Stake for Whom?

Whose stakes should we be considering in thinking about this manner of "sexing the globe"? Who decides what those stakes are? To avoid homogenizing the diversity of women's experiences, it is necessary to understand how local and global structures of power articulate in women's everyday experiences in order to understand what their key struggles are. Inderpal Grewal and Caren Kaplan call for feminist attention to address the concerns of women around the world in the *historicized particularity* of their gendered relationship to "scattered hegemonies," such as "global economic structures, patriarchal nationalisms, 'authentic' forms of tradition, local structures of domination, and legal-juridical oppression on multiple levels."[30] Ethnography that examines everyday-level micropolitics and connects to macrolevel structures helps us trace how power travels between personal, local, national, and global levels. As Chandra Mohanty suggests, in demanding that feminists rethink the assumption of Third World women as a homogenous social category, "(t)he experiential and analytic anchor in the lives of marginalized communities of women provides the most inclusive paradigm for thinking about social justice."[31] The messiness of reality generates the kind of nuanced understanding that helps us blur the binary understanding of subject/object, public/private, consent/force, aggressor/victim, and freedom/slavery that has structured much of our understanding about prostitution and sex trafficking. These binary frameworks have concrete effects on migrant women's lives. Their mobility and their sexuality are constantly reinscribed by states and activists to articulate those entities' various preoccupations with borders, gender, sexuality, and citizenship.

Going beyond the frame of sexual victimhood allows us to develop critical insights into the operations of power that go beyond individualized evils. O'Connell Davidson's stellar critique of the discursive construction of commercial sexual exploitation of children (CSEC) demonstrates its function in buttressing liberalism's ideas of autonomy, freedom, and the market. The rush to defend children as the essence of dependence, innocence and victimhood, and the last realm of human relations beyond contract "make[s] CSEC appear intolerable, and yet also encourage[s] us to tolerate the material inequalities and asymmetries of power that underpin children's presence in the sex trade."[32] The articulations of prostitution and trafficking are "not simply a process of description but a productive process that helps shape the cultural landscape and involves inescapably political questions about how, for instance, to organize sexuality, labour, and commerce."[33] Feminist scholars have critically engaged with issues of representation of sexual slavery, exploring the continuities that connect media coverage of white slavery at the turn of the twentieth century to that of sex trafficking in the twenty-first century.[34] Specifically, they have warned against the conservative gender and sexual politics buttressed by the formulaic villainization of alleged traffickers, an idealization of virginal victims, and the exaltation of reformers committed to end the trade in women. The sexual and moral panic that the news media have helped produce over the traffic of women, they argue, facilitates reinscription of gender roles, political maneuvers that reinstate the status quo, and the reification of a First World/ Third World divide.

My concern here is that if we project meta-analyses of structural inequalities onto human beings who breathe and live their lives as their own, feeling the freedom to challenge (although not necessarily the power to transform) their subordination, we risk erasing the agency, desires, and dreams of individuals, flattening and thereby losing critical insights into the diversity of human experiences. This ethnography aims to be a corrective to such a tendency.

Gijichon as Transnational Contact Zone

Gijichon is host to several groups of border-crossing people who have experienced different degrees and temporalities of dislocation. These include not only Filipinas and Americans—transient migrants who have crossed national boundaries to work in South Korea—but also the Koreans who make a living in *gijichon*, who can be identified as "internal exiles" in relation to dominant nationalist discourses. The present ethnography examines *gijichon* as a case of "transnationalism from below" and the individuals therein as transnational actors.[35] Interacting as consumers, mediators, and service providers within the political economy of the Asia-Pacific region, these actors conduct their exchanges at the intersection of international politics, colonialism, racial tensions, and cross-cultural imaginings. Borrowing from Mary Louise Pratt's examination of travel writing and transculturation, we could consider *gijichon* as a "contact zone." The notion of contact invokes "the spatial and temporal copresence of subjects previously separated by geographic and historical disjunctures, and whose trajectories now intersect."[36] Pratt takes a rather different approach to the metropolitan gaze from that of Mackie, asking how it is received and appropriated by the colonized and how these appropriations make their way into the metropolitan center. This perspective on power relations as mutual but unequal is, I suggest, key to understanding the dynamics of interactions in *gijichon*.

Putting the periphery in the center of history and the vitality and globality of marginal peoples at its heart, this ethnography of Filipina entertainers, in their interactions with GI patrons and Koreans working in *gijichon* clubs, is a study of what Anna Tsing calls the "friction" of global connections on the move—a coproduction of cultures whereby migrants, their relationships with each other and with their hosts and homes, constitute a part of "the awkward, unequal, unstable, and creative qualities of interconnection across difference" in globalization.[37]

Women's Migration, Agency, and Sexuality

As an ethnography of the Filipina entertainers in *gijichon*, I study these migrant women as both laboring and erotic subjects. To study women as desiring subjects in transnational labor migration is an attempt to open a space for conceptualizing women's migration, sexuality, and labor with some coherence. The current tendency to study sexuality and labor in migration as two distinct subtopics problematizes sexualized labor. To consider sexual-economic exchange immediately invokes, for some people, images of sexual violence, human trafficking, and organized crime, opening one to charges of dismissing women's victimhood.[38] Laura Agustín launched a cutting criticism of migration studies, transnationalism studies, and diasporic studies for not paying attention to women who migrate across borders to sell sex and thereby displacing the phenomenon to the purview of criminology, involving "victims of trafficking," and leading to the disappearing of the migrant category.[39] This discursive displacement puts women migrants within the framework of sexual victimhood, dismissing them as subjects and making their multiple desires and subjectivities invisible. Conversely, as Martin Manalansan observes, migration studies have focused on women as laboring gendered subjects, without a critical perspective on the fluidity of their sexuality across contexts. Manalansan argues that these studies unwittingly reproduce heteronormative and deterministic assumptions about gender, parenting, and affect.[40] Without denying that migrant women can be subjected to conditions of subordination and victimhood, this ethnography recognizes migrant women not just as laboring bodies but also as desirous and erotic agents, making space for their recognition as "desiring and pleasure-seeking migrant subject[s]."[41] Only in this way can we come closer to understanding the broad spectrum of women's experiences and struggles in migration.

Women's Migration and Agency

Do Filipinas migrate because of poverty, familial obligations, or their own ambitions? No single structural, cultural, or individual answer applies. "To make money for my family" may be the most immediate answer. However, understandings of self, gender, family, and sexuality are continuously reconfigured in displacement, not only because of changing perceptions of home from a distance but also as migrants come to realize their resourcefulness and its limits, as well as new possibilities at various junctures of their migration. As a localized context of social action for displaced people, *giji-chon* offers both opportunities and constraints in identity construction and reconstruction, making possible a wider space for identity formation and "made character" than would be predicted by social/structural inequalities and power/knowledge venues alone.[42]

An anthropological approach to migration emphasizes both structure and agency. We study people's capacity to make decisions, act, and strategize at the microlevel in relation to macrolevel structures (for example, historical processes of U.S. colonialism in Asia and responsive forms of nationalism, global migration flows, international protocols on migrant rights, border control) and mesolevel relational contexts (for example, social relations such as those of class, gender, and racial hierarchies and the local economies and cultural forms that tap into them).[43]

Agency, as understood in this ethnography, does not assume an autonomous individual with unfettered free will and powers. Sherry Ortner has articulated the challenge of conceiving this relationship between structure and agency as being able "to picture indissoluble formations of structurally embedded agency and intention-filled structures, to recognize the ways in which the subject is part of larger social and cultural webs, and in which social and cultural 'systems' are predicated upon human desires and projects."[44]

The analysis therefore takes into account a situated individual who has particular knowledge, desire, and imagination about what life could be; an awareness of the obstacles to achieving it; a sense of power to act toward realizing it; and a readiness to adapt and devise new tactics and strategies in the process. In other words, agency is power encumbered with constraints. A migrant's resources—in terms of qualifications, money, and network—shape the migration path she takes.

To decide to migrate as an entertainer is often a choice made within a particular set of limitations. Employment as a domestic helper or as a factory worker often requires exorbitant agency fees that have to be paid prior to departure (for domestic workers, these expenses ranged from nine hundred dollars for Hong Kong to seventy-two hundred dollars for Italy).[45] Most of the Filipinas I met had high school or community college educations and no ready access to either money or family networks overseas that would facilitate migration. Recruiters and employers of entertainers in Japan and South Korea have made it possible for such Filipinas to pay minimum or no fees before leaving the country, having the expenses of around eight hundred dollars deducted over three months after they start working. This has resulted in what some may refer to as a "debt-bondage" system that is commonly but not exclusively associated with migrant entertainers.[46] This is also the system in which a range of unfreedom arises—thus the notion of "bondage." However, for the Filipinas, sojourning as entertainers best suits their need to leave the country first and pay for the trip later. What is technically "debt-bondage" therefore becomes a practical and hopeful option for many of these women to pursue their projects of aspiration overseas.

How one perceives one's powers and constraints in relation to the world depends on the ontology of "self." Ethnographies have shown how the sense of self is fluid and interdependent and embedded within the collective in different contexts.[47] Caren Kaplan suggests that "travel produces the self, makes the subject through spectatorship and comparison with otherness."[48] The kind of travel I examine here involves spectatorship and comparison but also intimate encounters and desirous imagination. In their experience of displacement, migrants become, in part, what they aspire to be and also, in part, what others want them to be. Contradictory, multiple, and shifting modes of personhood and agency arise[49] and intensify in displacement.

For Filipina entertainers in *gijichon*, migration means not only disempowerment, alienation, and frustration but also liberation, excitement, and pleasure. They are structurally and culturally marginalized and susceptible to social and institutional violence with little protection of their basic rights as workers in a foreign country, and they suffer from the gendered stigma of their job as "entertainers"—often understood to mean "prostitutes"—which erodes solidarity with fellow migrant Filipino workers. As aliens, as laborers, as stigmatized women, they are isolated and vulnerable in multiple ways, and yet they attain a social and economic mobility often denied at home.[50] Their migration as part of the globalized sexual economy is fraught with contradictions that demand a nuanced analysis.

Migrant Women as Laboring Subjects

In the liminality of their migration, migrant women seeking personal transformation ultimately effect larger cultural, social, and political transformations. Studies of migrant Filipino domestic workers illustrate how migrant women challenge static views of gender.[51] With newfound economic and cultural capital, they negotiate new meanings of motherhood and roles in the family and mediate stereotypes of class, sexuality, and ethnicity, both at home and in their host countries.[52] They actively establish and expand transnational kinship networks and participate in transformative politics, challenging national borders and citizenship regimes.[53] Sarah Mahler and Patricia Pessar have proposed a theoretical model of "gendered geographies of power" to conceptualize gendered identities and relations in migration.[54] In light of these studies, which testify to the myriad ways that migrant women actively transform social life, cultural imagination, and political institutions, I examine how migrant Filipino entertainers both reproduce and challenge homogenizing discourses of nation, race, gender, and sexuality.

Women's imaginations, desires, and dreams for modernity have been important propelling forces behind the massive rural-urban migration since the 1980s and the transnational migration since the 1990s.[55] The pursuit of newly imagined identities—for example, modern woman, urban consumer, cosmopolitan traveler—is often as important as are family obligations or economic motivations in rural women's migration decisions.[56] Henrietta Moore has pointed out that "any approach to the analysis of agency must include a consideration of the role of fantasy and desire, both with regard to questions of compliance and resistance and in connection with the construction of a sense of self."[57] Media images, commodities, and people embody the glamour of the modern world, mediated by the national project of modernity ("development" and "progress"), making imagination a social practice.[58]

Women's mobility not only challenges their prescribed roles in the domestic realm but also threatens the symbolic investment of hegemonic nationalist discourse and the ideal social order. Women have often been a contested symbol of the nation, in terms of tradition and culture, progress and modernity, and national autonomy and sovereignty. Ethnographers have argued that the explosion of discourses about women's mobility, with a focus on sexual danger, is indicative of the ambivalence around women's changing social roles and increased mobility. Two main themes emerge in representations of migrant women: women as "pleasure-seekers," "prostitutes," and unfaithful wives, pointing up their sexual transgression of appropriate gender spheres; and women as victims whose sexual reputation and innocence have been sullied by evil recruiters and foreigners. Michele Gamburd points out how the emphasis on female passivity in this "horror story genre," as exemplified by sensational stories of rape and murder of overseas Sri Lankan domestic workers, encourages the reactionary legislative proposal of forbidding female migration.[59]

In media and activist representations that circulate in the Philippines, South Korea, and global arenas, migrant Filipina entertainers in *gijichon* have been described as "sex slaves" and "victims of sex trafficking" and alternatively as "prostitutes." Father Glenn certainly saw the Angel Club Filipinas as belonging more to the former category and sought compensation, while Korean immigration officers and police saw them squarely in the latter and ensured their deportation. The Angel Club Filipinas had their own understandings of their labor and migration and found these discourses irrelevant. Nevertheless, because women's agency and sexuality are central in the contested meanings of women's mobility in local, national, and international contexts, these discourses have concrete effects on their lives.

Obviously, migrant entertainers are sexualized on the job—they are required to perform certain ideals of feminine beauty and sexuality and to act out emotional and sexual scripts to generate heterosexual male desire in their clients. The club regime sexualizes them to maximize profits. Yet such sexualized performances may also serve as a site for them to explore their gender and sexual subjectivity in the liminal space of migration, as they can experiment with dress and behavior that they would not try at home. Sexualization as a form of labor discipline is by no means exclusive to such clubs or to erotic labor. Sexuality is both an integral part of factory management and a site for women's identification with modernity. Chinese factory managers invoke an "inherent" femininity and a future as mother and wife to induce docility in the laboring subject. However, female sexuality and gender ambivalence for both factory workers and domestic workers are strongly discouraged, if not prohibited.[60] Still, young rural women working in the city—whether Bangkok, Thailand, or Shenzhen, China—come to harbor an ambivalent desire for "individualistic" modern romance and a sense of alienation from the marriage practices in their home villages.[61] They acquire ideals of feminine beauty and assume new ways of presenting their sexualized selves, desiring to reconcile their alienation as laborers through such consumption practices. Reconfiguration of gender identities and sexuality is thus an essential part of migrant women's experience as their labor, desire, and consumption come to define them as modern gendered subjects.

Sexualization of migrant women workers is thus a feature of the disciplinary regime of transnational and private capital, be it on the shop floor, in the middle-class home, in consumer culture, or in the *gijichon* club. While this sexualization may differ in extent and language, the nature and purpose of creating such sexualized subjects is fundamental for wielding moral and economic control over women's bodies. These disciplinary measures, however, do not go unchallenged and may be productive of alternative desire and erotic practices.

This ethnography seeks to explore this nexus of sexuality and labor discipline in transnational migration. I draw on insights from scholarship on migrant women as laboring subjects to frame my analysis of migrant entertainers, developing a framework of understanding that goes beyond sexual victimhood while remaining mindful of their multiple vulnerabilities. Migrant women's bodies and labor are sexualized by capital, state, and nationalist imagination, regardless of their labor sector, but my purpose is not to homogenize experiences and conditions across different sites of labor. Rather, it is to understand the diversity of women's experiences within the macrostructures and macroprocesses of globalization without necessarily considering any sector to be exceptionally intolerable, while normalizing the structures that generate vulnerable migrant populations in the first place.

Ethnographic studies of migrant women set out to challenge the assumptions that women migrate primarily as dependents of men and that their experiences are ontologically similar to those of men. These studies argue for a recognition of migrant women as social and cultural agents. The problem, as feminist scholars have argued, has been due to a devaluation of women's work and the marginalization of women's experiences in understanding processes of globalization.[62] To rectify this, ethnographers have offered gender-specific insights into women's motivations, networks, patterns, and practices of migration. As a lesson learned from this feminist critique in mainstream migration and globalization studies, in this ethnography I also try to avoid reproducing a sexual hierarchy in which any particular type of women's work is devalued or the experiences of the women are marginalized. Women who migrate—into the sex trade or to other sites of labor—are political, economic, and historical actors. To deny this is to imprison migrant women in the very gender, class, and sexual orders that they must negotiate.

Migrant Women as Erotic Subjects

In the two years that I did fieldwork in *gijichon* and in my subsequent interactions with my Filipina subjects, during all the time that I have spent with them munching fried chicken in restaurants, eating chicken adobo in their bedrooms, walking in the market, and speaking on the phone, the subject of "boyfriends" easily aroused the most intense engagement and interest. I put "boyfriend" in quotes because it is a term that can mean a number of things in *gijichon*—a casual customer, a regular customer, one of a number of customers who identify as one's "boyfriend," or a "real boyfriend" with whom one is intensely emotionally attached. Discussions, comments, and gossip about each other's boyfriends, how to get a man's attention, how to manage the different boyfriends in *gijichon* and the Filipino boyfriend or husband in the Philippines, when and with whom to have sex, betrayals and breakups, and prospects of marriage are all consuming subjects in *gijichon*. Based on these observations, I focus on how romantic desires and maneuvers are important in these migrant women's self-making process and as means by which they take control of their lives, specifically in their relationships with men.

Romance is thus a key mode of agency for these migrant entertainers in GI clubs. This may sound paradoxical, as romance may be, for many readers, antithetical in an industry that commodifies female sexuality. However, in *gijichon* Filipinas' femininity, sexuality, and ethnicity are simultaneously the objects of consumption and the sources of their agency. To perform the role of a poor, virginal, and exploited oriental woman in need of protection is just one way to elicit financial and emotional support as well as the "love" of their American GI customers, and who knows where this "love" will take one? Sometimes, however, one does fall in love, and the Filipinas, as romantic and erotic subjects who entertain as many occidentalizing ideas about American men as American men entertain orientalizing ideas about them, do want romantic love. Romance in *gijichon* thus, on one hand, allows migrant entertainers to pursue social mobility as promised in their fantasies of transnational lives. On the other hand, as modern romance has its locus in the individual self, it allows migrant women, aware of their marginalization and stigmatization, to assert individual respectability and self-worth through genuine affection. "Love" is therefore always desirable, though the line between real and "performed" love sometimes becomes blurred.[63]

These romantic pursuits contribute to our understanding of transnational women's sexual agency. Women sometimes use migration, in gender and erotic projects, to challenge their gendered embeddedness at home. Nicole Constable's study of correspondence marriage shows that, contrary to most stereotypes of marriage between Chinese or Filipina women and U.S.-American men, some well-educated professional women may use migration to realize their dreams of marriage, rather than use marriage for migration. With regard to women from a different global and class location—a small population of professionally ambitious Japanese women—Karen Kelsky discusses how their erotic pursuits with "Western men" are embedded in an "emancipatory" turn to internationalism, in opposition to gender-stratified corporate and family structures in Japan.[64] I recognize migrant entertainers as desiring, erotic subjects who seek ways, through migration, to pursue pleasure and escape from their gendered entrenchment. As such, the particular ways in which mobile women deploy their sexuality illuminate the "scattered hegemonies" in which they are embedded and which they contest.

This is the first book-length ethnographic study of a group of women who have been identified as "victims of trafficking" and, I hope, opens fertile ground to explore the coexistence of victimhood and agency. While the main ethnographic sections are based on fieldwork in South Korea during the years 1998–2000, continual communications with some of the Filipinas and two follow-up field visits to South Korea and the Philippines allow the analysis to incorporate the effects of migration on their relationship with home and their own reflections about their experiences in *gijichon*. The migratory experiences of Filipina entertainers thus point to the effect that temporary migration has on migrants' sense of self in relation to the transnational field and to the diversity of meanings of female mobility and sexuality.

Research Setting, Methods, and Subject

As the opening story indicates, my role as a researcher in *gijichon* pulled me in different directions, sometimes by unexpected events that both challenged and illuminated my understanding. The research experience for this book demonstrates the serendipity of anthropological research.[65] I certainly did not expect that I would write about anything remotely resembling romance between Filipina entertainers and GIs when I first arrived in South Korea in August 1998. Nor did I plan to engage with the discourses of trafficking. The subject and arguments of this book have therefore developed out of fieldwork, with a focus that had not been intended in all the careful planning and reading beforehand. It is only appropriate, therefore, that I discuss how this project developed in relation to the research context and my research methodology. A detailed discussion of research methodology is provided in Appendix I.

In August 1998, armed with a research proposal to compare the experiences of Korean women working in *gijichon* and their counterparts in red-light districts in Seoul, I intended to examine how their distinctly demarcated clientele (American soldiers for the former and Korean men for the latter) might affect the construction and experience of their identities as "women" and as "Korean" in relation to dominant gender and nationalist discourses. I hoped that the comparison would yield a fruitful discussion of the intersection of sexuality and nationalism, the heterogeneity of women's experiences in sex work, and discourses of nationalism.

However, the introduction of Filipino migrant entertainers brought new layers of national and international conversations into *gijichon*. During my fieldwork the rise of activist, media, and research interest around the presence of Filipina entertainers in the clubs and their portrayal as trafficked women confirmed that I needed to steer away from my original plans. A crucial turning point was the collaborative research with Ms. Back Jaehee and with various other local individuals and organizations in their efforts to understand and assist these foreign entertainers (see Appendix I), through which I came to realize the salience of human trafficking (*insinmaemae*) in understanding these women. Kim Hyun-Sun, the director of Saewoomtuh, an organization for women and children in *gijichon* based in Dongducheon, described them as "victims of international trafficking" in her international presentations, which I helped translate. Korea Church Women United received funding from overseas and commissioned Back Jaehee and me to conduct our field research at different sites, and with data from that research, the group later produced "Fieldwork Report on Trafficked Women in Korea." The YWCA commissioned us for another small-scale research project on the Filipinas and organized a regional conference on "International Trafficking of Women in Asia." In other words, the Filipinas in this study had been crucial to Korean activists' defining the presence of "trafficking" of women into *gijichon* in particular and into South Korea in general.

These local interests made me realize that research on Filipina entertainers was timely, partly because they embody various challenges of globalization to South Korean society. The discourse of trafficking that Korean activists were building in particular intrigued me: its association with slavery-like practices did not quite fit with what I observed of Filipinas' lives in *gijichon* as I wandered around town and sat in coffee shops and restaurants with them. There were obviously abusive practices, such as the withholding of passports and salaries, and there was pressure to sell drinks and go out with customers, but was "trafficking" the best framework for understanding these abuses? I continued to consider these questions while I collaborated with NGOs to document these migrant entertainers as "trafficked" women.

After eighteen months of field research, in April 2000 I was set to leave South Korea and return to England to begin writing. However, as some of the Filipinas I had met early in the research were reaching the end of their one-year contracts around the time I was leaving, I decided to visit them in the Philippines in May. I made further research visits to South Korea in 2001, 2003, 2005, and 2006 and to the Philippines in 2003, and I have maintained contact with seven of the Filipinas over the years and traced their trajectories, most of which led to other countries. These subsequent experiences, however, are mentioned in this book only when pertinent to the discussion of the women's experiences between 1998 and 2000.

Doing Fieldwork

Fieldwork largely focused on the two U.S. military camp towns in Dongducheon and Songtan. These two *gijichon* were chosen because of the relatively large number of Filipina entertainers employed there. No service provider catered to these new arrivals, and I could not rely on local nongovernmental organizations to put me in touch with Filipinas working in the clubs. In fact, quite the opposite was the case, as I played a role in acquainting Korean NGOs with Filipina entertainers (see Chapter 6).

My initial channel for meeting Filipinas in *gijichon* varied for different sites. Two GIs in Dongducheon introduced me to Filipinas they knew, as well as GIs who had Filipino girlfriends. In Songtan an ex-*gijichon* woman introduced me to a club owner. Father Glenn, the priest at the Filipino Center for Migrant Workers, introduced my coresearcher and me to two runaway Filipinas (see Chapter 7) who were living with their boyfriends near Uijeongbu. I also actively struck up conversations with Filipinas and GIs in restaurants and coffee shops. In all these first encounters I introduced myself (and my coresearcher) as doing research on Filipinas in South Korea. In August 1999 my coresearcher and I helped Korea Church Women United distribute aid packages to all migrant women in Dongducheon, as businesses in the area were closed for two weeks due to serious flooding. After we had visited each club and had every migrant woman sign for the packages that they were happy to receive, we became recognizable to many in our subsequent visits to *gijichon*.

Positioning oneself is an epistemological act. As Roger Goodman points out, "the anthropologist is so directly the research tool" in fieldwork.[66] My positions in the field were important in determining the kinds of knowledge to which I had access—what Donna Haraway calls "situated knowledge."[67] As in the opening story, in the following pages I try to make explicit my position as interlocutor in the production of narratives in order to allow readers to evaluate how my presence, questions, and responses were always part of interactive processes. In practicing reflexivity as a researcher, I also state my experiences of incomprehension, struggle, and mistakes in the field.

Bearing in mind the intersubjective production of identities and interactions, I made a conscious effort to talk not only with Filipinas but also with GIs and Koreans. In addition to repeated (at least two) interviews with twenty-three Filipinas and interviews with seven GIs, this ethnography draws on my casual conversations and time spent with over thirty other Filipinas working in the clubs, as well as GIs, club owners, shop owners, and some undocumented migrant workers, such as manual laborers, independent vendors, and shop assistants in *gijichon*. I thus made a conscious effort to meet not only with Filipinas but also with the people who interacted with them. This approach allowed me to look at the interrelational dimension of identity along lines of gender, class, ethnicity, and nation and to situate their narratives within the multiple negotiations that they engage in on an everyday basis. I also conducted interviews with a journalist, NGO activists, a recruitment manager, members of the KSTA, and government officials at the local and national levels.

While my primary identity was that of a foreign researcher in South Korea, when interacting with more cautious Koreans in *gijichon* I made use of my association with various NGOs, declaring myself to be a volunteer for a women's organization at times and a student in Korean language at others, depending on the people with whom I talked. As ethnicity and nationality were heavily implicated in interactions in *gijichon*, my position as a Chinese female researcher from Hong Kong with British citizenship was significant in my interactions. Not being Korean, Filipino, or American allowed me a certain objectivity in the eyes of my informants, as I had little conflict of interest with them in terms of ethnicity. My identity as a foreigner served as a common basis for interactions with the Filipinas and GIs, while my knowledge of Korean allowed me to pose as a curious researcher of Korean society and to gain the trust of the Korean people I met. However, the anthropologist's potential to be a desiring agent and an object of desire in the field often mediates research. In the context of *gijichon*, competition for customers/boyfriends was fierce, and any ambiguity could become a source of conflict. As a single Asian woman, I had to be careful not to draw attention as a potential competitor, yet without appearing dismissive of the male acquaintances of the women. Whenever I met a GI through a Filipina, I always acknowledged the precedence of their relationship and informed the Filipina if I wanted to meet the GI independently. I also found myself downplaying my femininity. I had very short hair, no makeup, and largely androgynous dress—a sharp contrast to both Korean and Filipina entertainers in *gijichon*. The more the Filipinas and Koreans joked about me being "like a man," the less likely I was to be identified as a foe in the economy of desire.

This study is focused on the women's experiences of inciting heterosexual male fantasies as labor and as part of their sense of gendered self. All the women self-identified as having romantic and erotic desires for men, with the exception of Milla, who said that she had been a "lesbian" in high school and had a girlfriend but had begun dating men in college. During my fieldwork I heard of only one female GI paying a bar fine to take a Filipina out, but I was not able to confirm this. One Filipina said that, after being unable to find a job upon her return to the Philippines from South Korea, she "live[d] with a woman, a tomboy" in Manila for three months because she was receiving financial support from her.

A note on wording is in order here. The Filipina entertainers perform sexual labor as part of their jobs; this may include flirting, amorous interactions, erotic dancing, and/or sexual intercourse, and their clients may also be their "boyfriends" or "fiancés." The divide between commerce and intimacy is constantly blurred as part of their labor. It is important to note that the Filipinas considered here refer to themselves neither as "sex workers" nor as "prostitutes." As will be shown, women as well as men involved in *gijichon* clubs may object to both of these labels in their avid aversion to any implication of the sale or purchase of sex. The women sometimes use the term "entertainer" to identify themselves, but they have little need to do so since their lives mostly revolve around *gijichon*, where it is common knowledge that, as Filipinas, they work in the clubs. I use the term "migrant entertainers" to focus on their migratory status and their employment from an institutional perspective. This also allows for an approximation of the ambivalence that engenders the very negotiations about what is commodified and what is not in *gijichon* clubs and in the lives of the migrant Filipina entertainers in *gijichon*.

Structure of the Book

Readers will learn about different segments of the story of the runaway Angel Club Filipinas in each of the following chapters. This is a tribute to, and a variation of, Max Gluckman's "case study method," which emphasizes how close reading of a single event can yield pertinent social and cultural analysis.[68] However, I also draw on stories and data I collected over the long period of fieldwork, as the diversity of the women's experiences and of situations in *gijichon* deserve to be documented as thoroughly as possible.

The ethnography is organized to highlight the disciplinary regimes that migrant women are subjected to and subjects of in their migration journeys. Part II examines the political economy in which migrant Filipinas become mobile subjects in conflicting discourses about women's sexuality, nationalism, and modernity in both sending and receiving countries. In Chapter 2 the construction of migrant entertainers in South Korea is discussed with reference to state policies and two levels of cultural debates about the South Korean nation-state: What does globalization mean for the Korean nation and its people in the late 1990s? Where do *gijichon* Koreans stand in relation to the nation when migrant entertainers enter their midst? These contestations about the membership and boundaries of the nation through the bodies of Filipino migrant entertainers have important bearings on their legitimacy (or lack thereof) in relation to the South Korean body politic. In Chapter 3 the examination focuses on the conflict between dominant constructions of migrant entertainers in the Philippines that circumscribe them within particular gendered relationships with the nation-state and the women's own narratives of hope, desires, and dreams for self-transformation in migration that exceed such containment. I trace the delegitimizing effects of state policies and nationalist discourses on these migrant women's perceptions of their own migration.

In Part III two key ethnographic chapters examine the contested control over migrant Filipino entertainers' sexuality in the economy of heterosexual desires of *gijichon*. In tandem with the avid aversion to the label "prostitution" is an active deployment of the cultural symbols of "family" and "love" by Filipinas, Korean club owners, and American soldiers. Chapter 4 analyzes the club regime as a system of labor control and how Filipino entertainers come to inhabit this new habitus through a combination of accommodation, evasion, and resistance. It further discusses how the prostitute stigma is maintained as women seek to contest its effects. Chapter 5 explores romantic love as a discourse between GIs and Filipinas in their conflicting search for intimacy, sex, and money. Recognizing love as a weapon of the weak for the Filipinas, the ethnography also shows that the line between genuine desires and calculated performance, between the powerful and the powerless, is not carved in stone. It further shows how love is an integral aspect of both the ongoing negotiations in a transnational site and the process of transnational subject-making.

Part IV is set up to highlight the tension between migrant Filipinas' desires to assume a transnational existence and anti-trafficking nongovernmental organizations' drive to ground them in the name of protection. Examining the Filipinas' ambivalence about homecoming in their emergent transnational concept of self and the symbolic and material significance that migration has come to acquire for them and their families, Chapter 6 throws light on the increasing momentum for migration out of the Philippines. In stark contrast to the women's vitality of hope for self-transformation, anti-trafficking NGOs in South Korea and the Philippines seek to contain them within the singular identity of "victim of sex trafficking." The ethnography in Chapter 7 traces how NGOs deploy these women as symbols of female victimhood in their anti-trafficking campaigns and lobby for legislation that in effect further marginalizes the very women it tries to help. This chapter raises questions about how anti-trafficking activism may reproduce the masculinist state and a normative gender and sexual regime. Chapter 8 brings together the themes of the book through a brief review of some of the Filipinas' journeys after South Korea.

All the names of Filipinas, Korean *gijichon* women, and GIs are pseudonyms. The transliteration of Korean terms and personal and place names (except for well-established ones such as Kim Dae-jung and Seoul) follows the Ministry of Culture and Tourism (MCT) guideline.

PART II

Laborers of Love

A *Gijichon* Tour in 2000

"TDC," in the common parlance of GIs and Filipina entertainers, refers to Dongducheon (transliterated as Tongduch'on in the Yale-McCune romanization system), a city approximately forty kilometers south of the Demilitarized Zone. More specifically, it refers to a strip of land made up of two parallel streets in front of Camp Stanley and Camp Casey, the main installations of the Second Infantry Division of the United States Forces in Korea (USFK). What marks it as a military town is the occasional armored tank and military vehicle that drive by and the dominant presence of American soldiers in their combat boots and uniforms.

On the road immediately in front of Camp Casey, you can find a row of two- or three-story buildings with shops ranging from pizza places and burger joints to tailors, photo studios, Internet cafés, souvenir shops, and sportswear shops with sneakers and sweaters in vibrant colors and large sizes that would be rare in downtown Seoul. Walk across the rail tracks behind this road and you land on the main street, where most of the clubs are, under signs of AAA, Orion, Starz, Studio 52, Pan-Korea, and New House (see Figure 1). In between these clubs are small restaurants, mom-and-pop stores, and shops selling leather goods, clothes, dancing costumes, souvenirs, portraits, and paintings. To find common Korean fare, TDC is the wrong place to go. This is where "fusion" food with a colonial and neo-colonial twist is in vogue—instant noodles with sliced cheddar cheese, "Yaki" dumplings, hamburgers—menu items common only in camp-town restaurants. Since 1999 Filipino and Russian dishes and drinks as well as menus written in Tagalog and Russian have been available (see Figure 2).

The ethnic mix of Koreans; white, African American, and Hispanic GIs; young Filipinas and Russian women; as well as a few Amerasian adults and children is an uncommon sight in other parts of South Korea, as are the interracial couples. GIs are often seen with Filipinas, or less commonly with

Figure 1.　A club in Dongducheon (TDC)

Figure 2.　A *gijichon* restaurant with signs in Russian and Tagalog

Russian or Korean women, walking hand in hand or in an unmistakable "lovers' embrace" but sometimes side by side or in groups—like friends. In TDC a mixture of English and Korean appears on shop signs, and military jargon such as MP (Military Police) and PX (Post Exchange), is blended into the Konglish (Korean language with broken English phrases) spoken by Koreans young and old. You can easily hear basic Korean phrases interwoven into the conversations among GIs, Filipinas, and Eastern European women.

At night the club street in TDC comes to life in the gleam of the clubs' neon signs and with thumping music—mostly hip-hop but also country, metal, and rock 'n' roll—that pours out onto the street. GIs, in uniform or casual wear and usually in groups of two or three, ramble through the club street to look for the music, women, and alcohol that will help them wind down. A few middle-aged Korean women assail GIs in broken English, "Hey, you want nice lady? I got nice lady. Thirty dollars, thirty dollars. OK? OK?" Negotiations may take place, and an interested GI will be led to a room in a nearby alley, where a Korean sex worker provides a twenty-minute trick.

Most GIs, however, bypass these offers and continue on to one of the clubs, where they can enjoy the company, or simply presence, of younger, prettier, and more exotic women. Heavily made up in body-hugging attire, sometimes under coats if the wind is particularly forceful, these Filipino, Korean, and Russian women may occasionally stand outside their clubs to solicit customers. Some of these women manage to have a bar fine and may be barhopping with their GI companions for the night, while others head off to other venues for an intimate time. On Friday and Saturday nights, particularly those that fall on or follow the first or fifteenth day of the month—paydays for the GIs—the scene in TDC is doubly boisterous. The women have extra enthusiasm and urgency, the men are more generous, the shows are more exotic, and the music, alcohol, and money continue to flow into the early hours of the next day.

Some GIs also call the club street "downrange"—as for targets for shooting practices in the military. The phallic image is appropriate given the importance of the place for evenings with alcohol, female company, and maybe a bit of "spectator sex" during strip shows in some of the clubs (see Figure 3). After all, TDC is the most popular place for off-hours and off-base leisure, while GIs interested in more hardcore sex and female presence go to Tokkuri—an area of clubs up on the hillside behind Camp Casey—where Filipinas and Korean women perform "shows" and where those in-

Figure 3. A club in Dongducheon with a banner advertising strip shows

terested have easier access to "short-time" sex in the clubs. Curfew for the GIs on weekdays, however, ensures that none of them are spotted off-base after midnight. MPs patrol the streets and report offenders to the authorities—exceptions are those who manage to sneak into motels with their companions of the night before getting caught.

GIs are not the only customers in these clubs. Korean customers, though officially prohibited entry, do make their way into some of these *gijichon* clubs. Clubs in TDC have relatively fewer Korean customers compared to those in Songtan and "America Town" in the city of Gunsan, which rely on the generous spending habits of Korean men. Migrant factory workers from developing countries who work nearby in Gyeonggi Province also visit the TDC *gijichon* clubs. These migrant workers, from the Philippines, Pakistan, and Peru, have been arriving in South Korea since the late 1980s. Many have overstayed their visas to become undocumented workers. They normally show up after the GIs' midnight curfew and have become a regular source of income for some of the clubs in TDC. They, like the GIs, drink, dance, and talk with the women in a mixture of languages, and the TDC scene changes after the GIs retreat behind the gates of the base.

Figure 4. Wall writing outside a club in Songtan. Some of the writing says, "MAKE 'EM CRY TOUR 98" and "IT'S ALL ABOUT THE MONEY 'BABY.'"

Chapter 2
"Foreign" and "Fallen" in South Korea

Gijichon—U.S. military camp towns in South Korea—are not "really" what Korea is about, I was told a fair number of times during my two years of field research. For example, my twenty-year-old Seoul National University friend told me that I, as a foreigner, should not be going there because he felt ashamed of them; my sixty-year-old landlord just frowned and turned her face away the few times I talked about my trips to Dongducheon; and a senior Korean anthropologist asked me to study *chesa* (ancestor worship) and shamanism instead if I "really wanted to learn about Korean culture."

These reactions illuminated for me how *gijichon* symbolizes the antithesis of what the ideal Korean nation should be. From the perspective of Koreans who shared, in some ways, the triumphalist nationalist discourse of economic success and globalization in the late 1990s, foreigners who want to learn about Korea should do so either through its heritage (shamanism, ancestral rites), through its economic achievement in becoming one of the Asian miracles of the 1980s, or both. Politically, U.S. military presence in *gijichon* violates the ideal of national sovereignty. Culturally and socially, *gijichon* challenges the homogenous ideal of the nation that state and popular discourses promote. Katherine Moon has described *gijichon* as "neither America nor Korea"—"hybrid towns, possessing elements of America and Korea in the bodies of their residents, English and Korean language store signs, U.S. military slogans and logos juxtaposed with dolls garbed in traditional Korean dress."[1] In other words, their hybridity is inconsistent with the imagined nation. *Gijichon* Koreans—not just *gijichon* women working as hostesses in the clubs, but everyone whose livelihood depends on the presence and needs of the U.S. military—therefore become internal exiles. Geographically a part of South Korea, *gijichon* is politically, culturally, and socially a borderland, and *gijichon* Koreans are best kept on the margins of the nation.

From the perspective of the anthropologist, this common tendency in mainstream Korean society to demarcate *gijichon* as "un-Korean" and (therefore) a site of danger makes *gijichon* an illuminating site for the study of the constructions of Korean nationhood and contagion. Mary Douglas suggests in *Purity and Danger* that "ideas about separating, purifying, demarcating, and punishing transgressions have as their main function to impose system on an inherently untidy experience, certain moral values are upheld and certain social rules defined by beliefs in dangerous contagion."[2] *Gijichon* speaks neither to the pride nor the success of South Korea as a modern nation-state. In fact, it interferes with the dominant fantasy of a globalized, modern South Korea. What *gijichon* represents, therefore, is what needs to be purged from the Korean nation.

Foreign presence is a constant source of "internal cultural debates"[3] about the nation. In 2008 the world was surprised by the nightly candlelight vigils of millions in Seoul protesting the suspension of the ban against U.S. beef imports on the grounds of health concerns about mad cow disease. U.S. and Korean officials, including Secretary of State Condoleezza Rice, repeated scientific evidence that the beef was safe but were oblivious to the fact that the protestors' concerns went way beyond the beef: in 2008 "mad cow" symbolized South Korean discontent about both domestic politics and relations with the United States. Apart from accusations that the South Korean government kowtowed to U.S. demands to lift the ban in return for a Free Trade Agreement, the neoliberal principles of privatization and redevelopment championed by President Lee Myung-bak promised economic and physical displacement for many, at a time when the South Korean economy was reaching stagflation. The foreign threat of "mad cow disease"—a powerful metaphor of illness affecting the present and future of the Korean national body—incited South Korean citizens to contest what being Korean meant in terms of national pride, economic development, and democratic participation in this global era.

When research for this project began in 1998, South Korea was going through the IMF crisis. As South Korea went from being one of the four "Little Dragons of Asia" to being the recipient of the largest loan ($57 billion) ever given by the International Monetary Fund (IMF) to resuscitate South Korea's failing financial markets, "IMF" became a symbol of both South Korea's downfall on the international stage and the danger of the world outside, and it galvanized the nation to unite. Economic nationalism was thus at its height in the late 1990s. It has taken a range of forms, from the state-initiated industrial development of the 1960s, to the aggressive protection of native agriculture from foreign imports and the consumer nationalism of "Buy Korea" in the early 1990s,[4] to grassroots pooling of savings into "invest in Korea" funds to help the nation emerge from the 1997 debt crisis. Economic nationalism thus goes beyond the economy and operates symbolically, as the market is a site for the production and transformation of values, practices, and identities pertaining to the nation.

This chapter looks at the continuities and discontinuities of debates about the Korean nation incited by migrant entertainers who are constructed as both "foreign" and "fallen." On the one hand, it examines the reconfiguration of the body politic of South Korea, and on the other hand, it contextualizes the vulnerability of these migrant women, both phenomena being understood as interconnected processes in South Korea's struggles with the impact of globalization.

*   *   *

When Ajumma Lee was released from her nine-day detention in mid-August 1999, her son and daughter arranged for her to meet with the Filipinas. I was in their hotel room in Seoul where the Lees had put them up so that they could be ready for the meeting. Miss and Mr. Lee and Ajumma Lee were insistent that the meeting take place. The employer-employee relationship was not yet over—at least not for the Lees. The Filipinas were anxious, asking why they had to meet Ajumma and pleading with me to go with them. I agreed, even though I did not want to meet Ajumma Lee at all after hearing what she had done to make them run away—she had pressured them to go into VIP rooms, arbitrarily deducted their drink money, yelled at them, forbade them to sit down during work hours, and threatened to make them strip if they did not sell more drinks. We went to the Lees' apartment—apparently only one of their apartments—on the fringe of Seoul, traveling in the Lees' two cars, one a luxury Grandeur and the other a sedan.

I was surprised when I went into the apartment. Ajumma Lee looked extremely fragile and ill. She sat on the floor leaning against the wall, back hunched, crossed-legged, and covering her legs with a blanket. She looked like any other *ajumma* (a term for a middle-aged woman, usually married)—so ordinary that I could not match her face with the sinister image for which the Filipinas had prepared me. Kitty went forward and hugged her while the others sat down. For the next hour Ajumma Lee spoke of her difficult nine days in detention—how she wanted to die, and how she had not done anything that the police had charged her with. She insisted that she had treated the Filipinas as daughters, especially since her own daughter had experienced the hardship of being abroad (having studied English in Canada). The Filipinas just sat quietly in a circle—one of them actually sat with her back toward Ajumma—while she talked.

As I interpreted her "speech" about her sufferings and maternal love for the Filipinas, I kept wondering if she would put her own daughter in those VIP rooms and the neon bikinis she had made the Filipinas wear. But nobody openly challenged her. Ajumma Lee told the women that she did not hate them for putting her into jail—she hated the police for it. The Lees believed that the Seoul metropolitan police had framed them since they were club owners in *gijichon* and their association's chairman was a member of the opposition party. The meeting was concluded with Chinese take-out. Some of the Filipinas told me that they had never been given such good food when they were working in the club. I wondered if my presence had anything to do with this exceptional hospitality.

On September 10, 1999, immediately after the Lees returned from a trip to Australia for recuperation, Miss Lee called to tell me the "truth" that they had learned from one of the seven Filipinas—they had been framed by the two Filipinas who wanted to leave South Korea in order to marry their boyfriends (that is, Winnie and another named Joy): "At first we thought that the police were the bad guys. We thought that it was just a problem within our race (*uriminjok-kkiri-ui-munjae*). But it turned out that they [the Filipinas] were the ones who betrayed us. The police knew that they were bad girls. That's why, to be frank with you, the police told us not to pay them damages, just their salaries. They knew that they were lying a lot and that's why they expelled them from the country. They knew that they were bad, but we didn't."

Saying that they had initially believed it was a conspiracy by the Seoul police against *gijichon* club owners, the Lees wanted me to know that they now subscribed to the police's view that the Filipinas were "bad girls." The Lees said that they were the victims of the Filipinas' self-interested project to get married to GIs and suffered needlessly because of their naïveté in trusting in these Filipinas. Miss Lee's final verdict on the Filipinas was: "We won't have Filipinas (in our club) anymore. The character of their race is so bad. We are going to get Russian women. People say they are more pure (*sun-hada*)."

Ms. Lee sounded as though she genuinely felt deceived. Articulating the ideal of feminine purity as the yardstick for employing entertainers in the future, the Lees rejected Filipinas as scheming and ungrateful. Ajumma Lee took the phone, reiterated her innocence, and recounted her traumatic experience:

> I am still suffering from the shock of the whole thing. I was really hurt deeply, I was so miserable in jail. I didn't believe that humanity could be so degraded. We still fear danger, but we can't do anything but to start business again. . . . You know that I have raised the kids by myself, and just started the club a year ago. I really wanted to commit suicide, but my sons and daughter have given me support all along. My daughter has come back from Canada to help me, but she got to know about all this and it breaks my heart. . . . Please visit us at our club. We have had the fate to come to know you. You are so lovely and we treat you not like a foreigner, but like a Korean girl. Keep in touch and come visit us often in Dongducheon.

I was surprised that the Lees called me even after all the Filipinas had left the country, especially since I had never identified as someone who was there to "help" them. As Ajumma Lee's last words illustrate, as a foreigner who was "*like* a Korean girl," I became a mirror, like the Filipinas, but from a different side—a mirror in which the Lees wanted to see themselves as innocent and blameless victims for all the misfortune that had befallen them after their generosity toward non-Koreans.

In this narrative the Lees emerge from the incident as traumatized victims of the injustice of their foreign employees' ingratitude but with a stronger sense of unity with the Korean body politic, mediating their status as internal exiles in *gijichon*. Their original suspicion of having been targets of malicious attacks by the Seoul police because they were *gijichon* club owners was purged with the realization that they had been pawns in the Filipinas' scheme to marry GIs. The Us-vs.-Others divide thus shifts, in this narrative, from that between mainstream Koreans and *gijichon* Koreans to that between Koreans and Filipinas.

Ajumma Lee's narrative is immersed in mainstream social and cultural production of South Korean society and reflects South Korea's struggles with the impact of globalization, in particular the influx of foreign laborers. The melodramatic excess of emotions, claims of suffering and near-death experience, the recognition of the "true" evil villains (the Filipinas rather than the Seoul police) and of moral heroines (the Lees themselves, who had been betrayed for their generosity) echoes the "melodrama of social mobility" that Nancy Ablemann elicited from middle-aged Korean women's personal narratives. According to Abelmann, the multiple displacements in Korea as a result of Japanese colonialism (1911–45) and the Korean War (1950–53), as well as the "compressed modernity" of rapid development in South Korea, have generated melodrama as a popular convention in South Korean films, novels, and TV dramas. For women in particular, the excess allows the expression of tensions between tradition and modernity. Experiencing these tensions and the pronounced inequalities of South Korean society, women adopt melodramatic conventions to make sense of their lives and to dialogue with the larger society about issues of class, justice, and mobility.[5] In sharing her narrative with a foreign researcher, Ajumma Lee identified herself as a woman who had succeeded as a single mother on the fringe of Korean society, as was evident in the love and support her children gave her. Her victimization at the hands of the Filipinas, in this narrative, failed to blunt her commitment to be a good Korean and hardworking mother.

In the nation's project of globalization (symbolized by the hosting of the 1988 Olympics and the 2002 World Cup), the Lees' extension of kindness and generosity to me exemplified Koreans' hospitability to the world. External evaluation, ranking, and the country's image have been important in assessing the country's membership in the global community. Under the presidency of Kim Dae-jung (1998–2002), in the immediate aftermath of the Asian financial crisis, a vigorous campaign to restore South Korea's global membership was launched. Economic initiatives for rapid recovery and institutions for the promotion of human rights were introduced.[6] Beginning November 2, 1999, and continuing well into 2000, one of the two local English-language newspapers ran a front-page column entitled "Going Global in New Millennium." Foreign commentators and Koreans working with foreigners, from diplomats and academics to students, took turns writing on South Korea's globalization.[7] In the intersection with "going global," the various configurations of Korean identity assumed in relation to national Others determine the forms of reciprocity that are entailed and simultaneously reproduce and contest the hegemonic discourse of the nation.

The image of a people united not only by blood but also by the constant threat of hostile aggressors has occupied a central position in Korean historiography. In this metanarrative, the Korean nation survived numerous foreign invasions from Mongols, Japanese, and Manchus since the thirteenth century before being forced under Japanese colonial rule until the end of World War II and then under what some interpret as American semioccupation beginning with the Korean War. The Korean race is thus tied together by common sufferings because of foreign belligerence. Shin Gi-wook discusses how the modern political discourse of national oneness was born under Japanese colonialism (1911–45) [8] and was actively promoted by political leaders, as well as by opponents of the regime, for political and cultural legitimacy—most notably by President Park Chung-hee (1961–79), whose modernization projects launched South Korean economic development toward that of a world power.

The strength of this historiography was evident as late as 2007 in the South Korean delegate's response to questions about the use of the terms "pure blood" to describe Koreans and "mixed blood" to refer to non-Korean people in the South Korean report to the Committee on Elimination of Racial Discrimination at the United Nations (Geneva):

> Historically, Koreans had not differentiated between ethnicity and race. Faced with imperialist aggression in the first half of the twentieth century, the Republic of Korea had constructed its own concept of unitary identity. After liberation from the Japanese imperialists in 1945, the unity of the Korean nation was generally taken for granted. *The strong sense of ethnic unity and nationalism had been a crucial source of inspiration during the transition to modernity in the Republic of Korea.* Being sandwiched between great world powers, the development of a sense of cultural homogeneity had not been done as a means of aggression, but rather as a defence system to ward off the imposition of ideas of superiority by others. (My emphasis)[9]

Between global ambitions and fear of foreign encroachment, what does the entry of Filipino entertainers mean to the South Korean state and nation? What does it mean for *gijichon* Koreans that these arrivals meet their needs for labor but challenge existing ways of life—how do they maintain *gijichon* as they know it while incorporating migrant labor? I suggest that the struggles in *gijichon* reflected larger "internal cultural debates" about globalization, women's sexuality, and labor in South Korea at the turn of the twenty-first century. In discussing the nation as an "imagined community," Benedict Anderson argues that mass communications and mass migrations, closely linked to the rise of capitalism, are the main generating factors in the rise of nationalistic and ethnic unrest in the post-cold-war "disorder." Globalization processes engender a combination of "opportunities" and "threats" as the flow of human bodies "follow[s] in the wake of grain and gold, rubber and textiles, petrochemicals and silicon chips," but unlike these commodities, "they carry with them memories and customs, beliefs and eating habits, musics and sexual desires."[10] These human excesses of commodified labor are often constructed as cultural and social threats and are simultaneously harnessed to the reproduction of the hierarchy of race, ethnicity, nationality, and religion that distinguishes the migrants from their employers and represents the power relationship between their country of origin and their host country.[11]

Foreign Labor in South Korea

Foreign laborers enter the Korean labor economy as economic and social subordinates from the outset. Since the 1980s South Korea, hailed for its rapid industrialization and economic development, has recruited foreign laborers as "industrial trainees" to fill vacancies in "dirty, dangerous, and difficult" jobs abandoned by Korean nationals. The "industrial trainee system" was set up in the early 1990s as the official channel for migrant workers to work legally in the country—the idea was to provide workers from developing countries with the skills necessary for their own countries' development. These trainees, who worked for a three-year period on D-3 visas, received less than half the wages of their Korean counterparts, could not join unions, and had no insurance coverage. Many eventually abandoned their positions for better-paying jobs and stayed on as undocumented migrants. Their undocumented status generated human-rights abuses by employers as well as the state, which regularly perpetrated raids on illegal immigrants and deported them.

Debates and policies regarding migrant workers in South Korea in the 1990s embodied some major contradictions of modernity. Economic development created demographic and economic needs for foreign labor, and yet nationalist ideals engendered mistrust of culturally, socially, and morally undesirable foreign influences. Thus, while migrant workers were an important source of cheap labor, their employment raised poignant questions for the nation-state. Who should be included in the legitimate workforce? What should be the conditions of their stay, legal status, rights, and entitlement to residence and citizenship? What might the long-term presence of migrant workers mean for a nation often idealized as an organic homogenous whole with shared ancestry?

These questions became particularly difficult in the period following the 1997 Asian financial crisis in South Korea, a watershed in the country's development, when globalization and modernization revealed themselves to be double-edged swords. Migrant workers numbered 234,000 in 1997.[12] Yet almost overnight the unemployment rate for Koreans increased to a record level of 4.7 percent (1.25 million people) in February 1998, and real wages, which had been rising rapidly over the previous three decades, fell by 2.3 percent in the last quarter of 1997.[13] The issue of migrant workers became a symbolic one for South Koreans to reconsider their relationship with the world. The crisis led to the scrapping of an initiative for a "Foreign Worker Employment and Human Rights Protection Law" that had been introduced in 1996 by a coalition of civic and religious organizations and had received support from lawmakers and in key ministries.[14] The Asian financial crisis thus demonstrated the continuing vulnerability of migrant workers in South Korea to employers' abuses as well as to state violence.

In 2000, 85,000 foreign workers at 1,222 factories in South Korea reported that their wages had been unpaid for periods ranging from one month to three years, according to a report by the Joint Committee of Migrant Workers in Korea, a nationwide network of twenty-two counseling and education facilities for foreign workers.[15] Meanwhile, undocumented workers who participated in union activities and organized mass rallies to protest against government crackdowns and the abusive industrial trainee system were arrested, detained, and deported by the government.[16] In 2002, in spite of reports of human rights abuses and protests from organizations for migrant workers, the government advertised its project to extend the trainee quota for 2004 to 145,000 as a solution to the acute lack of workforce for small- and medium-scale businesses. In 2004, as a result of vigorous lobbying for improved conditions and protection for migrant workers, the Employment Permit System (EPS) replaced the industrial trainee system, giving those who enter through EPS the same labor rights as Koreans. In turn, the government asked all illegal aliens who had been in South Korea for more than four years to leave the country or risk being arrested, fined, and deported, beginning November 15, 2004. With these provisions for amnesty for undocumented workers, as well as for deportation, the number of unauthorized migrant workers decreased to 186,894 by 2004. By October 2005 more than 30,000 irregular workers had reportedly been deported.[17] However, the complicated procedures and strictly regulated number of jobs to be filled under the EPS made many reluctant to take advantage of the amnesty and instead drove them further underground. In addition, since the EPS bound migrant workers to their employers, employers reportedly seized official documents, including passports and work permits, preventing migrant workers from looking for jobs elsewhere and making them particularly vulnerable to detention and deportation to their countries of origin. Detention of undocumented migrant workers amounts often to prisonlike conditions, and those who are owed wages have few means to make their claims in detention. On February 11, 2007, locking in detainees to prevent escape led to the tragic deaths of twelve and injuries to fifty-five migrants in a foreigner detention center fire in Yeosu.[18]

In spite of various measures and mechanisms to protect the rights of migrants, the Immigration Control Act, which requires the deportation of "illegal immigrants," virtually overrides migrants' rights to compensation and due process. Rights to remedies are overshadowed by the need to remove the migrants from the nation. In other words, in spite of government efforts (for example, prosecutions of employers for nonpayment of salaries and noncompensation for injuries), migrant workers' activism (migrants formed their own trade union in May 2001), and Korean civil support for migrants' rights,[19] migrant workers' vulnerability continues to be a joint product of the principle of flexible labor and the exclusionary impulse of nationalism at the levels of state, capital, and everyday practice.

State Disciplinary Regime of "Fallen Women" in *Gijichon*

Within this larger context of migrants' conditions in South Korea, Filipina entertainers experience an additional layer of vulnerability because their occupation as migrant women working in *gijichon* clubs—and thus presumably "foreign prostitutes"—makes them deviant women and therefore targets of control, further distancing them from discourses of rights protection. Gender ideology in contemporary South Korea valorizes female purity, women's reproductive role, and the strict division of gender spheres. Purity, in this context, is the prescription of female sexuality exclusively within the context of marriage and childbearing for the husband's family. Women who sell sex, and thereby make their sexuality public for purposes other than reproduction, transgress the gender ideology and pose a threat to social order. The South Korean state, however, has played an active role in the regulation of these deviant women's bodies and sexuality for both the maintenance of the masculinist development state and the gender ideology that continues to marginalize these women.[20]

In postwar Korea, prostitution, though illegal, is also regulated by the state. The U.S. military government (1945–48) abolished the legal prostitution established by the Japanese colonial government (1910–45). The first antiprostitution law came into effect in 1961. The law defined commercial transaction of sex as a crime, legally referring to the act as "fallen behavior" (*yulla-kaengwi*). As elsewhere, and in spite of the gender neutrality of the legal provisions, in reality the onus often falls on the "fallen women" rather than on the men who pay for sex. In the masculinist perspective that privileges male sexual prerogatives, prostitution is a "necessary evil" (*piryo-ak*), and "fallen women" are therefore necessary. This attitude is found in the simultaneous criminalization and state regulation of the sex trade. Government policies regarding prostitution have focused on the regulation of sex workers by identifying locations where they may work and calling them "special districts" (*deukjjongjiyeok*), later known as "youth-protection zones" (*cheongso-nyeon bohojiyeok*). These are red-light districts commonly known as "private prostitute streets" (*sachangga*). The state also requires compulsory health checkups [21] and internment of women arrested for prostitution in "training centers" that are highly restrictive.[22]

State regulation of women's sexual labor in U.S. military camp towns (*gijichon*), however, acquires political-economic significance beyond preserving male sexual privileges. Facilitating the operation of the sex trade in *gijichon* fulfilled three important goals of the developmental state from the 1960s to the 1980s: (1) to ensure the continual presence of U.S. troops as a deterrent against the communist North; (2) to earn foreign exchange for further expansion of the economy;[23] and (3) to contain sexual excesses associated with the U.S. military outside of "normal" Korean society.

In the early 1970s venereal disease (VD) control became the main vehicle for regulating *gijichon* women. Katharine Moon has analyzed how VD monitoring beginning with the "Clean Up Campaign" gave club owners, government officials, and the USFK inordinate control over the women's lives and bodies. Women entertainers working in the clubs in *gijichon* were required to register themselves as "business girls" with local government; this registration system then became the basis for mandatory VD examinations and monitoring of the women's VD status. In the initial stage of this regulation, "mass round-up" of women, including "club prostitutes, waitresses, streetwalkers," for gynecological examinations and injection of penicillin took place.[24] If found with VD, women were put into "detention centers" (*suyongso*), sometimes for as long as a month, until they were cleared. The VD control system was developed not for the women's welfare but to ensure the health of the U.S. military.

Consistent with the disciplining of Korean *gijichon* women's bodies for relations with the USFK, the South Korean government continues to regulate foreign women with mandatory STD/HIV testing without provision for health education or counseling. In the 1990s deportation became the easy option for getting rid of foreign women found to be HIV-positive.[25] Migrant women thus remain objects of surveillance rather than subjects with rights to health information and services, and no accommodation has been made for their needs.[26] Clinic staff members speak only Korean, and very few of the Filipinas visiting these clinics know what tests are being administered. While treatment for STDs is provided free of charge, the Filipinas are not given any information on STD/HIV prevention, safer sex, or contraception, unlike their Korean counterparts. Instead, the information these women have commonly comes from those around them—coworkers and boyfriends. Many club owners refrain from providing condoms, as this would implicate them in the stigmatized and illegal business of prostitution. Any condom use appears to be initiated by clients; no Filipinas I met purchased condoms on their own initiative. Like Korean *gijichon* women, they enjoy neither privacy rights as patients nor access to information: club owners are informed of any STDs the women have contracted by keeping the cards after each checkup, and their health registration cards are processed in Korean, which means that they do not understand the records. No more glaring example of the instrumentalization of women's bodies for the health of both the U.S. military and the South Korean national body can be found than the treatment these migrant women receive.

While their sexual labor is being deployed, their sexual and reproductive rights are being violated in mandatory testing, in exclusion from health information and counseling services, and in immediate deportation for being HIV-positive. The HIV regulation of migrant entertainers therefore epitomizes the disempowering conditions of flexible laborers and sex workers in South Korea. The instrumentalization of migrants' bodies—including sex workers' bodies—in the maintenance of national health has persisted in South Korea. In the logic of both the state and capital, they are flexible and disposable labor whose regulation protects the economic and physical well-being of the nation. For migrant workers, this logic operates to exacerbate their vulnerability, forcing underground those in fear of deportation or institutionalization and compelling them to endure abusive working conditions.

Contested Place and Contested Bodies in Nationalist Discourses

Filipina entertainers are recruited to work in a place of poignant political salience for Korean nationalist discourses and to take the place of Korean women who have been targets of vehement nationalist debates. While this set of parameters does not necessarily have a direct bearing on their employment and life as migrants, it operates in such a way that public discussions of these migrant women's conditions in *gijichon* are often superseded by debates about the Korean nation. While open protests against U.S. military abuses of Koreans, especially Korean women, were muted under the authoritarian military government, the democratization processes and their cumulative results in institutionalizing civilian governments since 1993 have opened up a space for an anti-American movement. For many activists nurtured by the democratic student movements in the 1980s, *gijichon* is a symbol of multiple U.S. violations, from the overriding of Korean territorial and judicial sovereignty, as exemplified in the Status of Forces Agreement (SOFA), to environmental and noise pollution and the sexual exploitation of Korean women. *Gijichon* challenges Korean nationalism in political, economic, cultural, racial, and moral terms. In nationalist discourse the woman's body is often a symbol of the nation's sanctum, embodying the traditions and the future of the collective whole. The *figure* of the *gijichon* prostitute has become an allegory of Korea as a divided and subjugated nation in literary, political, and activist discourses.[27] The *person* of the *gijichon* woman, however, has become a target of exclusion from the nation proper for her gender and sexual transgressions.

In the rising tide of anti-American sentiments since the 1980s, *gijichon* has come to signify U.S. political and economic dominance in the country. While calls for the withdrawal of U.S. military forces from Korea used to be confined among a small group of leftists, in the late 1990s such calls came to express a more widespread sentiment, especially among the younger generations who had not been exposed to the North Korea bashing under Park Chung-hee.[28] In fact, a less hostile attitude toward the North was accompanied by a rise in anti-American sentiment after President Kim Dae-jung took office in 1998. Kim introduced his "Sunshine Policy"—a rapprochement toward the North Korean regime.

In this historical context, *gijichon* Koreans, and *gijichon* women in particular, find mainstream society threatening their ways of life and further marginalizing them in spite of the growth of a democratic society in South Korea. "They [the protestors for U.S. military withdrawal] are crazy. How are we supposed to live and eat if the U.S. military are gone?" asked a Korean *gijichon* woman who has worked in the areas of Dongducheon and Uijeongbu in the last two decades.

Given that women bear the burden of maintaining the national body physically and symbolically, "defiled"[29] Korean *gijichon* women pose two challenges to the nationalist ideal. First, they are the material representation of the collapse of boundaries between "us" and "them." Derogatory terms such as "Western princess" (*yanggongju*), "Western sexy girl" (*yangseksi*), and "Western whore" (*yanggalbo*) highlight *gijichon* women's sexual liaisons with foreign men—"Western" meaning U.S. here—and mark these women as outside the Korean nation.[30] Second, *gijichon* women's sexual liaisons with foreigners threaten the reproduction of the "pure" Korean nation for the future.

The offspring of relationships between Korean women and GIs are called "bastards of the Western princess" (*yanggongju-ssaekki*) and "darkies" or "niggers" (*kkamdungi*). Heinz Insu Fenkl's biographical novel gives us insight into the discrimination that these children of GI fathers and Korean mothers faced in South Korean society in the 1960s.[31] In "Different Blood . . . It's a Curse," an article on Amerasian children in South Korea,[32] most such children are "second-generation mixed-blood people"—the offspring of "miscegenated" parents. They are teased and discriminated against in school and have few job prospects other than in the entertainment industry or in sports. In effect, these children embody U.S. domination, the breakdown of the national boundary, and the fate of women who fail to defend themselves. Their marginalization preserves the "pure core" of the Korean nation.

In the more open political climate of the 1990s, a series of novels,[33] documentary reports, and videos about *gijichon* women, by Koreans and "overseas Koreans," emerged. Documentary films such as *Camp Arirang* and *The Woman Outside*, both by Korean American women filmmakers, portrayed the struggles and pains that *gijichon* women and their children experience and the direct articulation of their sense of nonbelonging to the Korean nation: a moving moment in *Camp Arirang* hits the audience when a Korean teacher asks a classroom of about ten Amerasian children, "Where will you live when you grow up? America or Korea?" The children answer, in enthusiastic union, "America!"

Great Army, Great Father: The USFK and Prostitution in Korea, a report published by Korea Church Women United, pointed to the failure of the nation as "Father" to protect *gijichon* women from the abuses in the clubs and at the hands of the U.S. military. In the late 1980s knowledge of the Japanese military's forcible recruitment of women for sexual servitude from the late 1930s to 1945 (the "comfort women") emerged. Korean women activists had successfully rallied around the cause and become part of an important transnational comfort-women movement by the late 1990s. Thus nationalism served as the women's movement's key instrument for mobilization and publicity. This alignment of the nation's fate with that of women in sexual servitude to foreign aggressors creates a milieu in which "fallen women" (*yullak yeoseong*) can be considered victims, albeit largely as a symbol of the nation's victimhood.[34]

As individuals, *gijichon* women are targets of exclusion because they embody the disgraced nation. As symbols, these women become the rallying point for outcry against foreign encroachment. This is well illustrated by Yun Keumi's iconic status in the Korean nationalist anti-American movement in the 1990s. Yun Keumi was a twenty-six-year-old *gijichon* woman who was brutally murdered by an off-duty GI, Private Kenneth Markle, on October 28, 1992. News of the manner of her death—she was found naked, bruised, and with various objects inserted into her body—triggered fury across the nation.[35] The Committee on the Murder of Yun Keumi by American Military in Korea soon developed into the National Campaign for the Eradication of U.S. Military Crimes (*juhanmigun beomchoe geuncheorundongbonbu*).[36] Despite her marginalization to the fringes of Korean society in life, Yun's brutal death transformed her into an allegory of the masculinist nation. A female member of staff at the National Campaign pointed out this drastic switch: "The men in the movement call *gijichon* women 'Western whores' when they are alive. But once they are killed by GIs, they immediately call them *urinara-ui-nu-ui* (the respected elder sisters of the nation)."[37]

Katharine Moon ("Resurrecting Prostitutes and Overturning Treaties") discusses how the plight of *gijichon* women and the *gijichon* movement have played a crucial part in rallying sympathy from diverse social groups and motivated organized efforts in the democratization and decentralization processes and in the anti-American movement in the 1990s. However, the sufferings of *gijichon* women become meaningful to civil society leaders only as "cases" to challenge the state and gain political capital in the process. Instead of reversing the marginalization or exclusion of these women and including them in collective action as equals, dominant social movements find political advantage in keeping these women on the margins.

Thus, while the state justifies the sacrifice of women for security and economic needs, the anti-American ethnonationalists borrow the women's "foreign-penetrated" bodies to symbolize the humiliation of the nation and to challenge the Korean government and the United States. Both paradigms instrumentalize *gijichon* women for the advancement of their respective agendas, with little regard for them as rights-bearing citizens of the nation-state. The entry of migrant entertainers, however, brought about changes not only in the political economy of *gijichon* but also in the signifying system of the powerful and the powerless, rendering derelict the old binary of Korea versus the United States. This invigorated a new wave of discussions about the relations between *gijichon* and Korea, and between Korea and the world. It also provided a discursive platform on which, by reiterating their humanity and patriotism, *gijichon* Koreans reclaim their membership in the nation proper. In this maelstrom of negotiations about Korean nationhood and national identity, however, the humanity of the Filipinas becomes insignificant.

Migrant Entertainers as Mirrors of the Nation

In news reports in the late 1990s, quarterly and yearly statistics on legal and illegal migrants became a barometer of Korea's prosperity. A new term emerged in these reports: "the Korean dream."[38] The term was used in the title of a Munhwa Broadcasting Company (MBC) documentary on the conditions of Filipina entertainers in 1999. Its genealogy is likely traceable to "the American dream" and, more recently, "the Nippon dream," terms used to describe significant immigration of Koreans to the United States and Japan, respectively, in pursuit of wealth. Most of the reports about migrants and "the Korean dream" appear sympathetic to migrant workers, portraying them as people from developing countries driven by poverty and facing different degrees of exploitation and problems in Korea. Yet they nonetheless help to confirm the inferiority of the migrants—"Korean dream" in this context, is an expression of the superiority of Korea in relation to the developing countries the migrants come from, as it represents the transformation of South Korea from a migrant-sending country to a migrant-receiving country—a "dream" destination for the aspiring foreign poor. A large portion of these migrant workers are from South and Southeast Asia, and their darker skin/phenotype marks them not only as laborers but also as poorer people from developing countries who have come to benefit from Korea's success. The term has been gaining currency, not only in public discourse but also in academic writing in Korea.[39]

This nation-class attitude is reproduced with specific reference to the entry of foreign women as sex workers. The term "inter-girls" (*intogol,* "international girls")—first used in clubs that employ Russian women and later appearing in newspaper headlines—projects a belief that the "internationals" have now come in the female form for the service and pleasure of the (male) Korean people, emphasizing and exaggerating the elevated status of the Korean nation. Their presence has been interpreted as a sign of the success of Korea's globalization project.

The first detailed report on the introduction of Filipina entertainers into GI clubs came in the May 1998 issue of the progressive magazine *Mal* ("Words"), which has featured reports of problems related to the U.S. military in South Korea. Oh Yeon-ho, a journalist well known for his anti-American activism, wrote the article "Filipino Women Imported into USFK Camp Towns" (Chuhan Gijichon-ae Su-ip-ttoen Pilipin Yeoseong-deul). According to Oh, a group of Korean women working in America Town (A-town) in Gunsan contacted him after a Catholic priest who heard their complaints recommended that they approach *Mal*. Three of the women met with him in Seoul to talk about the problems of HIV/AIDS caused by Filipinas and especially the recruitment of underage Filipinas. The women provided the journalist with a printed letter, which they circulated to students in a nearby university protesting the introduction of foreign women into GI clubs, asking to meet with the students. Oh visited A-town and Songtan the following week, visiting five to six clubs as a customer, and met with Filipinas, Korean women, and Korean club owners.

In the article Oh stated that, at its core, the problem of Filipina entertainers in *gijichon* was clearly a problem of human rights. Despite the interviews with Filipina entertainers that revealed employers' undue control and coercion, a close reading of his report reveals his anti-American and anti-globalization agenda. He questioned the granting of E-6 visas and the allowing of Filipinas to practice camp-town prostitution, criticizing the "conscience" (*yangsim*) of the Korean government and the USFK and writing that the Filipinas posed an AIDS threat as they engaged in illegal sexual transactions and were required to receive medical examinations only once a month, while Korean women had weekly STD examinations and blood tests and X-ray examinations every three months. This tacit approval of state control of *gijichon* women's bodies for public health revealed an approval of the instrumentalization of women's bodies for maintaining the health of the national body.

The language of the report revealed a strong subscription to the rhetoric of economic nationalist concerns. Oh repeatedly referred to the women as "national products" (*guk-san-pum*) or "imported products" (*su-ip-*

pum), echoing the consumer nationalist movement. Oh concluded with the following question: "Even if [we] put down all these issues, no matter how much of a globalization era this is, or liberation era this is, even if there is relative advantage of the commodities, do we have to go so far as importing prostitutes?"[40]

The language of human rights was gradually replaced by that of fears about foreign influx. This progression was also evident in the narratives of Korean women whom Oh interviewed. They were adamant about the harm that Filipinas brought to them and their nation, in terms of the outflow of foreign currency (U.S. dollars) and the women's seduction of Korean men who falter in their nationalist duty:

> Given our country's economic situation in this IMF era, do we have to give [U.S.] dollars to Filipinas? We Korean women are receiving money mainly from the U.S. soldiers—that is, it means that *we are [industrial] soldiers who earn U.S. dollars.* If it is the same price, why are [these Korean men] sucking blood from people of the same race? . . . But most of the Filipinas' clients are Korean men. It doesn't mean that these women like Korean people. It just means that they are sucking money from Korean people while giving their hearts to U.S. soldiers. These Filipino women charge Korean men about 300,000 won for a night out, but they give [it] free to US soldiers. That's because they want to immigrate to the States by catching one of these soldiers. (My emphasis)[41]

In my interview with Oh, the author of the article, he made it very clear that he did not agree with the women's claims of patriotism and had reported them only as expressions by the women. Marginalized by mainstream society for their transgression of the ethnonationalist ideal of feminine purity, these women's active deployment of the developmental and nationalist rhetoric of the 1960s and 1970s suggests the alternative modernity that economic nationalism promotes.

Though the term "industrial soldiers" is not usually associated with prostitution, South Korean authorities on various occasions had referred to *gijichon* women as "patriots" and "industrial soldiers" in the 1960s and 1970s.[42] By the same logic, the *gijichon* women from Gunsan mentioned above highlighted their importance in earning foreign exchange for the national economy during the difficult IMF era. They portrayed themselves as nationalists superior to Korean men, who betrayed their own people and further undermined the nation's financial well-being. Constructing the Filipinas as the scheming Others who had no love for Koreans and Korean men as betraying the nation by paying for sex with Filipinas, they reified the Us-vs.-Others divide of Korea's ethnonationalism that marginalized women like themselves as "Western whores" in the first place.

In asserting their membership in the nation proper, these Korean *giji-chon* women highlighted their role in protecting the nation through their sexual labor. When asked if prostitution itself should be done away with, one of them was quoted as saying, "Originally, there should not be prostitution. But if it were not there things like rape would occur even more. They [the U.S. military] rape even when there is prostitution. What would it be like if there were no prostitution? Wouldn't the rape of our country's women in the surroundings of military bases increase? We are the breakwater (*bangpajae*) that stops these things from happening. We should not be despised for what we are doing."⁴³ In other words, they are prostituting *for* the nation. Through their complaints about the harm they suffered from migrant women's entry into *gijichon*, they demanded that the government and the nation recognize their contribution—thus actively reinscribing themselves as legitimate members of the nation-state.

Gijichon women were not the only ones who adopted the developmental rhetoric to speak against their marginalization. The president of the Korea Special Tourism Association, Kim Kyung-su, was arrested on August 22, 1999, as a result of the Angel Club Filipinas' report to the police. A flurry of electronic and print media reported his suspected involvement in trafficking and forced prostitution of foreign women. Kim spoke defiantly on a September 16 television news broadcast about Filipino entertainers' plight in *gijichon*: "The national pride that we people, who have continued to engage in [*gijichon*] business, have is as strong as the insult and coldness that we have received [from Korean society]. We on one hand serve as *industrial soldiers* and on the other we engage in this work as a way of making a living [my emphasis]."⁴⁴ Using the language of cost-effectiveness, Kim side-stepped the accusation that he was bringing in prostitutes and criticized immigration and labor policies that restricted migrant women's entry, especially as regards the paperwork and attendant costs of bringing in "entertainers": "If the government permitted hostesses other than entertainers and women waiting staff to be imported, we could have imported [the women] at a much lower price than the market price now."⁴⁵

The linguistic code used here echoes the military jargon and patriotic fervor of what Seungsook Moon calls the "militarized modernity" of the developmental state under President Park Chung-hee (1962–79), whose authoritarian military regime brought the nation from ruins to riches through intensive industrialization and modernization projects. Moon argues that this rhetoric has shaped the trajectories of gendered political subjectivity for men and women. While Korean men were pushed to support their country as breadwinners and soldiers, Korean women were called upon to be dutiful mothers and rational household managers to ensure healthy families. While both Korean women and men working in factories were hailed as "industrial soldiers" (*saneop-yeok-kkuun*) who helped develop the export-oriented industries in the 1970s, women were segregated in gender-specific industries such as textiles with much lower pay, reaffirming their primary role as reproducers and homemakers. This gendered discourse of "industrial soldiers" reappears in Korean *gijichon* women's arguments concerning the patriotic role their sexual labor played in defending the nation and in Kim Kyung-su's call for recognition of his entrepreneurial devotion to economically empower the nation.

Using the entry of Filipino entertainers as a springboard, both the journalists and the *gijichon* Koreans have thus engaged in a dialogue with mainstream Korean society about the responsibility of the state to the Korean nation in the era of globalization, and especially since the Asian financial crisis. *Gijichon* Koreans in particular use the motif of Koreans working hard for the nation in speaking against their social marginalization and in asserting their own patriotic contribution as legitimate members of the Korean nation. To speak of Filipino entertainers in the language of imported goods, commodities, and immoral Others gives weight to the ideal of the Korean people as having a common set of status, interests, and essence in relation to these foreign Others, and thereby to the claims they make on the nation-state.

* * *

Carrying the magazine article from *Mal*, I paid a visit to Gunsan in March 2000, hoping to see if what had been expressed in the article was a general opinion among Gunsan *gijichon* women. My discussion below does not presume to present the "authentic" voices of the women. I take these narratives as representing self—performativity and not just performance, because personal narratives are always fluid across interpersonal contexts, always serve a political function, and often express the interests of competing groups and subject positions.[46] In the narratives the social is articulated and contested, constitutive of identity and experience, with reference not only to the historical processes of nationalism but also to the micropolitics of *gijichon*.

Sujong, a thirty-four-year-old Korean woman, had been working in America Town for seven years after working for two years as a dancer in Songtan. She had a petite frame and a slightly plump figure, with skin like ivory and long, straight hair. I had met her three months earlier in her club, and she had offered to put me up if I visited America Town again. She was well respected in A-Town, because of her relative seniority and her position as the local gang leader's mistress. She continued to work only as a "drinkie-girl," serving mostly Korean customers. She enjoyed much freedom in her working hours and in the clubs where she worked.

We were sitting on the floor of Sujong's room when I expressed my curiosity about the impact of foreign women entertainers on Korean women. She said immediately, "Of course they affect us a lot (*yeonghyang-i-manji*)." I showed her the article in the magazine, and she read it in silence, nodding her head at times and underlining parts of it. She also added with a sigh, "But our club has decided to bring in six to eight Russian women, because we have no customers. Customers are not coming in if we don't have foreign women. Now we have four dancers and three other women. Business is no good. Because there are no Korean women, we have to bring in foreign women." Before we had time to discuss the article further, she took me to the club where she was working, and there I met the dancers and other hostesses and showed them the article.

Yoonjung was twenty-nine years old. She had been in Gunsan for ten years and worked as a dancer. She was a young-looking woman with a very slim and tall figure, beautifully made-up and dressed. She struck me as being very confident and pretty. Sitting across from me on the low faux-leather couch behind the small glass table in the club, with legs and arms crossed and with her long silky dyed-brown curly hair flowing down to her waist, Yoonjung looked straight at me with her big brown eyes. She was quite quick to dismiss the bad influence Filipinas were accused of, saying that without these foreign women the clubs would all close down: "They come from a poor country. They have come to Korea to make money; that's good. So there's nothing bad about it. They bring in customers; without them all the clubs would be closed. They have come to make money, just like the many Korean women who went to Japan and the States to make money before. I don't see any problem in it."

Equating Filipinas' migration with Korean women who have pursued their American dreams and Nippon dreams with the identical goal of making money, Yoonjung thus not only expressed an appreciation of the Filipinas' presence, proclaiming a laissez-faire attitude toward her foreign counterparts in the club, but also implicitly suggested her own competence in benefiting from the customers they bring in. When I asked about the women who sent the protest letter and talked to the journalist, Yoonjung dismissively said that those women were in fact the problem themselves, since they took drugs and had long left America Town. By this, Yoonjung was suggesting that competition in *gijichon* was fair play and that losers were eliminated from the game.

When we left the club, Sujong realigned herself with Yoonjung's position and elaborated on the failure of the protestors in *gijichon*: "These women are on drugs . . . they never show up for work consistently and take every other day off. Of course the club owners do not treat them well. They don't just take one or two days off but do it continuously. Even when they show up for work, they don't do their job properly. They can't make money, and of course the club owners wouldn't lend them money, given their poor work performance."

Other Korean women I met were also eager to distance themselves from the "victim" image that the magazine article so eagerly portrayed. They defined themselves in contradistinction to these complainants by claiming their sanity, their strength, and their ability to stay on top of the game in *gijichon* despite the influx of foreign women. Sujong's abandonment of her initial complaints about the foreign women and her joining in the critique of the protestors was understandable in this light—she too was unscathed by the competition of migrant women. Opinions about Filipinas therefore become an expression of these Korean women's competitiveness and status in the economy of desire of *gijichon*.

To say that one is doing fine in spite of the competition is one thing. To distinguish oneself from one's competitors is another. Many of the *gijichon* Korean women said that the foreigners were poor women from a poor country who were brought in simply because they were women of a "different color" (*saek-kkari-dallida*) ("color" here refers not only to skin color but also to variety). They countered charges of forced prostitution by suggesting that the Filipinas willingly prostituted themselves for the money, sometimes even using sex as an instrument for other ends (for example, marriage with GIs), without mentioning that Korean women may engage in the same pursuits. In *gijichon* common comments about Filipinas in the clubs were not only that they were women from a very poor country, where the basic club salary of $250 was already a large sum, but also that they were liars and lazybones, ready to make use of any opportunity for easy money. This narrative of the Filipinas' moral flaws as a people thus allows *gijichon* women to claim their Koreanness, with its connotation of the virtues of the moral rectitude and industry that have helped South Korea succeed as a nation-state.

*   *   *

Ajumma Lee accused the Filipinas of betraying the Lees and running away just because two of them wanted to marry their GI boyfriends, thereby bypassing the obvious questions, Why did they have to "run away" in order to do so? And why did others run away with them? For the Lees, the sole focus was on how the Filipinas' own romantic and erotic pursuits were incompatible with their role as migrant labor subjects and their moral obligations to the Lees, without whom they would probably be jobless and penniless. Discussion of workers' rights, employers' contractual obligations, and formal negotiations are muted subjects in employment relationships between migrant workers and Korean employers in general and in the sex trade in particular. Migrant entertainers in *gijichon* embody this disarticulation from a "rights" discourse. The regulatory impulse of both the state and capital is directed at the women, whether for public health reasons, border control, or the accumulation of profits. The celebratory nationalist discourses of South Korea's ethnic homogeneity and economic success, embodied in the motif of the hardworking Korean, harness foreign workers to reproduce the hierarchies that place South Korea above migrant-sending countries. In this perspective, foreign workers are dependents rather than rights-bearing subjects. Within the institutional and discursive contexts that circumscribe the temporality and legitimacy of migrant workers in South Korea, *gijichon* Koreans who confront the arrival of migrant entertainers seek dialogue with the larger society about globalization, women's sexuality, and their membership in the nation. They revived the gendered subjectivities and rhetorics of the developmental state to assert their Korean identity against their marginalization and their resilience in the midst of globalization. The political economy of the Asia-Pacific region that has engendered cross-border travel and migration has facilitated this marginalized group's project to renationalize themselves by articulating their own predicament and aspirations with those of the nation as a whole.

Gijichon women are not a homogenous group, in spite of the very salient discourses that construct their symbolic value to the masculinist nation that flattens the diversity of their experiences. In fact, they occupy different and changing subject positions in the economy of desire of *gijichon* according to age, physical attractiveness, and mode of making a living—and, with the entry of migrant entertainers, ethnicity.

In spite of their similar structural relations to the U.S. military and Korean club owners as women entertainers whose femininity and sexuality are commodified for male consumption, the ethnic divide that is actively reproduced in the identity politics of *gijichon* undermines any effective solidarity between women of different nationalities in *gijichon*. The silencing of migrant women in Korean women's organizations' activism for "*gijichon* women" confirms this nationalist preoccupation. At an international symposium on "*Gijichon*: Women, Nation, and the Military" hosted by Hansori, an umbrella organization of antiprostitution groups, as recently as on October 16, 2008, the main focus was on the South Korean government's responsibility for the plight of Korean women who were mobilized as patriots to serve American soldiers. *Gijichon yeoseong* (literally, *gijichon* women), therefore, is far from a neutral term referring to "women in *gijichon*" but has specific nationalist overtones that by default exclude national Others.

Nationalism is far from obsolete. Filipino entertainers' entry into *gijichon* illustrates how the arrival of foreign workers has generated intersecting projects to renationalize Korean borders. Filipino entertainers thus find themselves not only within the marginal space of *gijichon* but also in the chasm of contradictions of modernity in South Korea. The internal cultural debates that they invoke about the nation and globalization, in turn, reinforce their invisibility as migrants and workers, circumscribing their legitimacy and resources in the context of their reception in South Korea. The next chapter examines how these entertainers are rendered similarly illegitimate and invisible in the Philippines.

Chapter 3
Women Who Hope

On the day of their departure I was standing with Winnie and the other Angel Club Filipinas near the gate at Gimpo International Airport.[1] Winnie, the woman who provoked the death threat by roaming with her fiancé Johnny in the clubs, gave me her fiancé's phone number upon my request so that I could interview him. She said that Johnny was going to visit her in the Philippines, where they were going to get married before moving to the United States.

S: What are you going to do back home?
Winnie: I want to go to Cyprus.
S (surprised): Cyprus? I thought you were going to marry Johnny.
Winnie: Yes. But if he doesn't come [to marry me], I will go to Cyprus (turning halfway and starting to walk toward the gate with the others).
S: Cyprus? (perplexed, following her toward the gate).
Winnie: Yes, Cyprus. My friends say you can make good money there. Good-bye, Sealing. Thank you for all your help. Please tell Johnny that I love him very, very much. I will wait for him in the Philippines. Please tell him for me. OK?
S: Yes. Of course. Take care. Bye.
Winnie: Bye-bye!

As Winnie turned and disappeared through the gate, I waved good-bye, partly amused and partly astonished by her ease in juxtaposing her plan A (of romance, marriage, and moving to the United States) with plan B (of making money in Cyprus). Winnie obviously had no plan to wait like a damsel-in-distress for Johnny and was preparing herself for work overseas again if the marriage plan fell through. Apart from Winnie (who did eventually marry Johnny and move to the United States), at least four of the Angel Club Filipinas left the Philippines again within the next two years, either through marriage or for work. One of them, Angie, returned to South Korea as an entertainer in 2001.

*   *   *

Going home only to want to go somewhere else reveals a subjectivity predicated on the idea that mobility is a desirable, if not necessary, way of life. As scholars of women's rural-to-urban as well as international labor migration in Asia have suggested, this subjectivity is produced as a local response to state modernization projects as well as through media popularization of a global consumer lifestyle.[2] Discourses of progress, development, modernity, and cosmopolitanism inculcate this subjectivity, which desires to achieve these values through participating in modern modes of consumption and production, in modern city spaces, and in the transnational circuit of migration. As Lisa Rofel notes of postsocialist China, affective, sexual, cultural, and material desires are what neoliberal subjectivities are made of, propelling multiple and conflicting quests for modernity at different locations and contesting what post-Mao China could be.[3] With particular reference to migrant labor, the cultural production of this subjectivity of desire is central to the economic production of surplus value dependent on flexible labor.

Individual Filipinas' migration desires, decisions, and trajectories are therefore neither natural nor inevitable. Saskia Sassen has argued that "migration is not simply an aggregation of individual decisions but a process patterned and shaped by existing politico-economic systems."[4] As Winnie's distinct plans for the United States and Cyprus illustrate, she was aware that the two destinations require essentially different connections (Johnny or friends), capacities (love or work), and goals (marriage or money). Both the desire to migrate and the consciousness of the gendered and racialized geography of Filipino migration are shaped by aggressive state actions to facilitate labor out-migration since the 1970s, and the social, economic, and political networks linking the Philippines with foreign labor markets. International migration has thus become a necessary path for the Philippine state as well as individual Filipino citizens' participation in modernization and globalization. Winnie and other migrant women show us that to desire mobility is to be hopeful for a better life.

The Filipina entertainers who are the subjects of this ethnography embody three distinct developments of Philippine labor out-migration in the 1990s. First, women became the majority of land-based migrants. In 1994 land-based female overseas contract workers (OCWs) overtook males and accounted for 60 percent of the total land-based OCWs newly deployed that year—up from 30 percent in 1975 and 51 percent in 1991.[5] The women migrants were mostly entertainers, domestic workers, or nurses. About 95 percent of all migrant entertainers and domestic workers and 92 percent of nurses were women.[6] Second, economic growth in Asia made the region an increasingly important market for Filipino labor migration, with countries such as Hong Kong, Taiwan, and Japan becoming destinations for Filipino migrants as domestic helpers, factory workers, and entertainers, so that Asia overtook the Middle East as the main destination for Filipino overseas contract workers in 1997.[7] Third, circular migration became the norm, with increasing numbers of migrants who renewed their contracts abroad. This migration was encouraged by the state: in the late 1990s the Philippine government lifted bans to countries that failed to provide adequate protection for Filipino overseas workers, and this encouraged migrants to renegotiate and renew their contracts.[8]

Migrant women entertainers also occupy a uniquely ambivalent position among OCWs from the Philippines. This ambivalence springs largely from the assumption that they are mobile prostitutes and thus gender and sexual deviants. As such, female overseas entertainers not only encapsulate the general anxieties about the negative effects women's migration has on the social and moral fabric of the family but also personify the suspicious sexuality of migrant women, whose travels and travails take place outside the domestic sphere. In the 1990s female migrant entertainers became a key symbol of the Philippine state migration policy gone awry, especially following the controversy over the death of Maricris Sioson in Japan in 1991. Sioson went to Japan on an "entertainer" visa in April 1991 and worked as a dancer in a club in Fukishima. Five months later she died at the age of twenty-two. The official cause of death was listed as fulminant hepatitis. However, an official autopsy in the Philippines showed that the cause of death was traumatic head injuries. It was widely believed that she was murdered by her employers.[9] Critics attacked the state for promoting a labor export industry and the degradation of Filipinas abroad. Sioson's body, construed as one coerced and ravaged by foreign sexual aggression, has become a gendered symbol of the state's willing subjugation of the nation within the world political economy.

My analysis in this chapter is threefold. First, I examine how dominant constructions of migrant entertainers in the Philippines—as "willing victims" in state discourse and "victims of sex trafficking" in nationalist discourse—are debates about national progress and modernity, national autonomy, and state responsibilities toward its global citizenry. Together, they express ambivalence around female sexuality, women's changing social roles, and increased mobility. Their focus on sexual deviance and sexual danger also creates a drive for reactionary policies and gender politics that seek to limit women's mobility. Second, I juxtapose these discourses with migrant entertainers' narratives—as desirous, purposeful, and hopeful subjects in spite of overwhelming uncertainty—about their migration decisions, their jobs, and their dreams. Third, the discussion teases out the ways dominant constructions and bureaucratic procedures marginalize and delegitimize these migrant entertainers, in turn shaping how migrant women express their migration decisions and evaluate their experiences. This calls for the inclusion of women's narratives in any attempt to understand these migrant entertainers' experiences, and highlights the violence of imposing preconceived notions about their agency and suffering.

Modern-Day Heroes in the Philippines

Hailed as *ang mga bagong bayani ng bagong milenyo* (our modern-day heroes) by the Philippine government, overseas migrant workers have become an essential part of the nation's economy and global profile.[10] The economic imperative to maintain labor migration is evident in an overview of the country's economy. By 2000 the Philippines had an outstanding foreign debt of over $52.06 billion, while its GDP was a mere $22.59 billion in 2000.[11] In 1998, 70 percent of the GNP was channeled to debt service. This debt burden is a legacy of the country's reliance on foreign borrowing for development since the 1960s and grew from $2 billion to $24 billion between 1970 and 1983.[12]

In 2000, 33.7 percent of Filipino households were estimated to be living below the poverty threshold.[13] Polarization of wealth continues to worsen.[14] The Philippines received $29.1 billion in remittances in 1995–99, second after only India ($45.9 billion).[15] Remittances have become imperative in keeping the Philippine economy afloat, amounting to $6.05 billion in 2000, $8.55 billion in 2004, and $10.7 billion in 2005.[16]

Labor migration began in the 1970s as a stopgap measure to deal with excess labor and to pay debts. The Labor Code of 1974 promulgated by President Marcos recognized the potential of overseas employment to deal with excess labor in the Philippines. In the 1980s overseas employment became part of the government's debt-management policy. President Aquino (1986–92) further relaxed regulations on overseas employment. For 2004 the official estimate of overseas Filipinos was 8 million—of which 3.6 million were documented and 1.3 million were undocumented migrants.[17] In order to regulate the overseas employment industry for the purpose of capital accumulation and to sustain its legitimacy by acting as an arbiter of the interests of private recruiters, overseas workers and their families, and the government, the Philippine state established a set of institutions and organizations to regulate population mobility—what James Tyner calls the "state migratory apparatus."[18] A chief institution in this apparatus is the Philippine Overseas Employment Agency (POEA), set up in 1982, the first of its kind in the world to regulate overseas migrant workers.

Euphemisms of State Legitimacy: Entertainers, Professionals, Willing Victims

"The function of euphemistic labels and jargon is to mask, sanitize, and confer respectability. Palliative terms deny or misrepresent cruelty or harm, giving them neutral or respectable status."[19] Legalistic language that appears to recognize human rights concerns is much more difficult to counter than outright denials. While the outflow of Filipina entertainers has become increasingly significant since the 1990s, the long-standing association between entertainers and prostitutes has opened the Philippine state to much criticism for exporting Filipinas to prostitute. This was also the period during which state discourses in migration endorsed "neoliberal, free trade thinking underpinned by the notion of deregulation."[20] The Philippine state has deployed administrative procedures and practices (professionalization) as well as discursive construction to maintain its legitimacy in regulating the continual outflow of migrant Filipina entertainers, while attributing all responsibilities for harm to women who have chosen to take the risk of prostitution as "willing victims." This operates to erode migrant entertainers' sense of entitlement to state protection of their rights as citizens, migrants, and workers.

Entertainers, but . . .

When sex work is criminalized, state regulation of commercial sex is often performed under an elaborate set of euphemistic labels to mask, sanitize, and confer respectability on the authorities while marginalizing those engaging in sex work. While entertainers, guest relations officers (GROs), hostesses/hosts, and escorts are legally recognized professions in the provision of hospitality services, the government also demands regular health checkups for STD/HIV for these workers, both male and female.

Government monitoring of the STD status of women in the "hospitality business" began as early as the 1930s in the city of Cebu.[21] The Philippine state, like its South Korean counterpart, also maintained mandatory testing for women working in R & R facilities for the U.S. military stationed in the country until 1992, after U.S. colonial rule ended.[22] In the 1970s tourism promotion was a major part of the Philippine government's development strategy,[23] and "hospitality girls"—including "women employed as hostesses, masseuses, waitresses, and dancers employed in nightclubs, cabaret, bars, and similar establishments"[24]—served in establishments catering to foreign tourists as well as locals. The flow of tourists grew dramatically from 166,431 in 1972 to 1,008,159 in 1980. Many of the male tourists, especially those from Japan, were suspected to be on package sex tours.[25] The growth of these tours soon attracted large-scale protests in Japan and the Philippines and led to an appreciable decline[26] in the number of Japanese tourists in the early 1980s. Nevertheless, the number of licensed "hospitality girls" who took regular health checkups and were given health certificates showing them free of diseases increased from 1,699 in 1976 to 7,000 in 1986 in Manila alone.[27] The provision of sexual services, therefore, is presumed, muted, and actively regulated, and yet it is criminalized as part of the Philippine state developmental project.[28]

Criminalizing prostitution is part of a disciplinary regime targeted at female sexuality. It validates "notions of appropriate sexual, gender, and racial behavior in [the] identification of prostitutes as immoral."[29] Policing, arrests, and the penalization of prostitutes are not merely effects of the legal system but productive of the Othering and marginalization of sex workers. The "whore stigma"[30] thus operates to reify ideal female sexuality (in the home, monogamous, reproductive, noncommercial) while threatening those who defy these ideals with legal and moral sanctions. Subsuming the regulation of sex work under a set of euphemisms sustains the criminalization of prostitution, reinforces the stigma against sex workers, and subjects others to the stigma, while allowing those with political and economic privileges to benefit from the trade and evade moral and legal sanctions.

The ambiguities inherent in the category of "entertainer" mean that, although an "entertainer" might not necessarily be engaged in sex work, she will very likely be subject to the stigmatization of prostitution. Lisa Law, in her examination of the sex work and HIV/AIDS discourse in the Philippines, found that her informants experienced "shame" in a variety of ways and that this sense of shame "has spatial coordinates: they map life histories, and affect the way they move through the everyday space of the city and neighbourhood."[31] Such spatial coordinates of this shame may also propel entertainers to embark on overseas migration.

Bella, a seventeen-year-old Filipina who needed a job partly to make money to help pay her mother's debts and she hoped, for her own college education, said, "I don't want to work in the clubs in the Philippines. If I work in a club, if I don't have a choice, I need to go far, where nobody knows me." Anonymity overseas thus mediates the stigma that one would have experienced at home—most Filipina entertainers in *gijichon* in South Korea tell their families that they work as waitresses or factory workers "because they won't understand," "because my mom would think that I do bad things," or "because I don't want them to worry." Of the women I met, only one, a twenty-three-year-old, had told her mother she was an "entertainer," but she had strongly emphasized that she was not doing anything "bad."

Professionals, and . . .

The demand for Filipina entertainers overseas emerged in the 1980s with the increased ease of cross-border travel and the "flexible labor" emblematic of neoliberalism. Between 1981 and 1987 the number of Filipino overseas contract workers deployed to Japan increased from 11,656 to 33,791, 93 percent of whom were female entertainers. Between 1992 and 2000, 76 percent of the 458,819 professionals deployed overseas were women; in 2000, 85 percent of the total of 67,454 female professionals deployed were entertainers (the percentage for male professionals was 18 percent).[32] In the late 1990s migrant Filipina entertainers found their way to the Middle East and Europe and became fixtures in countries as diverse as Singapore, Malaysia, South Korea, Australia, Cyprus, Iran, Iraq, Israel, Spain, Italy, Greece, Belgium, and the Netherlands.[33]

The association between entertainers and prostitutes continues in this women-dominated migration flow. Maruja Asis found, in her interviews with Philippine policy makers and NGO activists, that "most respondents are aware that the majority of entertainers work as hostesses in Japan. There is also the nagging suspicion that many women end up as prostitutes."[34]

However, migrant entertainers who leave the Philippines legally are classified as "professionals," belonging to the subcategory of "overseas performing artists" in Philippine state statistics. According to the POEA, "overseas performing artists" include dancers, composers, singers, and musicians. "Illegal" migrant entertainers who fail to comply with state standards and procedures, whether by failing to leave the country under the proper designation or by engaging in work other than that specified by the designation, are therefore excluded from the legitimate purview of the state.

This professionalization of the category took place in the 1990s, when a series of incidents involving overseas Filipina workers,[35] including Maricris Sioson's death in 1991, provoked a crisis of legitimacy for the Philippine state. In 1995 the RA8042 (the Migrant Workers and Overseas Filipinos Act) introduced specific reforms for migrant entertainers. These included specific training for overseas performance artists, academic and skills tests for Certificates of Competency, and final endorsement by the POEA in the form of the Artist Record Book (ARB). The protection that the Philippine state thereby offered was limited to monitoring the propriety of training and the quality of the entertainers. These provisions failed to address recruitment procedures, conditions of work, and other circumstances that render entertainers vulnerable overseas. According to James Tyner, this professionalization of entertainers as "overseas performing artists" gives tremendous legitimacy to the Philippine state migratory apparatus; yet "[d]iscursively, it is apparent that the exploitation and abuse of female performing artists has, at the government level, been framed as an issue of *legitimacy, morality,* and *proper behavior* of the women themselves."[36]

The practical effects of the new regulations and procedures for prospective entertainers involve greater costs and obstacles to leaving the country and mean that migrants are personally responsible if they run into any trouble overseas. While Japan was considered the best destination for many prospective migrant entertainers, mainly because of better income, South Korea became a good fallback option, as the requirements of the South Korean government were less stringent and did not include possession of an ARB.

It was also possible, and not uncommon, for Filipinas to go to South Korea with passports other than their own, as recruiters and managers provided a network of support for organizing the documents necessary for migration, including forged passports. Ira, for example, had planned to go to Japan initially. She passed the academic test but failed the dancing-skills test four times. Without the qualifications for an ARB, necessary for entry to

Japan, Ira decided to go to South Korea. She auditioned and was immediately picked by a Korean club owner. Instead of using her own passport to apply for a visa, Ira agreed to use the passport of someone else who, according to the manager, had backed out from the recruitment but had already received a visa for South Korea. Another Filipina, seventeen-year-old Bella, had entered with a passport that had belonged to a twenty-five-year-old. She related how she had seen her own mother's passport, which her mother had sold some years previously, inside the check-in station at the Camp Casey U.S. military camp.

However, as I learned from conversations with Filipinas, those who arrived in 1999 found it necessary to take a detour to Hong Kong or Bangkok in order to get their E-6 visas, reflecting the increasing difficulties of getting the visa in the Philippines. By engaging in this operation, both the recruiter and the woman were "test[ing] the limits of fate through patent gambles and unhedged bets against the international state system."[37]

"Willing victims"

In my interview with the labor attaché of the Philippine Embassy to South Korea, Mrs. Alfonso, in 2000, I discussed my experience with the Angel Club Filipinas and other Filipina entertainers in South Korea. Mrs. Alfonso, in her mid- to late forties, struck me as a much-muted version of Imelda Marcos in terms of her fashion sense and accessory choices, as well as in her very elegant and measured pace in speaking English—very unlike the Filipinas I was used to meeting in *gijichon*. After some discussion of the difficulties of having a sustained working relationship with the Ministry of Culture, Mrs. Alfonso commented on the situation of Filipina entertainers in South Korea. She acknowledged that some of them had received false information from recruiters, "but some of (the Filipina entertainers) are really *willing victims*. Some of them have already been to Japan, but still, they are *willing* to come to Korea (my emphasis)."[38] In Mrs. Alfonso's narrative, women's experience and knowledge of prostitution as part of their job as entertainers are coded in the word "Japan"—the implication being that such women were no longer innocent and therefore could not legitimately make claims for state protection. The term "willing victims" in fact appears in state discourse that specifically refers to migrant entertainers who run into trouble overseas because of prostitution. It first appears in the 1995 Senate report on the death of Maricris Sioson. The report concludes that the entertainer who encounters abuse can be considered "a willing vic-

Figure 5. Boarding pass for a Filipina entertainer who transited in Hong Kong on her way to Seoul

tim": "to make ends meet, because [the entertainer] has accepted pay rates lower than that stipulated, and because of the pressure from her family at home, who are counting solely on her to deliver them from their economic hardships, she would in the extreme, turn to the easiest way of making money—prostitution. And hence, she herself becomes a willing victim."[39]

To emphasize women's "willingness" (as Mrs. Alfonso did) amplifies women's agency, intent, autonomy, and therefore responsibility, while diminishing the accountability of the state in addressing their vulnerabilities to abuse. This discourse of willing victim has the curious effects of both recognizing the vulnerabilities of migrant Filipina entertainers overseas *and* abrogating state responsibility for any harm that they suffer. The discourse of "willing victims" allows the state to actively shift all responsibilities to migrant women. It further precludes consideration of the more fundamental issue of migrants' rights and safe migration.

In teasing out the discursive strategies of the media and various agencies of the state following the death of the entertainer Maricris Sioson, James Tyner has observed that initially Sioson's death was framed by the larger context of the exploitation and oppression of migrant workers in general. As the months passed, however, the causes of exploitation were placed squarely on the "backs" of abused women migrants, and particularly those who supposedly epitomized a dangerous and/or deviant female sexuality.[40] The task for the state, in this logic, becomes preventing women of questionable values and morals from migrating overseas as "entertainers."

Contract, Knowledge, and Disempowerment

Off a narrow winding road amidst the paddies in Gyeonggi Province, the provincial area surrounding Seoul where a large number of undocumented migrants work in small factories, was a tin-roofed hut of about 180 square feet, where Katie, thirty-two years old, and May, nineteen years old, were living with their Filipino boyfriends. We first met in March 1999 through Father Glenn, the Filipino priest who ran the Filipino Migrant Center in Seoul and held Mass in cities with large numbers of Filipino migrants.

A single mother, Katie used to run a mom-and-pop store at her family home in a small town near Pampanga, but business was not good and she did not make money. She then moved to Manila to work in factories, leaving her three-year-old son with her family. Three years later a friend at work introduced her to a manager, who offered to help her go to South Korea. The job would involve "serving drinks and talking to customers." Her sisters and mother were already working abroad, but sour family relations had prevented her from seeking their help for overseas employment. The opportunity to go to South Korea gave Katie the chance to be independent and a good mother to her son by making more money.

A manager recruited May from a small village near the city of Baguio. She had just finished high school. She decided to leave home and go to South Korea because "there was nothing to do at home," and she "wanted to see the world."

When I met them, the two women had run away together from the club in which they had been working in mid-1998 because the club owner had planned to set up their quarters for prostitution. They had then tried to get factory jobs but were not successful. They were being supported by their Filipino boyfriends who had entered South Korea as industrial trainees and then overstayed as undocumented migrants. Neither of the women had told their families about their jobs. They talked about how their recruiter in the Philippines had not said that prostitution was part of their job.

S: If you go back to the PI, would you go to your Filipina manager [recruiter]?

(May and Katie laugh.)

Katie: NO! Because they told us, "If you break the contract, if you run away, you have to [pay a] penalty; you have to pay $5,000 as penalty for breaking the contract."

S: That's why you won't go back? And you won't tell the police?

Katie: No. We are scared.

S: Of what?

Katie: I don't know. I am just scared. I don't know what to say. Because it's still my fault.

May: Yes. Because we wanted to come here.

Katie: Yes, we wanted to come here. We agreed easily. They just talked nicely, and we just grab [sic] it.

What Katie and May communicated is an awareness of the illegitimacy of their own migration decision—taking the risk that selling sex might be part of the deal entails relinquishing claims on the state or on general sympathies. First of all, their "fault" was to have "wanted to come" to South Korea—a transgressive desire to go beyond their gendered station at home. Second, they had "agreed easily." Most overseas Filipinas have learned tragic stories of other Filipinas' overseas migration, whether from friends or the media.[41] Katie, who had watched the film *The Flor Contemplacion Story* and learned about her mother's dangerous experiences overseas, was not stopped from leaving the Philippines by such knowledge.[42]

The contract, which embodies the modern liberal ideal of individual autonomy and civil equality between the contracting partners, comes to acquire very different meanings for the migrant entertainers.[43] The employment contract for Filipina entertainers (see Appendix II) that the Filipinas sign with the Korea Special Tourist Association was emphatically a means of control to protect employers' interest against "wilful disobedience" and other events that prevent employees from working, including "escape," pregnancy, and marriage. The contract states that any entertainer who "escape[s] from the club" to other (work)places or "escape[s] for living together with the guys [*sic*]" will be reported to the police and Immigration as a criminal case. For Katie and May, as well as other Filipinas, clause 9— specifying that they need to pay a compensation of $3,000 if they leave the job before termination of the contract—effectively stops them from quitting. In some cases they may find customers who would pay the compensation to release them from the job; in most others "escape" is the logical alternative.

The contract lays out employment conditions such as hours of work, number of days off, and compensation. However, as will be discussed in Chapter 4, club management differs significantly from what is laid down in the contract. Most of the Filipina entertainers knew that their job required the performance of feminine sexual appeal to entertain the customers. Yet those who knew that they would be "serving drinks and talking to" male customers did not know of the quota of drinks they were expected to fulfill, those who knew of "sexy dancing" did not know of some clubs' "naked" dances, and those who expected to have sex for money did not know of the arbitrary rules and penalties that undermine their physical and financial autonomy. The exact conditions of their jobs were subject to individual club management, and different individuals handled these unexpected demands in different ways.

While Katie and May saw themselves as liable to be penalized according to the contract for running away from the club, they did not see themselves making a legitimate claim against recruiters and employers who did not fulfill their contractual obligations. They incorporated their awareness of the risks into the contract and held themselves responsible—just as state and recruiters wanted. The power differentials between them and the club owners and recruiters were too great. Running away rather than negotiating with club owners as equals or seeking help from law enforcement as legitimate plaintiffs is therefore a common way to deal with unsatisfactory working conditions. The very regulatory structure that taps into the ambiguities of the term "entertainers" reproduces the moral sanction against prostitution and the gendered operation of sexual stigma that disempowers those it claims to protect and "professionalize."

A Sign of the Nation—Entertainers as Victims

In addition to the Philippine state discourses, journalistic, academic, and activist discourses interacted with each other in representing and making claims about Filipinas in prostitution overseas. While these representations try to communicate the conditions of migrant entertainers' vulnerabilities overseas and take the government to task, the emphasis on the victimhood of migrant entertainers has the reverse implication on female agency as it empties the women of any agency and complexity in their migration. Entertainers figure in these discourses as symbols of the subordinate position of the Philippines in the new global order and as evidence to accuse the state of failing in its responsibilities.

News reports with titles such as "150 Pinays Sold as Sex Slaves in Africa"[44] have become common refrains in the Philippine print and online media since the mid-1990s. The famous Philippine director Lino Brocka, whose realist films deal with subjects of poverty and the culture of the masses, portrays the labor-related sexual subordination and abuse of Philippine migrant entertainers as a product, as much as a symbol, of the nation's powerlessness. These female figures embody "the feminized position of the Philippines in the newer global division of capital and labour."[45]

In the late 1990s "sex trafficking" became a powerful shorthand for expressing these concerns in the NGO sector. GABRIELA, the Philippine national women's alliance, has charged the state with participating in the "sex trafficking" of entertainers: "Among recruiters, bar owners, matchmakers and pimps, the government itself is a vehicle for the continuing and worsening incidence of sex trafficking. The government plays the tormentor's accomplice in this unending tragedy."[46] In these discourses that construct entertainers as victims of "sex trafficking" or "sexual slavery," narratives about migrant entertainers have three common elements: first, they are *poor women* who migrate out of desperate poverty; second, they are *innocent women* who are ignorant of the risks of working as "entertainers"; third, they are *powerless women* coerced into sexual servitude. I do not claim that these are untrue or nonexistent situations. However, if we leave these assumptions intact as generalizations of the experiences of all migrant entertainers, we are liable to (1) miss a great deal of the complexity of these women's migration projects, erasing their subjectivities and voices in the process; and (2) reproduce the structures that seek to inscribe women into particular gender and sexual regimes, dismissing their efforts to search for alternative avenues to power and freedom.

Nerferti Tadiar has powerfully critiqued the nationalist discourses that treated the bodies of overseas Filipina domestic helpers—especially those who experience exceptional violence—as mere signs in contested constructions of the national body. The consequence, Tadiar warns, is confining political struggle to global juridical reform, expanding state powers of regulation, reaffirming bourgeois democratic ideals, and preventing a critique of global capitalism.[47] Tadiar suggests that Filipina domestic helpers are capable of "dreaming other worlds in other ways"—ways that differ from those of scholars who write about their suffering, exploitation, and oppression, who are "trapped by fantasy-ideals of critically-conscious, sovereign subject-agents of heroic resistance and change."[48]

This critical reflexivity and emphasis on migrant women's agency and alternative visions, however, is disappointingly absent in Tadiar's analysis of Filipina migrant entertainers. In her discussion of the masculinist state promotion of regional trade in pursuit of the "Asia Pacific dream," Tadiar describes "the international economy of forced prostitution" through which Filipina entertainers are recruited to Japan.[49] She concurs with the Filipina feminist activist Liza Margoza Maza in identifying this movement of Filipinas as "modern-day slavery of women brought about [by] 'imperialist globalization.'"[50] Here, Tadiar embraces activist discourse about migrant entertainers without a trace of the reflexivity that she proposed for understanding Filipina domestic workers' agency. Does the conception of women's agency and alternative visions stop when they participate in sexual-economic exchange?[51]

I agree with Tadiar that we need to examine migrant Filipinas' "practices of living that attest to *who* they are as creative forces rather than *what* they might be for others,"[52] and I propose that we do not exclude migrant entertainers in this project.

Desire, Dreams, and Hope in Migration

Labor migration has long been an exit strategy for women from their gendered subordination since the 1980s in Southeast Asia.[53] In the Philippines, even though the percentages of women who enroll in primary, secondary, and tertiary education are equal to or higher than those of men,[54] fewer women are employed, and those who are employed find themselves in lower-paying[55] and less prestigious jobs than their male counterparts. In 2000 only one-third of the labor force in the Philippines was female.[56] All but four of the twenty-three Filipinas I had regular contact with were high school graduates, and some had received two-year college diplomas, but only ten had ever had a paid job, and six of them had worked only as entertainers/hostesses. A woman's prime responsibility is seen to lie with her family, and her public role is typically subordinate to her family obligations. As in many other countries, a woman's access to economic assets is indirect and mediated through her husband. Furthermore, eleven of the twenty-three women were single mothers, five of whom had had children with men to whom they were not married, while the other six had been married to their children's fathers. Most of the married women had experienced some form of domestic violence that drove them to leave their husbands well before they came to South Korea.[57] One woman's husband had run away after the birth of their third child two years prior to my interview with her, and another woman's husband had died within a year of their marriage. As single mothers and married women, these women could hardly find jobs that could sustain them and their children, and they suffered the additional stigma of living in a Catholic country that idealizes female purity and prohibits divorce. These are important social contexts within which entertainers migrate, but it is to their desires, dreams, and hopes that I turn in the following pages.

Janet was working at one of the clubs in Songtan when I met her in March 1999. Twenty-four years old, she was a single mother of a two-year-old daughter. She had completed computer studies at a two-year college and had had an office job before she came to South Korea.

S: Why did you come here?

Janet: For money, of course. ∴ . . . I have come here to make money for my family and my daughter. I don't want her to grow up like me.

S: Were you very poor when you were a kid?

Janet: Well, not very poor. But if we wanted to buy something we like [*sic*], we couldn't because we didn't have the money. Now I make money and I send [*sic*] them [my family] so that they can buy whatever they want.

The modern consumer desires Janet expressed suggest that it is a relative poverty that has propelled many to pursue the opportunity to work abroad, so that one and one's family could "buy whatever they want."[58] Like other migrant women, entertainers spend much of their money on consumer products (for example, PlayStations, television sets, brand-name sneakers), gold jewelry (which could be pawned in times of need), sending children to private schools, and parents' visits to private hospitals, rather than just feeding the family. Migration is the opportunity for these women to fulfill their aspirations for upward class mobility, or approximating it for themselves and their family. Janet's response throws critical light on the "poverty" argument that is all too commonly used to explain migration decisions.

Migrant Filipina entertainers make and remake the meanings of their migrations often between two different sets of social relations and cultural values: gendered familial obligations and personal aspirations. These are not necessarily mutually exclusive considerations and often combine to propel migration. "To make money for my family" is usually the first response to the question, "Why did you come to Korea?" *Utang na loob,* a Tagalog term that literally means "debt of the inside" and may be translated as "an individual's indebtedness to her or his family," is frequently cited as the cultural force for Filipinos' labor out-migration and a primary reason for women's migration.[59] Yet like other migrant women, some of the Filipina entertainers in *gijichon* had left for South Korea against parental advice, harboring particular desires for travel, consumption, and adventure. Their migration was often a pursuit of self-making.

What I propose here is an understanding of the vitality of hope in migration. Migrants leave home hopeful, with dreams of fulfilling both familial obligations and personal pursuits of modernity and with only a vague idea of what is in store for them. The migrant Filipinas arrive in South Korea and develop an awareness that their migration could be a watershed moment in which they may have the opportunity to reshape their lives. Migration is both the object and a site of hope, for it opens up new alternatives to what life could be. Hirokazu Miyazaki reminds social scientists to incorporate hope into their investigations and critiques. It takes courage of the mind for hope to become a method, prompting the search for alternatives.[60] Migrant entertainers, I would argue, embody both this courage of the mind and the hope that animates a search for alternatives and possibilities.

Bella: It's my decision [to come to South Korea]. I want to explore a new life. I want to help my mother. I can't find a job in the Philippines—

that's why I come [*sic*] here. I thought maybe if I go . . . because my mother told me I would get a lot of money in Korea. That's why I came—because I thought I could go to college next year, and I could help my mom.

S: Do you think you would still go to college next year when you go back?

Bella: Yes. Even though I didn't get a lot of money here, I can still be a working student. I love school—I want to have a degree, to finish college. I don't want to be old and you don't have knowledge, you only are a graduate from high school. I want to work in an office, I want to have a business. . . . If I get a HRM [hotel and restaurant management degree], I will get a restaurant; if I take computer [engineering], maybe working; and when I have enough money, my mom loves to cook, maybe we'll have a restaurant.

From college graduate to white-collar office worker to computer engineer to a restaurant owner with her mother—Bella was on a roll with dreams about her future. While these dreams may appear ordinary to middle-class women in both the First and Third Worlds, these fantasies of what they could become constitute an important practice for these Filipinas in their migration. This conversation with Bella took place three months after she arrived in South Korea. Six months later she was telling me about plans to marry her GI boyfriend, move to the United States, finish college, and become a GI herself one day.

In fact, marriage to a GI is a dominant theme in the lives of Filipina entertainers in *gijichon*. I met the five Filipinas working at the Pussy Cat Club when their contracts were ending, and they were about to return to the Philippines. They said that their experiences in South Korea had been very good because the club owners treated them like "daughters." They had come to make money for themselves as their families did not depend on them for remittances. In fact, a few of them said that they had never sent money home while in South Korea. I asked my usual question about what they wanted to do back in the Philippines, since they were leaving in two weeks. They said, with a remarkable lack of enthusiasm, that they intended to return to school or to find another job. I decided that I would ask them what they would like *most* to do. They laughed together when someone said, "To get married and go to the States!"

S: Why the States?

Brenda: It's a dream for us to go to the States. But it's hard to go there. We always want to do that.

S: What do you want to do there?

Brenda: To work. People say that it's easy to find a job there. And you can get a lot of money even just by working for three hours, like serving [in a restaurant], or work at a McDonald's. It's a dream for many people.

Their "American dream" has a specific political and cultural resonance with the Philippine history as a U.S. colony (1898–1948) and related migration.[61] In spite of the country's declaration of independence in 1948, the dominance of American culture and institutions in the Philippines remains pervasive. The United States continues to be viewed as *the* land of opportunities for many. As Deirdre McKay observes in her discussion of international marriage between Filipina domestic workers and Canadians, "Filipina women form their own identities within colonial histories that privilege a particular form of Americanized modernity and imaginary of romantic love. . . . 'American' men (a category that includes Canadians and all Caucasians) are seen to be good providers, romantic lovers, and unlike Filipino men, not given to keeping mistresses." The hope that Brenda and her fellow entertainers expressed, with laughter, just before their departure from Korea contrasts with their lackluster responses about returning home. When what they want "most" is to realize the "dream" to get married and "go to the States,"[62] we see an agitated hope generated specifically after working for a year entertaining American GIs in *gijichon*, amidst the generalized anxieties of returning home to be "emplaced" with no opportunity to leave.[63] This also reflects the gap between the idealization of the United States as a land of opportunities and iconic modernity (McDonald's) and the poor opportunities for attaining such ideals in the Philippines.

Migration is therefore a site of hope—in addition to being a site of exploitation, abuse, discrimination, and alienation. The concept of hope allows us to focus on the future-oriented approach that migrant entertainers employ in shaping the meaning of migration. People who decide to migrate are motivated by expectations for material and immaterial rewards that migration could bring for oneself and one's family: money, consumer goods, adventure, and social status. Yet these expectations are riven with anxieties about the risks and dangers of the alien environment. In the migration site, new experiences and social relations allow the exploration of new subjectivities, as migrants acquire new knowledge about their power and vulnerability, limitations and potentials, desires and dreams.

Violence and Trafficking—in Her Own Words

Most of the Filipinas I met between 1998 and 2000 had not heard of "trafficking" or had only a vague idea of it (as a "crime"). Bella was the only exception. As her entertainer training in the Philippines had involved only sitting and drinking with customers, she was not prepared to be placed in a club where she was pressured (with the offer of one hundred dollars per month on top of her three-hundred-dollar base salary) to perform naked "water-and-whip shows" and sell sixty ladies' drinks per week. After less than a month she ran away with four other Filipinas from the club. She wanted to work in a factory, but since there was a crackdown on undocumented migrants in factories, she decided to work in a club again. Her Korean manager found her a new club, but then she and another Filipina were caught by the club owner and his assistant from the first club, beaten up, and then taken to the TDC police station. At the police station, with the person who beat her up acting as interpreter (Bella could not speak Korean), the owner gave them three choices: they could pay a five-thousand-dollar penalty and go free; go to jail; or continue working for him. Bella and her friend then "decided" to go back to the first club. The police made Bella and her friend apologize to the club owner and sign an agreement that they would not run away again or they would have to pay five thousand dollars each, and that they would not seek help from GIs. She was angry with the police for siding with the club owners. Two days after Bella returned to the first club, however, the club owner asked the Filipinas' manager to take them away. In a new club Bella had to do only "sexy dance," and there was no drinks quota. She "liked it better here."

S: Have you heard of "trafficking" in the Philippines?

Bella: You mean human trafficking? I know that they are doing human trafficking because they use different passports. For example, I didn't use my own passport. I used the passport of a different name. They wanted me to leave quickly; they got the passport of someone else's [*sic*]; I used a passport that said I was twenty-five years old.

S: And you know that this is part of "trafficking"?

Bella: Yes. Because they brought Filipinas here, and they explained differently [working conditions are different from what they said]. Like you can get a lot of money here, you don't need to work—like cleaning the clubs, etc., you just have to dance. It's just different words. When we came here, it was very different. Because some clubs want you to have sex just to get money.

Bella rightly identified the criminality of false documents and fraudulent claims as constitutive of human trafficking. Yet the relevance of the discourse and criminality of trafficking stopped there for Bella. She did not feel the need to be rescued from *gijichon*. She also never expressed regret that she had come to South Korea as an entertainer. In fact, she insisted, "It was my decision to come." In addition, we had learned about her series of dreams for the future. Her "worst experience" was neither the "water-and-whip show" nor the fact that she was being beaten up; it was that "no one helped" her while she was beaten on the streets. The club owner told the two GIs who walked by that Bella was being punished for stealing money. She was too shocked to refute the claim. The episode epitomized for her the extent to which she was Othered and marginalized as a migrant entertainer, and the illegitimacy and isolation that resulted.

Yet neither the state discourse of "willing victims" nor the activists' proclamation of her as a "victim of sex trafficking" would address these problems. For the well-meaning activists who believe that the cause of Bella's suffering is having to get naked, the ultimate solution is to rescue her from the club, bring and keep her home,[64] and stop other women from leaving as entertainers. The general vulnerabilities of migrants, their working conditions, their access to channels of redress for violation of their basic rights, the discriminatory attitude towards migrant populations in the host country, remain remote subjects when the gaze is set on the naked body.

*   *   *

This chapter has tried to illuminate the fissure between dominant constructions of migrant entertainers and migrant women's aspirations. Knowledge about migrants—definition, categories, and numbers—does not merely reflect an external reality but is productive of the meanings of this mobile population and confers legitimacy and authority on those who have the power to produce such knowledge. Tyner has suggested that the focus on sexuality allows the "sexual elements of these women's employment to overshadow all other attributes, characteristics, or subjectivities of the entertainer concerned."[65] With this preoccupation with sexual deviance and sexual shame, the subjectification of migrant entertainers in both state and civil society discourses in the Philippines makes invisible the multiple meanings and aspirations that women invest in their migration projects.

The discussion further seeks to illuminate the politics of knowledge production in understanding migrant women's bodies and sexuality and the concrete effects these discursive constructions exert on their sense of self. The human-rights lawyer and scholar Alice Miller asks the crucial question, "How do we ensure that our interventions focused on stopping harm against women do not unknowingly reinscribe and reinforce the idea that the most important thing about a woman is her sexual integrity (formerly known as her 'chastity')?"[66] Both state and civil society discourses reproduce the stigma of prostitution that ultimately disempowers women who perform sexual labor and undermines their sense of legitimacy as rights-bearing subjects.

In spite of the uncertainties and the exploitative conditions in *gijichon*, most of the women constantly engage with the possibilities that migration offers—not just in financial terms but also in social, physical, sexual, and romantic arenas. They do not see themselves as "professionals," "prostitutes," or "victims of sex trafficking" but rather in terms of their multiple subjectivities and possibilities in migration, encapsulated in their sense of "self." Migration allows these women to defy their gendered subordination at home and search for new possibilities abroad, but it also subjects them to a different gender and sexual ordering with which they need to contend.

Bella complained that GIs call Filipinas "juicy girls" and "butterflies." I asked, "What do you want them to call you?" "Nothing!" she replied. "Just, if they don't know me, just smile. If they know me, they can call my name." In Bella's terms, ignoring her would be better than calling her by just any name that one sees fit to use. The demand for acknowledgment and respect in asking for a smile and for recognition of her as an individual with a name may also apply to others who try to address women like Bella. Imposing the category of "victim" on them is as much an interpellation as GIs calling them "juicy girls." Both produce the women as subjects in one's ideology/fantasy, failing to recognize their self-making projects and their search for and practice of alternatives in migration. It is to this vitality of hope and agency, and the ability to negotiate and strategize in spite of their marginalization as migrants, as prostitutes, as deviants, that I turn in the next section.

PART III

Transnational Women from Below

A Day in *Gijichon*, December 1999

I met Ira and Lou from the Mermaid Club at the Olympic Restaurant in TDC at 1:00 P.M. There really was not much choice besides the Olympic—Ira and Lou liked fried chicken and spaghetti, and few restaurants near TDC served these dishes. Many other Filipinas and GIs were regulars at the Olympic. We usually met around noon. I generally started my journey from Seoul at 9:00 or 10:00 A.M., about the time they got up.

Neither of them had a date that day. They usually tried to meet up with their customers/boyfriends in the daytime. If one of them had a date and the other did not, the two of them would still go out together. It is common for GIs to pay for the meals not only of their dates but also their dates' friends. If I did not ask to meet them, they would probably cook. Their ten-thousand-won food allowance per week did not allow them much meat, which was very expensive in South Korea. The difficulty of getting meat in their diet was one of the Filipinas' frequent complaints about life here. In spite of their complaints, however, many of them gained weight after coming to South Korea. They tended to have snacks after work in the early hours. Sometimes GIs would get food for them from the base. They cooked "milk fish" last week—I had never tried it before. They said they had it in the Philippines, and the commissary on base was the only place to get it in Korea. I asked Ira if she paid the GI for the fish. She answered, "No, I don't pay him. I just tell him what I want and he will get it for me"—just like the phone cards, shampoo, conditioner, chocolate bars, spaghetti, and cooking sauce that their GI customers/boyfriends would often provide.

After lunch I asked them to help me move some of my friend's belongings. We walked past a video shop on our way. Lou, as I expected, asked me to rent some videos for them. To thank them for helping me, I did. If they were not with me, they would probably be sitting at home, going through their photo albums or listening to CDs their customers had copied for them. It was not payday (every first and fifteenth of the month, like those of GIs), and they would not be shopping in "second market"—the nearby market area where they could get clothes, makeup, and stationery. They picked two out of the range of Hollywood movies available in the shop. We went back to their room behind the club. Four of them shared the two double beds in the same room. Bella was lying in bed talking to her boyfriend on her mobile phone. Candy was out, apparently drinking with her Filipina friends at the Montana Club. Filipinas who never drank in the Philippines (a gendered taboo) might take up serious drinking in Korea—especially popular was the strong and cheap Korean liquor soju—and have drinking parties in the afternoon.

They played the movie *Enemy of the State* on the VCR-TV. The owner of their club, "Daddy," had been very generous to provide them with the equipment; not many Filipinas had such luxury. They chatted to each other and to their customers on the phone. Ira called two of her customers and asked if they would visit her at the club that night. Jamie, her "real" boy-friend, was in field practice for two weeks. Drink sales were really bad in the club for everyone except Candy. Candy had many drinks, they said. For one thing, Candy was the only one who regularly went into the VIP room with her customers.

At around 5:00 P.M. they started getting ready for work. They took turns taking showers in the kitchen, as there was no separate shower room. Then they changed into their "working" clothes—they decided that the theme was going to be jeans and T-shirts that night. They put makeup on and went into the club just after 6:00 P.M. It was a very big club with almost seventy seats and a pool table. There was also a small stage as well as a dance area. "Mommy," the mother of the club owner, was already sitting at the bar. She did not speak a word of English but took care of cleaning the club. Onni ("elder sister" in Korean), the bartender, was a Korean woman who used to be married to an American. Her husband died, she said, and now she lived alone in TDC. Ajumma—the Korean waitress in her midfifties—also came in at around 6:30 P.M.

I sat around with the Filipinas on the crimson faux-leather seats in front of the stage. The club was dimly lit. Lou demonstrated some of the moves she had learned in the club where she previously worked, where the women had to perform dance shows every night. I tried to copy some of her gyrating moves, but without much success. Here the stage and the pole were more for decoration. They had been installed in all the clubs hiring Filipina entertainers to prepare for checkups by the Immigration Office—

for according to immigration laws, the women were entertainers recruited to dance and/or sing, not to sit with customers.

There was not one customer when I left them at 7:00 P.M. Normally more GIs would start going "downrange" at around 8:00 P.M. December was not a good month for business because GIs saved money to buy and send gifts home and had less money for spending in the clubs. Moreover, Ira had heard the previous day that "girls in Mermaid" had a bad name for being "stuck-up" because they would not go on bar fines (other than with their "real" boyfriends). It was to be another long, quiet night for them until the club closed at midnight.

Chapter 4
The Club Regime and Club-Girl Power

When the seven Filipinas returned to TDC with the Lees the evening after the seven-hour negotiation, they did not get to just pick up their bags and meet up with their boyfriends as they had hoped. Annabel, in a phone conversation with me after she had returned to the Philippines, said that the Lees, in order to help get Mrs. Lee out of jail, locked the doors and made them testify on videotape that there had been no forced prostitution.

> Onni [Ms. Lee] made us speak on videotape. First, she asked us, "How are you?" She then said they wanted to prove that the police were wrong. They wanted us to tell the police that the *ajumma* didn't push us to have sex. I was really nervous. They locked us up in the house. They wanted to go back to the police (with the tape). On the tape, all of us talked. I didn't say what they wanted at first. The other girls were mad at me. They wanted to get out. Their boyfriends were waiting for them outside. . . . For me, it was not right. I think I said, "She pushed me to have sex with a Korean." Then Onni said, "Annabel, I want this to help my mother to get out of jail." Other girls said, "Annabel, we want to get out!" So I said, "Yes, she didn't push us to have sex." Then for the first time, they gave us good food, very nice food.

By locking in the women while appealing for help, instead of explicitly threatening them, the Lee siblings exercised a blend of coercion and emotional appeal, with good food as a reward. The Filipinas, however, had different reasons for compliance. Instead of protesting in unison against being locked up, they complied with the Lees' request because it was much more important for them to meet their boyfriends. What the Lees planned to do with the tape mattered little to them—they would never have taken the case to the police if Father Glenn had not talked them into it. Annabel gave in not so much to Ms. Lee as to peer pressure. Their compliance thus seems to have been a result of relative indifference, with the investment of energies in more valuable pursuits.

*   *   *

This chapter examines the ways labor control operates in *gijichon* clubs and how Filipina entertainers respond to the regulation of their bodies, labor, and identities through a combination of accommodation, evasion, and resistance. The marginal status of Filipina entertainers in relation to the Koreans and to the Philippine state means that Korean club owners can wield enormous power over the migrant women who work and often live on club premises, and who are largely dependent on their employers for everyday living. It is uncommon for Korean club owners to lock up Filipina entertainers, but although what the Lees did was exceptional, it bespeaks the power they can exert on their employees.

Club owners commonly deploy a familial discourse in the clubs, establishing themselves as benefactors while maintaining control over their migrant women employees. As Foucault suggests, "Power is tolerable only on condition that it masks a substantial part of itself. Its success is proportional to its ability to hide its own mechanisms." The disciplinary regime in the club that seeks to control the women's bodies and their emotional, physical, and sexual labor is often implemented in terms of parental concern for "daughters" who need guidance and discipline. Within this disciplinary regime, Filipina entertainers comply while creating space for maneuvering. They resist club owners' attempts to contain and profit from their bodies and sexuality by actively seeking out crevices and openings in the operation of power to pursue their own migration projects of independence, adventure, romance, and other promises of modernity. In vulnerable positions as migrant women, cheap foreign labor, and prostitutes in *gijichon*, Filipina entertainers are not the docile bodies that a structural analysis might presume them to be. Laboring in the twilight zone of legitimacy between state regimes, with little recourse to rights protection and vulnerable to employers' abuse, migrant entertainers actively deploy what available resources they can—narrative, gestures, silence—to attempt to control their migratory experience and make it personally meaningful.

Regulating "Other" Bodies

A capitalist logic informs the regulation of bodies and emotions in the club. Studies of female factory workers in China have detailed the microlevel control of women's bodies—not only through skills they need but also through their daily routines, including their working time, meal times, and even the frequency and duration of bathroom breaks—all for the maintenance of an efficient and productive assembly line. Such a spirit for maximizing profits could be observed in *gijichon* clubs.[2] More interesting to our present discussion, however, are the cultural logics underlying the club regime, which are informed by and deploy gender, family, and ethnic identities and interests to exercise control over the migrant entertainers.

On a general level, *gijichon* club owners subscribe to the dominant view that migrant workers are from an inferior nation-class. Club owners' narratives about Filipina entertainers construct them as "poor," "stupid," and "ungrateful," reinforcing the club owners' own sense of ethnic superiority as well as legitimizing unsympathetic control of these ethnic Others. Different clubs adopt different modes of familistic discourse to elicit the active cooperation of the workers, with varied success. In addition to providing an understanding of the diversity of management regimes in *gijichon*, I examine them as regimes of subjectification to consider how they produce Filipina entertainers as particular ethnic, gender, and sexual Others and shape the ways they accommodate, resist, and negotiate labor control with their Korean club owners.

Construction of the Philippines and the Filipinas in *Gijichon*

It did not take long for Filipina entertainers to learn that they were treated differently and often more heavily regulated than their Korean counterparts in the clubs. Some clubs explicitly prohibited communication between Korean and Filipina entertainers, using a divide-and-rule approach to prevent conflicts, on one hand, and ensure division, on the other. The Filipina entertainers were aware that Korean entertainers received five dollars rather than two dollars for each drink they sold, had greater mobility (few of the Koreans stayed on club premises), were not subjected to a comparable system of fines, and generally had greater autonomy in the clubs.

Hanna was a seventeen-year-old who worked in Horizons Club, known by Filipinas in TDC to be very strict, with a lot of rules and penalties. She complained that while Korean women were allowed to take GIs upstairs for "short time," Filipinas were prohibited from doing so. Filipinas who worked alongside Korean women were thus aware of their second-class status in a foreign land. Hanna and other Filipinas felt that their work performance and behavior were constantly under watch, not only by the club owner but also by the bartender-cum-manager and even the Korean entertainers. Another Filipina Milla complained that while Filipinas were forced to dance wearing bikinis with no stockings, Korean women could dance wearing one-pieces and stockings. "This is their land, that's why," she said.

"Daddy"—this was what the five Filipinas who worked at the Mermaid Club called him—was a club owner from 1997 to mid-2000. His father had been a club owner since the 1960s and employed as many as sixty women at one time. Daddy's family lived in Seoul, where Daddy attended university while his father ran the club in Dongducheon. Daddy went into the business after the tenant who took over the club after his father's death declared bankruptcy. Although his club was one of the largest in TDC, it had only five entertainers, and business in his club was never as good as in the others. He neither pressured the women to sell many drinks nor imposed bar fines. "I don't like to sell women's *back back* [vaginas, a reference to *ari ng babe* in Tagalog], so I have no profit," he said. He sold the club after he had failed to find replacements for four Filipinas who finished their contracts and left in May 2000. He said that he was "the only university graduate among the club owners. Most of them didn't even finish elementary school." He found it difficult to adapt to life in Dongducheon.

I met Daddy again in May 2001, and we went together to visit one of his ex-employees, Lou, who was having a lot of difficulties working in a new club. The pressure to sell sex was mounting. She was drinking every day, and her penalties for getting into fights with club owners or coworkers were piling up. She had not received her drink-money pay since arriving at her new club three months earlier. Lou was resolutely trying to avoid becoming a "prostitute" and was planning to run away. When I asked Daddy in different ways about his thoughts on the new club owners' pressure on Lou, he said, "You know, the Philippines is a very poor country. $250 [basic salary] is already a lot of money for them. . . . It's their fortune. [Pause] They don't have brains. They don't think [*mori-ga-op-so, saeng-kak-op-so*]. . . . All Korean clubs expect Filipinas to sell their '*back back.*' All Koreans are the same. All men are *loco-loco*. [What is a *loco-loco*?] You don't know? It's Filipino [language]. It means a man crazy about sex. All Korean clubs want their women to sell their '*back back.*' All men like sex."

I was taken aback by Daddy's comments. He had opted to sell his inheritance rather than continue his father's club business. It was also clear that he cared about Lou—he had driven two hours from Seoul just to see her, and he looked genuinely happy when they met and bothered when Lou told him about her situation. He gave her five thousand won when we left. However, this did not mean that he was immune to the dominant view of Filipinas in *gijichon*. Refraining from passing any judgment on Lou's club owners, he expressed his sympathetic yet fatalistic view of the Filipinas' situation—their (mis)fortune as Filipinas, born in a poor country with no jobs and no money to feed its people, and their responsibility for being "stupid" and failing to foresee what working in a Korean club would entail, as all clubs tapped men's uncontrollable desire for sex.

Perceiving them as women from a lower-class nation dependent on stronger countries such as South Korea for jobs, club owners believed that Filipinas should be grateful for the opportunity they had and the money they were making in South Korea, both of which were beyond the reach of many in the Philippines. Filipinas themselves sometimes participated in reproducing this image of themselves as the "have-nots." At her meeting with the runaway Filipinas from the Angel Club, Ms. Lee laughed at Diane (the Filipina who had her passport and returned to the Philippines before the other six), when she got excited over winning a mere two dollars from gambling. Winnie pleaded, as if for Ms. Lee's sympathy, "But Onni, two dollars is already a lot of money in the Philippines. One dollar is already enough for us to live for one day."

Ms. Lee's reaction confirmed my alarm at this ill-timed comment. After initial astonishment, her face darkened; she was possibly led to feel that if life was really so hard in the Philippines, they should all the more be grateful to the Lees for giving them jobs in Korea, rather than putting Ajumma into jail. If emphasizing one's powerlessness when faced with the powerful is an attempt to trigger pity and thus action to ameliorate the gap,[3] Winnie had chosen the wrong moment to do so. Her expression, however, illustrates the readiness of Filipinas to emphasize their powerlessness, and that of their country.

Criticisms of Filipinas' ingratitude and laziness abounded among the club owners. The *ajumma* of the Wild Horse Club gave up employing foreign women in 2000, after having had Filipinas for the previous two years: "Filipinas are headaches. They lie all the time. I worried about them. I made sure that they eat well. *I told them we are a family.* I told them, 'You came here skinny and with no money. Now you are not skinny, you eat well. You look much better. And now you don't work'" (emphasis added). However, the Wild Horse *ajumma*'s invocation of familial discourse failed to instill a sense of moral obligation among the Filipinas. Sally and Maria, two Filipinas at the Wild Horse, explained why the *ajumma* said they were "hard-headed": "Because if she asked us not to go anywhere, we still go. She wanted us to stay home all day, but we can't."

The Filipinas' goal in Korea was not limited to making money. As discussed in Chapter 2, Filipinas' migration projects are multiple—to see the world, meet people, and have fun. Conforming like good "quasi-daughters" within a Korean family was just not part of their dream in Korea. Filipinas therefore responded selectively and creatively to Korean club owners' familial discourses. While club owners tried to subjectify them as dutiful daughters, the Filipinas negotiated the club owners' disciplinary powers and moral claims with their own migration and self-making projects.

The Family in the Club

The club owners' control was naturalized according to different degrees of familistic behavior, a phenomenon that has been studied by scholars in corporate culture in Japan and South Korea.[4] Oh Ji-yeon has found that family rhetoric became common in *gijichon* clubs in the mid-1990s.[5] This was a time when business was falling and a shortage of entertainers made ineffectual the oppressive mode of control that had previously characterized *gijichon*. Oh pointed out how club owners actively assumed the role of protectors to maintain the women's loyalty. Not only did they ask the women to address them as maternal or paternal figures, but they also sought to give the women a sense of stability and belonging. This sometimes worked very well with women who had been shunned by their natal families as "Western whores" and were eager to retain a "familial" identity and loyalty. The club owners' humane treatment of the women therefore succeeded in effectively controlling them, by helping to create a "quasi-family" within the club.

When Filipina entertainers were first introduced to their "families" in *gijichon*, they were taught to address the club owners as *ajumma* (auntie), mommy/mama, or daddy/papa. All Korean women would be referred to as *onni* (elder sister), while any younger Korean man working in the club, such as a DJ, would be *obba* (elder brother). The Filipinas adapted well to the use of these kinship terms in the club. They also learned to call Korean women and men in shops and restaurants *ajumma, onni,* and *obba,* as appropriate. While it is common in South Korea and the Philippines to call women who are older than oneself "elder sister"—*onni* in Korean and *ate*

in Tagalog—the extension of this familistic naming to the club owners humanized the system of labor control in the clubs.

Obviously, a familistic atmosphere could not be generated simply by the use of kinship terms. It was always up to the club owners to make the women feel "part of the family." Below, descriptions of three different club regimes using the familistic model provide a glimpse into the diversity of labor controls and the responses they generated.

Regime 1: Authoritarian Parenting and Bad Daughters

The management of the Angel Club might be called authoritarian—the club owners set all the rules, and there were more orders than requests; penalties were many, and there was little space for discussion. This was not uncommon in *gijichon*. The club was family-owned, with Mrs. Lee running it with her son, Mr. Lee, occasionally assisted by her daughter. The Lees adopted a form of familism in managing it. The seven Filipina entertainers addressed the Lees with the appropriate kinship terms. On the day that the Filipinas ran away from the club, the Lees were planning to take all of them on an outing to the nearby national park for a picnic.

Obviously, the familistic rhetoric had failed to engender a sense of belonging to the club among the Filipinas. The major complaints of the Filipinas were undue pressure to sell drinks, demands for physical control and the control of mobility, and arbitrary penalties.

Drinks were important for the generation of profits in a club. A club owner said that in order to make hiring a Filipina worthwhile, she had to sell a minimum of 150 drinks a month. Club owners sometimes set the quota as high as 500 to maximize profits. A woman got a ticket for each drink sold. Each woman at the Angel Club had to sell a quota of 150 drinks on Friday and Saturday nights. Those who failed would be made to mop the floors immediately after work at 7:00 or 8:00 A.M. Annabel never had a day off during her two-month employment at the Angel Club because she never fulfilled the drinks quota.

Besides selling drinks, women got tickets for accompanying customers into a VIP room or on bar fines. Mrs. Lee's constant exhortation of women low on drink sales to go into the VIP room and go out with customers— implying that they should perform sexual services—created much discontent. Those who refused or failed to comply with Mrs. Lee's bidding risked being penalized as much as fifty dollars. The last straw was when Ajumma threatened to make them strip if they failed to make better sales. The women ran away the next day.

The regulation of physical mobility was important to the *gijichon* club regime generally. The Filipinas could usually leave their club only between 11:00 A.M. and 4:00 P.M. Mobility control was threefold in purpose. First of all, club owners wanted to make sure that interactions between GIs and entertainers did not go unmediated by the capitalist logic of the club. Measures to limit contact between GIs and Filipinas ranged from restricting free time, to the prohibiting of mobile phones, to not allowing any days off. Bar fines were sometimes imposed on Filipinas meeting with GIs in the daytime. In some clubs bed checks were carried out by the club owners or caretakers of the Filipinas after closing hours, and sometimes in the morning as well, to ensure that all the women were inside. Fines of as much as two hundred dollars could be levied on women who were suspected of having met GIs outside of the club. In other words, the club owners had the power to incorporate the social lives of the Filipinas into their business operations.

Second, controlling their mobility, and thus their sexual accessibility, helped to avoid or minimize problems of pregnancy, which were a nuisance to the club owners, who had either to persuade and assist the women to have abortions (at the women's expense) or send them back to the Philippines. Third, controlling the social life of migrant entertainers could prevent them from either running away or building personal relationships with GIs who could help them escape. In fact, many Filipinas had received help from GIs to run away. Some GIs provided technical support, some gave money, and some went as far as finding accommodations or accompanying them to their embassy.[6] Regulating the movement of Filipinas thus was an attempt to isolate migrant entertainers from any significant support network outside of the club.

The extensive bodily and financial regulation that Mrs. Lee imposed alienated the Filipinas. Mrs. Lee made them perm and dye their hair and wear "uniforms" of neon bra tops and miniskirts at the women's own expense. At work they were not allowed to sit unless they accompanied a customer ("We were treated like robots, we had to stand all the time and could move only when they ask [sic] us to"). Many other club owners were also eager to maximize the erotic appeal of the women to lure customers and sales—hair, makeup, and body weight all came under their scrutiny.

In addition to arbitrarily imposing penalties for being late and not obeying orders, Mrs. Lee ate into the women's earnings in other ways. Tips from customers were turned into drink money (meaning that only one-fifth of the amount would go to each woman), so that the women often hid the tips in their bra tops or panties. Gifts from customers also became "taxable" in the Angel Club. One of Joy's customers gave her a gold bracelet and a stereo CD-cassette player on her birthday. Mrs. Lee demanded that she "pay tax" for one of the gifts, so that, in spite of the fact that Joy had fulfilled the drink quota every month, she was penalized for gaining from this particular customer's patronage without benefiting the club proportionately.

The Lees were clueless about the collective resentment of the Filipinas, as was evident in their plan for an outing to the national park on the very day they ran away. The Lees clearly subscribed to the familistic discourse much more than the Filipinas did. During the three weeks of our communication about the runaway Filipinas, the Lees reiterated that they treated the Filipinas like a family. This point was made most dramatic when the women and I were chauffeured to meet with Mrs. Lee after she was released from detention (see Introduction).

This meeting provided insight into how the Filipinas responded differently to such familial discourse. When we arrived at the Lees' apartment, Kitty went up to hug Mrs. Lee right away and then sat next to her. Annabel commented afterward, "Kitty kissed Ajumma—she is so plastic. After all that happened, she kissed Ajumma?! It was not right. She talked [*sic*] so many bad things about Ajumma and then she kissed her. I know she told Ajumma that she didn't want to run away. That's why they like Kitty. [The rest of us] talked about it afterwards." Indeed, in the subsequent phone call from the Lees after they had returned from Australia (Chapter 2), they were eager to tell me that Kitty said running away had been the idea of two of them who were "really bad" and had lied to the Lees. Although it is not my concern to verify the truth of any of these claims, from Kitty's performance with the Lees we can see that the emotional discourse that club owners deployed did not always go unreciprocated. While other Filipinas did not hug Mrs. Lee, some of them felt guilty at seeing her so frail and sad. Yet they reminded themselves, and me, that Mrs. Lee was not as harmless as she looked. After expressing their guilt, Angie said, "She can be nice, but when we work, she becomes very different."

The familistic rhetoric allowed the Lees to reinscribe themselves as good guardians who had been unlucky in hiring ungrateful and scheming Filipinas. For the Filipinas, the authoritarian control justified their running away.

Regime 2: Familistic Hegemony and Good Daughters

Ching Kwan Lee, in "Factory Regimes of Chinese Capitalism," highlights a "familistic hegemony" model characterized by covert and inconspicuous labor control. This is an apt description of the management of the Winner Club. Joy, one of the Angel Club Filipinas, returned to Korea in March 2001. In May 2001, nineteen months after I had seen her off at the airport, she greeted me in Songtan with a radiant smile. She said that she was doing fine, and then she introduced me as her "best friend" from Hong Kong to her Filipina mamasan,[7] "Ate Tammy." She looked excited and happy.

S: Were you not afraid that your new club owners might be the same as [at] Angel?

Joy: Yes, I was. That's why I was so scared when I first arrived. But they are not. They are really nice. I am really lucky. You know, before in Angel, we are [sic] not allowed to sit down—we had to stand up all night. If we sit down—"Penalty!" Ajumma would say. And if we said that we were cold, Ajumma said, "Shut up." But here, if we tell Papa that we are cold, he says, "OK, OK" and he goes and turns on the heater. If we say, "Papa, *pae-go-pa* [we are hungry]," he would go to Burger King and buy each of us a hamburger! They are really nice. Before, in Angel, they never gave us nice food. Only vegetables, and dried fish and rice. Here, they are really nice. Papa is a really nice person.

It was payday, and Joy said that I could join them for the barbecue lunch that the club owners were treating everyone to. I hesitated but was dragged along by her coworkers on their way to the restaurant. At the restaurant almost twenty people were already seated at two long tables. In addition to the nineteen Filipinas, some of their GI boyfriends were also there. The middle-aged Korean couple sitting at one end of the first table were obviously the club owners. This sumptuous Korean barbecue meal, as I learned from Joy, was a treat on every payday—the first and fifteenth of every month.

At the meal the entertainers would also get their pay envelopes. Written on each was the total amount of money for drink sales for each entertainer for the previous two weeks, minus the expenses she had incurred. Joy's envelope listed items such as "rubbish bag," "water," "lights" (electricity), "coffee," and "Winner T-shirt," which Joy had requested in addition to the one she had been given. She was paid 480,000 won in total for the two-week period, after a 60,000-won deduction for expenses. Each entertainer at Winner was required to make 1 million won every month—upon which she would get a 150,000-won bonus. Since a woman got 2,000 won for every $12 drink she sold in 2001, fulfilling the quota would bring the woman 1 million won while bringing the club owners more than 6 million won (the exchange rate for Korean won to U.S. dollars was 1,300:1 in June 2001). If all nineteen women working in the club fulfilled the quota, after paying the salary of 250,000 won, the maintenance of around 100,000 and the 150,000 won quota bonus per woman, the club owner might make a net profit of as much as 124 million won ($95,000) from the women's drinks alone.

At this lunch I learned about the family tragedy of nineteen-year-old Joanne, who had been in South Korea for three months. Joanne's widowed mother had been killed in a car accident three days previously, leaving three young children behind. What surprised me was that the club owner was not only willing to let Joanne go home for a week for the funeral and settle family business but also was willing to pay for her air ticket. It had all been arranged with her manager, and she was due to leave in four days. This was the first time I had heard of a club owner letting a newly arrived entertainer go home for a week, not to mention paying for her air ticket plus the cost of getting a multiple-entry visa. Club owners frequently feared that once an entertainer—for whom thirteen hundred dollars had been paid as a recruitment fee and a further three hundred dollars monthly as an agency fee—left the club, she would not come back and the investment would be lost. Not allowing a woman to return home in the middle of her contract was the norm. Familism at the Winner Club thus went beyond mere rhetoric, as the management actually accommodated the Filipinas' family-based identities.

According to Joy, being made to leave the club was a dreaded penalty for anyone's failure to fulfill the one-million-won drink quota. "Some of the girls cry when they find out that they have to move to another club, because it's so nice to be in Winner," she said.

By extending to the Filipina entertainers kindnesses uncommon for employees (in *gijichon* and in general) and assuming the image of "parents," the Winner Club owners successfully subjectified the Filipinas as "good daughters" for whom they wanted to fulfill parental expectations. Joy and other Filipinas at Winner constantly worried about the number of drinks sold each month.

Coethnic Management of the Filipina "Sisters"

Ate Tammy, as every Filipina in the Winner Club called her, was the official mamasan of the Winner Club. In her early thirties, she was the eldest of the group and was entrusted with the job of managing all the Filipinas and liaising with the club owners. She had been working in South Korea for four years, almost two of those in another club, the Apache. For example, she might report to the club owner a fight between two Filipinas, who would then be fined ten dollars each. However, at times she would act as a representative of the other entertainers. By giving her special authority, privileges, and gifts, the club owner sought to rally her loyalty and rigorous assistance in regulating the behavior of the other women. She had the privilege of having an air-conditioned room which she shared with Joy, while six other Filipinas had to share three bunk beds in the other room with just an electric fan.

Ate Tammy had written a "smile" message in black permanent ink on the door that divided the Filipinas' rooms from the main kitchen (see Figure 6). Not only did Tammy seek to ensure that her coworkers maintained "cheerfulness," but she also sought to promote a harmonious atmosphere among the "sisters" by appealing to their common identity as Filipinas as a basis for love and mutual respect. Tammy played her role as mamasan—as both representative of the club owner and "sister" of the Filipinas—well. Unlike notices she had written in Tagalog on the bathroom door, which concerned everyday-life details, she had written the key notice in English. Since the door opened into the kitchen and could be seen by anyone who entered the house, Ate Tammy made sure that everyone—in particular the club owners—knew that she was doing her job properly.

The appointment of a Filipina as mamasan to mediate between the club owners and the entertainers—a coethnic to cushion the effects of power that the club owners exercised and to manage conflicts between the Filipinas—exemplifies the Korean club owners' keen awareness of the politics of ethnicity. However, Ate Tammy was sometimes a coconspirator in undermining the club owners' interests. For example, Joy and other Filipinas regularly sneaked out at night to meet their boyfriends after soliciting Ate Tammy's complicity. Control could never be absolute.

Regime 3: Maternalism and Good Mothers

The Wild Horse was a small club with, at its peak, four Filipinas working in it. The *ajumma* had not forced the women to go on bar fines but complained that they did not work hard. She did not like the Filipinas to have

Figure 6. "SMILE" notice for Filipina entertainers

serious GI boyfriends. "Don't trust the GIs. Don't trust men" became one of her dictums to the women (and to me).

I have already discussed the fact that club owners were cautious about interactions between GIs and Filipinas and were eager to mediate between them. Yet they were also aware of the emotional play that is necessary for a woman to maintain and develop a clientele (see Chapter 5). Club owners attempted to guide women away from developing strong bonds with their customers in two ways: 1) by appealing to their family responsibilities; and 2) by warning them of the dangers of emotional involvement. Both were expressed as the benign concerns of a maternal figure.

Sally, a twenty-three-year-old single mother with two babies, was the favorite of the Wild Horse *ajumma*—she sold the most drinks and seemed to have a continuous flow of customers, with around four or five bar fines every week. She had lied to the *ajumma* that she had been to college—presumably to gain her respect and trust and to distinguish herself from most of the other Filipinas in the clubs. I asked Sally and Maria to tell me the most memorable thing their club owner had ever said to them:

> Sally: She said, "You have come here to make money. Use here [pointing to the head], not here [pointing to the heart]."
> At this point Maria interjected: "And use here [pointing to the genital area]."
> Sally (continuing her quotation from her club owner): "Make lots of money so that you can send [money to] your babies."

What is important here is to see how the *ajumma* emphasized the need for rational calculation rather than emotional involvement and discouraged romantic exploration. She then emphasized Sally's identity as a mother. Speaking as woman to woman, and as a mother herself, the *ajumma* counseled that money for the family was the key to fulfilment.

Maria's interjection, which Sally had ignored, reveals Sally's narrativization of her distinction from other Filipinas who exchanged money for sex. She often emphasized that she slept only with people for whom she had feelings. These were often GIs with some rank (sergeant or above) and faithful regulars. An eloquent speaker with a calculated composure that belied her young age, Sally had managed to go out on "no sex" bar fines[8] more than once—something that pleased the *ajumma*. Sally often exuded a strong pride in her ability to manipulate the ambiguity of a bar fine and set the terms for her services, as well as earn the *ajumma*'s recognition: "Yes, other Mamas would tell their girls, 'Make them [GIs] happy.' My Ma doesn't. If she heard that I didn't sleep with them, she said, 'Good.' Many GIs complain about me, but I don't care. They want to have the money back, but my Ma would never give them back the money."

As I found out later, Ma asked after each bar fine if the woman had had sex and would give them morning-after "tablets" to prevent pregnancy. In fact, Ma sent the Filipinas to the local clinic for "tests" (for pregnancy and STDs) every two weeks, much more frequently than the three-month interval that was the norm. Her approval was thus more about the avoidance of pregnancy than Sally's abstinence from (cheap) sex. However, in Sally's appropriation of Ma's utterance of "good," this became supporting evidence of her unyielding attitude with her customers. Respect for her had to be demonstrated adequately in financial terms and, ideally, a rank in the military commensurate with her desired standing among fellow Filipinas. Sally put it succinctly: "I want myself high, not low."

In Sally's narrative the maternalism displayed by the club owner allowed her to establish control over her job and distinction from other Filipinas.

In these three different club regimes, we can observe a few common themes. First, the familism in the club allowed club owners to locate themselves as the rightful protectors—and also controllers—of the women they employed. By masking the employment relationship as one of parents and daughters, the relationship between the entertainers and their employers was transformed into a "legitimate" one of reciprocity between inferiors and superiors beyond the exchange of labor for money. The emotional management this allowed achieved widely different degrees of success, depending on the extent to which club owners carried it beyond rhetoric, as well as on the Filipinas' abilities to balance their desire for the club owners' approval with their desire for adventures and romance.

Second, while it could be said that the club regime was a joint project of the club owners and the entertainers, it was vexed with obvious power differentials and paradoxes. In spite of the familistic rhetoric, the relationship between Filipinas and club owners remained ambivalent, riddled with tensions and contradictions, as discourses of familial harmony clashed not only with the capitalist logic of the business but also along ethnonationalistic lines.

It was common for the Filipinas to develop a parallel use of kinship terms among themselves in Tagalog. In the Mermaid Club the four Filipinas who arrived one year after a woman named Theresa soon began to call her "Mommy." She was respected because of her discipline, maturity, and the composed guidance she always had for other women in the club. Lou, who arrived in Korea for a second time to find herself working in a far more abusive club than her previous one, found consolation in having a Filipina who was thirteen years older than her as a best friend. They shared the same bed in their quarters, and Lou called her "Nanay" ("Mother" in Tagalog). The everyday use of Tagalog, through which the Filipinas could communicate, gossip, and plan to subvert the club owners' powers (for example, by running away), helped cement them as a group, and the use of kinship terms helped consolidate that group.

Third, I found that the family metaphor was far more compelling for Korean club owners and Korean entertainers than for the Filipinas. The Filipinas might perform a modicum of compliance to avoid getting into trouble and to gain the trust of their club owners, but the metaphor rarely went beyond the rather superficial performance of playing family. Unlike corporate employees, who might actively deploy the familistic discourse to criticize their employers, Filipina entertainers in *gijichon* clubs rarely held their club owners accountable to their claims to provide parental protection. The demands for moral reciprocity largely failed to have an effect on the Filipinas, not only because of the mediation of ethnic and class differences but also because the Filipinas were more concerned with their own projects and goals in and beyond Korea. As flexible labor, the women were well aware of themselves as itinerants and had little interest in building long-term familial relationships with the club owners, especially when they could be investing in a range of other opportunities for the future (such as marriage with GIs; see Chapter 5).

Fourth, Korean club owners' management style and method, which set up both ambiguities and boundaries, are important to the Filipinas' management of their own gender and sexual identities. The club owners operate within particular legal and moral parameters about prostitution, and few can openly demand that the Filipinas sell sex. They must leave the women to deal with the ambiguities of the bar fine and the VIP room and instill a sense of control among the women to manage their sexuality with GIs. Within the context of the club regime, in which the Filipinas' incomes, bodies, and mobility are under different degrees of control, the ability to make decisions about their bodies and to resist appropriation or subjugation becomes an important factor in constructing and exercising their identities in *gijichon* clubs.

The question persists: "Who is a prostitute?"

"I am not like those girls": Stigma and Respectability

"You are a Filipina? How much for one night?"

The latter is a question that almost all Filipinas have in one way or another confronted while working in *gijichon* clubs. All of them are colored by the stigma of prostitution, but the ambiguity also means that no one would identify as a prostitute, so that a constant negotiation of the stigma is necessary to maintain one's respectability. Erving Goffman discusses the importance of information control for a stigmatized person who is discreditable but not discredited: "The issue is not that of managing tension generated during social contacts, but rather that of managing information about his failing. To display or not to display; to tell or not to tell; or let on or not to let on; to lie or not to lie; and in each case, to whom, how, when, and where."[9]

In order to maintain their respectability, Filipina entertainers in the clubs use a variety of strategies to distinguish themselves from "other Filipinas." Below I discuss how club regimes deal with the stigma of prostitution and argue that Filipinas deal with the stigma in two main ways: by distinguishing oneself from "others" who do prostitution; and by couching sexual-economic exchanges in emotional terms. Yet such struggles for respectability ultimately reinforce the stigma of prostitution and reproduce a particular ideal about female sexuality, buttressing the sex hierarchy that marginalizes them as "prostitutes" in the first place.

The majority of *gijichon* clubs actively avoids the label of "prostitution." According to the club owners, the bar fine is a "penalty" that a woman, or her customer, has to pay for taking time off from the club. In other words, a bar fine was not money for sex, and the club owners were not engaged in the prostitution of the women. In fact, Ms. Lee claimed that they had made the Filipinas sign an agreement that they would not engage in prostitution. This was therefore proof that they did not force the Filipinas to sell sex, as they had been charged with doing and for which her mother had been detained. The Filipinas were thus left to their own devices, desires, and negotiations with their clients. Yet there were also clubs that, while strictly forbidding the Filipinas from selling sex, facilitated a range of sexualized performances and interactions with clients. For example, Filipina entertainers in the O Club had to lap dance, perform topless shows, and work in VIP rooms but were strictly warned against having sex with customers, while their Korean counterparts continued to do "short time" and "long time." One explanation offered by local activists for this cautious attitude toward prostitution was that the chairman of the Korea Special Tourism Association, who was also a local councillor and thus had a vested interest in maintaining the image of himself and his association, had warned fellow club owners against prostitution, in particular by Filipinas who had been brought in through the recommendation of the association. The club regime—for legal and moral reasons—thus transferred the stigma of prostitution onto the individual women.

How does one make good money in the club without becoming a "whore"? As Marit Melhus argues, gender is a vehicle through which morality speaks, and while the masculinity of men is perceived as a continuum—you are either more or less a man—women are perceived as dichotomous—you are either a good woman or not.[10] Since Filipina entertainers' main source of income is their public performance of femininity and sexuality, they are battling against both the virginal ideals of modest femininity and the stigma of prostitution. Being too quiet and reserved does not get one customers, and yet having sex for the money marks one unmistakably as a prostitute. Ambivalence becomes a woman's best defense.

Yet ambivalence also facilitates the circulation of rumors and gossip. Rumors are public tales with uncertain origin and validity that are ways for people to express and cope with anxieties and uncertainties about how the world works, while gossip consists of communications about individuals within a group that has shared interest or common history. Gossip therefore defines the intimacy and boundary of a group and can also serve as a tool of social control to evaluate and regulate the behavior of group members, as well as to maintain and contest hierarchy within the group.[11] For example, as there is intense competition between women over customers and sexual reputation in the clubs, gossip about the HIV/AIDS status of certain women would undermine the business not only of the women but also of the clubs in which they worked. I have heard of no equivalent rumor about GIs.

The displacement of the prostitute stigma operates on a cascading scale, allowing one to continuously maintain superior status in relation to others: those who claim to have never participated in prostitution mark their distinction from women who provide manual relief by hand or mouth for money; those who claim to provide manual relief mark themselves only from those who have sexual intercourse for money; and those who go out on bar fines repeatedly (and at least some of these occasions involve sexual intercourse) mark themselves from women who have sex cheaply and without emotion. These narratives illustrate the importance of sexual reputation in *gijichon*, the level of anxieties that the prostitute stigma engenders, and the making of a sex hierarchy that constructs some sexual-economic exchanges as legitimate and others as less so or as illegitimate.

Filipina entertainers at the King's Club said that their club owner did not allow VIP rooms, "short time," "long time," or bar fines and had also driven out GIs who wanted sex with her Filipina employees. Empowered by their club owners to turn down these advances, some Filipinas responded likewise to unwelcome advances from GIs ("No! We don't do this here. You go to XXX club!"). Ira told me with pride that GIs thought that Filipinas in her club, the Mermaid Club, were "stuck up" because they turned down GIs' requests for sex by responding, "Go fuck yourself!" and "Don't you have hands yourself?"

One afternoon Sally, Maria, and I were meeting in a first-floor coffee shop in Songtan that had large windows overlooking the buzzing shopping street. Sally discussed how she managed her sexuality while getting four or five bar fines a week. More important, she was also telling Maria and me her opinions on what "other Filipinas" were doing:

> GIs buy my ticket, but it doesn't mean that I have to have sex with them. We can just go bar-hopping [on a bar fine]. *I can't sleep with someone if I don't have feelings.* Excuse me, I am a Filipina, but I am not like many Filipinas. I have customers who want to sleep with me. I asked, "Do you think that because I work in these clubs, that means I am that kind of girl?" They said, "Yes." I said, "Sorry, but they have their lives, I have my own. I am not that kind of girls [sic]. *I respect myself, so please respect me.*" That's why my Ma loves me more and more. I get customers, I get their money, but I don't sleep with them. One customer bought me a drink. Then I asked him to buy me another one, he said, "OK, but what next?" I asked him, "What?" "Sex." [She straightened her back, rolled her eyes and raised her voice to show her outrage.] Two juicees [sic], he wanted to have sex with me for two juicees! I am not like other girls—people buy them shampoo, lotion, jeans, shoes, and they sleep with them—for free! What's in a pair of shoes? What's in a shampoo, a lotion?! (My emphasis)

Delivered with self-assurance and genuine contempt for "other girls" who have sex with men for mundane consumer products, Sally articulated how she maintained her respectability in the club. "Feelings" were necessary for her to have sex—though she did not specify what exactly these feelings should be—but not enough. Adequate material benefits including hard cash were a must—having sex for mere consumer goods was equivalent to giving it out for free. "My opinion is—if they use your body, you use their money. This is fair. They use your body and they don't give you anything, that's not fair!" However, she did not believe that money should give a man access to her body, even if he had paid a bar fine and she had gone to a hotel room with him. Sally has told me with pride how she ran away from men who were left naked and ready for sex in hotel rooms. Instead, her idea of fairness was that a woman *could* have sex with a man if he gave her money, but it was not a must. In this narrative Sally echoed the dominant sexual ideology that a woman's sexual accessibility determines her respectability, but she also emphasized that sexual-economic exchange is always part of the deal.

Women who have sex with men for mere pleasure are frowned upon in *gijichon*—for they defy both the feminine ideal and the economic rationality of the clubs. Filipinas have a reputation among Korean club owners and entertainers for "selling themselves cheap" or even having sex with GIs for free. Between Filipinas, disapproval of sex for pleasure is not uncommon. Annabel pointed out that it was a condom found by police in the VIP room that nailed the Angel Club owner:

Annabel: Kitty, Winnie, maybe even Joy . . . Kitty saw a cute guy. I don't know why they were doing it . . . I didn't agree with what they did. I found out that they were having sex with GIs that they wanted, because they found them cute only.

S: Don't they also get money out of it?

Annabel: No, you remember Kitty? They stayed in the hotel. She paid for the bar fine. She got money from other GIs. But if she really liked the guy, she would do it.

This account of Kitty's active sexuality—a radical reversal not only of gender norms in heterosexual relations but also of gender and ethnic roles in the economy of desires in *gijichon*—speaks to the potential of the club for female sexual expressions. Voicing her disapproval of such aggressive female sexuality, Annabel preserved her own respectability. In the Mermaid Club, Ira and three of her coworkers always referred to Candy as "crazy," not just because of her vivacious demeanor but also because she would do "crazy" things that gave her the top drink sales. According to them, out of her own initiative Candy improvised strip dances and in the middle of one performance opened a beer bottle with her vagina onstage, to the cheers of the audience. She also took customers to the VIP room. I asked if Ira knew why Candy did all these things without requests from the club owner. Ira frowned, "I don't know. Because she likes it." Ira did not even mention the possibility that Kitty might need extra cash. Enjoying the public display of sexuality and engaging in sexual-economic exchanges with multiple men made Candy a "crazy" woman in the eyes of Ira and her coworkers.

My interest here is in Annabel's expression of dismay and Ira's disapproval of Candy. Their remarks delineate a very narrow space for legitimate sexual behavior for women—one must not have sex with men for pleasure or money only.

The constant efforts to affirm who does the nastier or cheaper things reflect the anxious awareness of the Filipinas of their position in a narrow zone between the "discreditable" and the "discredited." Bella, the seventeen-year-old Filipina who had worked in two different clubs, met a female GI who offered to accompany her to the church on base. She started to go but was teased by other Filipinas in the club for being "stupid." I asked Bella why. She answered, "I work in the club and I go to church. They said it sounds stupid. Because what we do in the club, teasing and temptation like that, and I go to church . . . I go to church to worship, because I am a different person in the club, even though I didn't do bad things, you know. And I just want to go to church. Inside the church, it's a different feeling."

Going to church thus was Bella's attempt to allow her different subjectivities as both temptress and God-fearing believer to coexist. She was aware that what she did in the club might be pushing the boundaries of Catholic womanhood, but since she "didn't do bad things," it was still legitimate for her to go to church. Others disagreed. Those who thought that Bella was "stupid" for going to church were well aware of the distinction between the moral domains of the club and the church. In *gijichon* clubs women are distinguished by what kind of sexual-economic exchanges they participate in, but outside of the *gijichon* clubs, they are categorically "bad" women, far removed from the "good" women who have a rightful place in the church. Thus, by putting down Bella's choice to go to church, the other women were unwittingly also propping up the sex hierarchy that stigmatizes them.

On the other hand, Filipinas identify prostitute "others" to challenge the discourse about entertainers in *gijichon* that homogenizes them as prostitutes. By doing this they mark their individual moral distinction and demand respectability from other Filipinas, GIs, and the anthropologist. However, in this attempt to identify their location within the complex web of meanings for the term "entertainers," they simultaneously consolidate the stigma of prostitution, in effect reproducing the general cultural intolerance of women's participation in sexual-economic exchanges.

Sexy Women, Interrupted

To be "sexy" is part of an entertainer's job. Each day Filipina entertainers take about two hours to shower, put on makeup, do their hair, and get dressed for work. At clubs with shows, the women spend hours learning and practicing their steps and moves. Their bodies are the primary sites of club owners' discipline for the generation of profits. Being sexually attractive will get the men to pay.

It is commonplace to argue that these practices reflect and perpetuate the patriarchal and capitalist objectification of women. Yet if we agree with this structural diagnosis too readily, we risk turning the women into mere effects of structural forces. Do they insert their own subjectivity into performances that necessarily present images different from those the club owners and clients have of them? Can their performances of female sexuality in the club be acts that disrupt, mimic, and exceed the powers that seek to appropriate their bodies and sexuality?

"Where there is resistance, there is power."[12] Abu-Lughod's reformulation of Foucault's pronouncement puts forward an understanding of resistance as a "diagnostic" of changing relations of power and highlights the contingent and flexible nature of resistance. Below, I follow this suggestion and identify four separate moments of bodily resistance that constitute an assemblage of protests against the structures of power in *gijichon* clubs. The performance of aggressive female sexuality can be a form of female rebellion. To illustrate this point, I situate these Filipinas' understanding of their newly acquired bodily practices within the transnational social field—in particular, in relation to the conservative ideals of female sexuality in the Philippines. As Steven Pile argues, spaces of domination can be different from spaces of resistance, and resistance may involve spatialities that lie beyond "power."[13] This approach to resistance necessitates a conception of power as "transient, flexible and ambivalent."[14] This is particularly true when the subjects are in dislocation and thus embedded in a transnational field that goes beyond a single site. The directionality of specific acts or speech may be comprehensible only when analyzed in the larger social and political-economic context, and since oppression can be multiple, a single act of defiance might also be multivalent.

The Nails

A little ritual took place among the Angel Club Filipinas on the evening immediately after the negotiations. We were standing in front of a convenience store next to the KFC where the negotiations had been finalized, waiting for Mr. Lee to come back with a photocopy of the agreement. Two of the Filipinas disappeared into the white glare of the convenience store and came back out with two nail clippers. The seven Filipinas then stood in a circle in the middle of the street in central Seoul and took turns clipping their long and well-manicured nails under the illumination of the white and red neon signs. I had spent hours watching Filipinas manicure and pedicure themselves and each other in their rooms and inside the club—it was an important part of their physical upkeep—but why were they making a point of cutting short their nails here and now? "We don't need [our nails] now. We don't work anymore," Diane said. But why had they needed their long nails at work? Diane explained that when a customer got nasty in the VIP room, she would use her nails for self-defense, usually targeting the face and neck. She had done this twice during her one-month stay in the Angel Club. Now that their departure had been formalized with the agreement, the excision of this instrument of bodily resistance symbolically marked their exit from the club. I had always thought of long, manicured nails as a conformity to consumerist definitions of female beauty and an inconvenience in everyday life. Little had I suspected that behind those glossy colors were instruments for self-defense.

The Look

Bella was trained to do the "water and whip" show (pouring bottled water on her body while whacking a whip) soon after her arrival at the No. 1 Club, from which she ran away after two months. She and four other "new girls" had been enticed into dancing naked by the club owner with the promise of an extra hundred dollars per month. When asked how she felt when she first went on stage naked, she said, "I felt very shy, because there were so many men down there. I wanted to cover my face with a piece of paper." However, instead of covering herself, Bella assumed a much more defiant posture. Rather than submerging her shame or accommodating the voyeuristic pleasure of the audience and the profiteering of the club owners, Bella was uncompromising in her resistance to smiling:

> I was crying inside. I wanted to cry on the stage. I never smiled. Even though I danced. But I never smiled. That's why the Korean got mad at me—"You scare the GIs!" I put on dark makeup, dark lipstick, as if I have an evil face. Then I never smiled. They got mad at me, "Why you scare the GIs? GIs run away because of you!" [laughs] I said, "I didn't do nothing. GIs told me that I look good today, so I don't care."
>
> Some GIs are really scared of me. If I go to the GIs and ask, "Can I sit here?" "No, no, don't sit here, I don't like you." [laughs] You can see

from their face [*sic*] whether they are scared or not. But some GIs talked to me because I never smiled. Like when I didn't have a customer, then they came to me and said, "Smile, baby." [laughs] I hate smiling when I am in that club. I never smiled.

Bella was apparently very pleased with her defiance. The club owners became impotent to make her smile or assume a demure posture. Their regime managed to undress her but failed to program her facial expression or the look in her eyes. Bella's body was simultaneously the object of appropriation and the prime site of resistance. The club owners' domination of the women proved even more incomplete when Bella found support among some of the customers for whom the show was staged. Through her eyes, her resistance to smiling, and her makeup, Bella performed but refused to please. Her dance helped create a fantasy of change, escape, and achievement within the mundane and oppressive environment of the *gijichon* club. The seventeen-year-old was naked but far from powerless.

The Word

Lou, Ira, and I were in the room when Daddy, the club owner, came in and handed Lou her money before sitting down on her bed. We were all waiting for the Filipino manager to come and take Lou, a twenty-two-year-old, to the airport. Lou was leaving Korea after fifteen months in Dongducheon.

Daddy: What are you gonna do when you go back to the Philippines?
Lou: Fuck.

She said the word with such clarity—with a slight pause between the "u" and the "ck"—that echoes of it filled the room as she turned her head and looked straight at Daddy with a cheeky smile while swinging her legs, which were dangling from the edge of the bed. Daddy was reclining on one end of the bed, expressionless. Still looking for a reaction from Daddy, Lou repeated with greater emphasis, "I am gonna fuck."
    Ira and I were resting on the other bed in the room, watching the exchange. We giggled but tried hard not to laugh out loud. The word "fuck" was by no means a rare expression among the Filipinas; Daddy and the Filipinas used it regularly in their daily conversation. However, it assumed a particular valence in this context—especially in view of Daddy's relatively serious enquiry—which Ira and I found amusing.
    After a long pause, Daddy said, "If you come back to Korea and you

want to come back to this club, tell Mr. Ahn, OK? Do you have his phone numbers?" Lou gave up waiting for Daddy to respond to her challenge, probably content with her own apparent victory as revealed by Daddy's change of subject.

To make sense of Lou's utterance, one has to understand the significance of the moment (her departure from the club), her experience in South Korea, and her pending return to the Philippines in the context of her relationship with Daddy. Working in the club had not been entirely pleasant for Lou, nor is it for most Filipinas. Earlier on the same day I had asked if she was happy that she had come to South Korea, and she had answered reluctantly, after a long pause, "Fifty-fifty." The money had been helpful, but club work had been difficult. Her request for a transfer from the club she had to strip dance in had taken her to Daddy's club. She sometimes used the provocative body movements she learned in the first club to get more drinks, and yet she had ruled out any sexual services beyond them. She never went into a VIP room and did not take bar fines except for her "real" GI boyfriend. Though she had a boyfriend and a few good friends from the military, her sexuality had constantly invited unwelcome solicitation if not outright humiliation from men—GIs, male migrant workers from the Philippines and Bangladesh, for example. Though Daddy did not pressure her to sell sex, the *gijichon* club system had nonetheless positioned Lou and other women at a vulnerable juncture—they had to decide whether they would sell sex, and if not, they had to fend off comments and requests that equated them with "prostitutes." It was more a *juncture* than a *position* because when money was running low, the option of selling sex was always open. It was subject to continuous negotiation, with an awareness that prostitution would amount to an unmitigated transgression of the feminine ideal.

To Lou and other Filipinas, this club system had an ethnicity—Korean. Daddy, being a club owner, was part of this system. Therefore, the remark was targeted at Daddy—as a man, a club owner, and a Korean—who embodied the multiple oppressions that she had had to deal with for the past fifteen months. Knowing full well that Daddy was eager to have her back at the club when he asked the question, Lou was aware of her relative power over him and what he symbolized. She effectively silenced Daddy with *the* word in a moment of symbolic victory, in the style of David over Goliath.

The confident utterance was furthermore a reclamation of her sexual subjectivity. The club system had turned her body and sexuality into potential objects for sale. Denying the sexual availability that customers constantly projected onto her body had been an unpleasant preoccupation for Lou. She had told many a GI to "go fuck yourself" when they asked for her "price." Now that she was about to leave and reunite with her boyfriend in the Philippines, she was ready to say the four-letter word not as a denunciation but as a proclamation.

Lou's utterance might also be read as an expression of her uncertainty about going home. Earlier that day I too had asked Lou what she was going to do at home. She had given me the same answer, "I'm gonna fuck," more jokingly and much less provocatively. "Just sleep, eat, and fuck" was Daddy's expression for having nothing to do. It is a common belief among Korean club owners that the Philippines is a poor country with little future. "I am fucked" and "fucked-up" were also part of the inventory of common expressions in *gijichon*. Daddy did not hesitate to express his belief that Lou and others come back to work for him because there were no jobs in the Philippines, and Lou knew that this was not entirely untrue.

The Kiss

Lou, Bella, and Ira frequently hugged and kissed each other on the lips when their customers were around but never when only the club owners, Filipinas, or I was around. As we went through her photo album featuring some pictures of these mock-amorous moments, I asked Ira why they liked to kiss each other in the club:

Ira: We don't know. Just fun. Fun to kiss.
S: Do you do that when other people are not watching?
Ira: No. [Pause] Even if they are watching, if the guys are there, we will do it.
S: Yes, but you do it because other people are watching?
Ira: [Smile] Yes. 'Cause [pause] they are gonna think that "Who is the lesbian of that girls [*sic*] . . . of those girls?" They are gonna get confused. So that's good.
S: That's good?
Ira smiled as she nodded.

The desired effect of the "lesbian" kiss was to shock and mock in solidarity the heterosexual hegemony that has generated the club culture, their subordinate position as entertainers, and attempts to appropriate their female sexuality into the servitude of male desires by managers, club owners and customers alike. They found the performance amusing because of their ability to disturb the male onlookers. The public performance itself made the act significant and legitimate. Its meaning would differ significantly if committed in private. The statement "Even if they are watching . . . we will do it" expressed their fearless determination to challenge the sensitivity of the "guys." This kiss, therefore, was different from the erotic acts performed between women onstage for the voyeuristic gaze of male customers—for its purpose was not to please but, in Ira's word, to "confuse." The women attained pleasure by successfully disrupting normality in the clubs.

Club-Girl Power

The club is one site; the body, however, is another, and the nails, the look, the word, and the kiss represent its polyphony. Foucault wrote that the power and resistance of individuals are exercised from innumerable points at a particular historical moment in world history and that identity politics is an interactive and multiple process.[15] The seemingly disparate gestures considered in this light take on a collective value for the entertainers who defy, challenge, mock, and disrupt their inscription as objects of desire in the club. In their compliant performance of their femininity and sexuality, they simultaneously refuse to please.

In her study of the struggles of women factory workers in China, Pun Ngai proposes a "minor genre of resistance" with her analysis of the diabolical powers of experiences on the edge, such as screams, dreams, and bodily pain: "A minor genre of resistance has only one aim: to allow movement, as a nomad, into the odyssey of radical human freedom, to break through the boundaries that block the flows of transgressing desire, to provide the experience at the edge, of freeing oneself and actualizing oneself in the world."[16] Painfully aware of their subordinate status and marginality, of the silencing of their voices as migrant women, cheap labor, and prostitutes, Filipina entertainers seize the opportunities and means by which their defiance becomes known and transgressive desires are felt. These bodily tactics are not struggles for autonomy, for they operate in what Michel de Certeau calls "the space of the other. Thus it must play on and with a terrain imposed on it and organized by the law of a foreign power. . . . It operates in isolated actions, blow by blow. . . . In short, a tactic is an art of the weak."[17]

This genre of resistance is also manifest in a transnational field, on a scale entirely different from that of the club but with the similar goal of movement and freedom. In *gijichon* the Filipinas actively deploy their sexed bodies as instruments of resistance in manners inconceivable at home. Feminine ideals of bashfulness and purity are still strong in the Philippines. Back home Bella would not have made herself up or stripped, Lou would not have said the four-letter word with such facetiousness to a man of Daddy's age, and they would not have kissed women on the lips in public. While these acts would have been publicly condemned in the Philippines, they gave these women potency in carving out their subjectivity and identity against their homogenization as "drinkie girls" in South Korea. The dislocation allowed the women to be different, in a place where they had no biography. In fact, many of them seized the chance to assert their independence from the moral and religious prescriptions that restricted their autonomy at home, asserting their newfound liberty where they could. They might smoke, swear, laugh, and talk loudly in the streets; wear hot pants, miniskirts, and heavy makeup; or pierce their noses and tongues without hearing (or understanding) a word of criticism. As Ira noted, "Here it's OK because everybody knows that we work in the clubs. In the Philippines, if you smoke, people would say that you are a club-girl. . . . [laughs] I didn't use to look like this in the Philippines. I had black hair [rather than dyed brownish hair with red highlights], straight [rather than curled]. . . . [Here] I become more [of a] flirt. Because of my job, I need it."

She felt that she was freer in South Korea: "Maybe because it's a more modern and liberal society?" *Gijichon*—conflated with Korea for Ira and other Filipinas because it was the only Korea they knew—had incidentally allowed these Filipinas to explore and reclaim their sexuality and bodily autonomy in manners impossible at home. It was in where they were not, more than in where they were, that these Filipinas found a new sense of freedom.

Their dislocation, which made them vulnerable in an alien land, freed them from conventional forms of authority at home. While the "club-girl" label had to be avidly avoided at home, it was fastened to their bodies by default of their nationality as they walked the streets in *gijichon*. This unwelcome but unavoidable tag gave them the license to transgress and challenge the feminine ideal. Though the regime of control circumscribed their freedom and autonomy, they waged their guerrilla attacks on the system that sought to categorize, subordinate, and appropriate their bodies and sexuality. Though incorporated into the structure, these attacks constitute an important, yet often unnerving, part of the whole, maintaining a fluidity that prevents closure. When they succeed in disturbing the order of the system by transgressing their subordinate roles as female entertainers, they experience power and pleasure.

*   *   *

Located in the territory of the Other, laboring in the economy of heterosexual desires mediated by *gijichon* clubs, Filipina entertainers are nomads who find themselves in intersecting zones of cultural, economic, and sexual friction. In particular, they are regulated by the club regime that seeks to localize their labor and sexuality for profits through the familistic discourse while averting the label of "prostitution." Within the capitalist and patriarchal logics of control, Filipinas labor to be *not* "one of those girls who do those things" in a club system that is premised on the commodification of their sexuality. They continue to pursue their migration projects while they are subjects of overlapping webs of disciplinary powers that subordinate them.

Just as their bodies are the main targets of club owners' regulation, they also serve as a key site for the Filipinas' resistance. To suggest that the Filipinas navigate their way through the maze of the club regime is not an attempt to romanticize their resistance. It is true that the Filipinas, in their careful aversion of the label "prostitute" and in their attempts to resist appropriations by club owners and customers, simultaneously resist and participate in their own oppression by reinforcing the sex hierarchy that marginalizes deviant sexualities. Dorinne Kondo has suggested, "That people inevitably participate in their own oppressions, buying into hegemonic ideologies even as they struggle against those oppressions and those ideologies—a familiar fact of life to women, people of color, colonized and formerly colonized people—is a poignant and paradoxical facet of human life."[18] While these everyday practices of resistance are unlikely to effect any significant change in the structure of power, they can be read as expressions of the Filipinas' awareness of the possibility of freedom and resistance and as insistent efforts to practice this possibility. These are their means of negotiating with the norms and structures that frame their lives in order to demand recognition as more than just malleable objects of fantasies and docile bodies. This concept of resistance highlights the poignancy of these inarticulate yet potent expressions of their subjectivity beyond their subjectification by the state, capital, and the heterosexual economy of desires in *gijichon*.

Chapter 5
Love "between My Heart and My Head"

I had to laugh at the symphony of "Honey, I love you," the phrase that the Angel Club Filipinas uttered into their mobile phones, which echoed in the otherwise empty first-floor coffee shop. It was the day I convinced them of the need to retrieve their passports from the Seoul police station so that they could leave Korea as soon as possible for their safety, as club owners were upset with them for getting the president of their association put in detention. After the two-hour train and subway ride from Dongducheon to Seoul, we were told to return in an hour for the police officer in charge. In the August heat we found an air-conditioned refuge in the coffee shop—the type young Koreans visited in the late 1990s for its ambience rather than for its very weak and expensive (around twenty-five-hundred-won) coffees, just before Starbucks arrived (in 1999). It had large windows and white linen-covered couches and was usually visited by customers hoping for quiet conversation. However, the place was far from quiet. Most of the women were talking on the phone almost continuously, finishing each call with "Bye, Honey, I love you," while others giggled on the side. My guess was that they were talking with their "boyfriends." I asked why they never used other terms of endearment for different men—such as "honey." After a pause there was a burst of laughter. The answer was that using different terms with different men might lead to confusion, and the guys would find out that they were talking to other men.

I came to realize that the Filipinas did not share my anxiety that they might not get back their passports that day (they did not), delaying their departure and possibly endangering their safety from the angry club owners in TDC. Annabel was the only one who did not make a call. She had been in South Korea for only two months and had made barely any money, so it made sense that she did not have a mobile phone. She was sitting there very quietly, as if deep in thought. I wondered if, being one of the two older women of the group, she was anxious, as I was, about their passports. I asked Annabel if she was OK. She responded, "I want to go back to TDC. We have many customers, you see. They said that they would give me money if I quit my job and go back to the Philippines. They said they would send me money. I need to go back and ask them, to confirm [their promise], you know. I need the money." I was given the impression that she did not have a "real" boyfriend and wanted to meet her customers to get some guarantee for financial help upon her return to the Philippines.

Annabel was radiant when I met her and the other women the following week. I asked where she had been for the past week. She gave me a contented smile and said, "With my boyfriend. He got a pass for Friday, Saturday, and Sunday, so we stayed at a hotel, and he paid for the room too." Annabel then told me excitedly about her boyfriend Philip, a twenty-year-old American from Kentucky. They had met two months previously at the club, when she had just arrived in South Korea. Annabel was emphatic that he "respected" her (because he would not take her into a VIP room) and that he was a virgin. The first time they dated, she tried to seduce him in his room, but he refused and said, "This is not the right time. I really like you but we should be doing this only after we get married." I asked why she tried to seduce him. "Because I like him," she replied. She then said that they would be getting married.

Thus, within one week, and away from the club, Annabel had found herself a man who not only was willing to pay for their stay in a hotel and had bought a remote-control model race car for her son but had also decided to marry her. My sense of the compression of time in military camp-town relationships reached a new height. Annabel's sullen face of the previous week had been replaced by a beaming smile. A future had been secured. A dream had come true.

*   *   *

The preoccupation with "love" among the Filipina entertainers in *gijichon* cannot be exaggerated. This is not just represented by the careful, yet game-like usage of "Honey, I love you" with different customers, but also by the material gifts and frequent discussions about the prospects of marriage that "love" brings. As Annabel's experience showed, customers could be a source of financial, social, and emotional support for the entertainers—romantic love may be idealized as a pure emotion in modern society, but scholars and laypersons alike are aware of the give-and-take in its practice.

Within the regulatory mechanisms of the club regime, "love" became an important instrument that Filipinas wield to influence their customers, whose numbers, loyalty, and generosity determine their well-being. Within their aspirations for personal, material, and social advancement, the romantic love rhetoric is important to them as a means of getting financial and material assistance, getting social support and respect as an individual, and securing a future through marriage. These goals might overlap or be realized separately—not every Filipina leaps at the first opportunity to marry a GI—although the key to attaining these goals is the women's "labor of love."

Sexual posturing and flirtation do not remain within the four walls of the club but extend to everyday life for both Filipinas and GIs.[1] Mediated by the idioms of romantic love, money and sex are not matters of simple transaction in *gijichon* clubs. In a context where "boyfriends" have become synonymous with "customers," "I-love-you" is a daily utterance, and marriage proposals are weekly occurrences, relationships in *gijichon* clubs assume a complexity that challenges the dichotomous "male domination–female subordination" model put forward in most studies of the commercial sex.[2]

I do not claim that love erases the power differentials between Filipina entertainers and their GI customers. Rather, I try to show that love is an integral aspect in both the ongoing negotiations within this power relation in a transnational site and the process of transnational subject-making.

Anthropologists have contributed to the understanding of "love" as a cultural discourse by showing how its expression and communication are embedded in larger social structures and cultural processes of modernization. L. A. Rebhun, in her study of the centrality of *amor* as a romantic passion and a sentiment of social affiliation in Caruaru in northeast Brazil, argues that emotional love serves as a "lens" for understanding specific forms of social and economic organization, as well as cultural differences. Projecting this lens of love onto the "ethnoscape" (Appadurai, "Global Ethnoscapes") of cross-cultural encounters, a number of anthropological works argue for the diverse ways in which "love" is both an emotion and a discourse for negotiating the effects of and opportunities in globalization. Denise Brennan discusses how Dominican women sex workers "perform love" for male tourists to pursue the possibility of overseas migration, while Nicole Constable (*Romance on a Global Stage*) examines relationships in "mail-order marriages" between American men and Filipina and Chinese women to show the possibility of romance and intimacy. In Padilla and others' volume *Love and Globalization*, the authors demonstrate in diverse settings how "love" as an emotion is embedded in historical, political, and economic structures and serves as a discourse for modern subject-making. Lieba Faier argues from her study of Filipina migrants in rural Japan that "love" is a term for "global self-making" and points to how women seek to transform themselves and their lives through their global encounters. However, the style of "love" between the Filipinas and their regular GI patrons is specific to the economy of *gijichon*, constituting a particular discourse of morality and pattern of intimacy.

I examine the discourse of romantic love between Filipina entertainers and GIs as constituting what Lila Abu-Lughod and Catherine Lutz's term "pragmatic acts and communicative performances"—as a social practice, negotiated and reproduced in the politics of desire in *gijichon*. The term "politics of desire" is used to refer to the negotiation of desire within the webs of significance of gender, ethnicity, and class that are shaped by the politico-economic context of the Philippines and the United States (compare Constable, *Romance on a Global Stage*). The affective and erotic desires expressed and experienced in *gijichon* thus need to be understood within the orientalizing and occidentalizing tendencies that have their roots in U.S. colonial history in the Philippines. Political economy is therefore crucial to understanding love and its practices in *gijichon*.

In *gijichon* clubs "love" is the fulcrum where work, play, and identity intersect. As a marginal site in the transnational field, *gijichon* is what Gloria Anzaldúa calls a "borderland," where "two or more cultures edge each other, where people of different races occupy the same territory, where under, lower, middle and upper classes touch, where the space between two individuals shrinks with intimacy."[3] The pursuits of "love" by the Filipinas can usefully be interpreted as commentaries on local and regional hierarchies.[4] These "border crossings" thus comprise multiple "sites of creative cultural production."[5] Individual articulations of the emotion of love, and subsequent maneuvers of these articulations, challenge and are circumscribed by these social and cultural constructions.

This chapter explores romantic love as a discourse that genders moral agency in a transnational field. The discussion has three purposes. The first is to illustrate love as a discursive instrument toward an end—a meeting of social and economic unequals. The economy of desires in *gijichon* engenders performances of love in what Filipinas and GIs call the "game." This game requires the presentation of self according to gendered and racialized scripts of romantic love in order to get what one wants—money, gifts, sex, and so forth. Affective demonstrations become integral to and instrumental in social, material, and sexual pursuits. It is important to look at the everyday lives of marginal groups who have little access to institutional and political channels of redress. Where there is little space for political organizing or collective actions, it is all the more important to attend to the mundane aspects of life to understand their social and cultural agency—exercised as challenges and as attempts to transform subordination.[6] Love is therefore a "weapon of the weak" used by Filipinas to manage their sexuality, labor, and vulnerabilities in migration and to open up possibilities to pursue their migration projects for their families and themselves. This part of the analysis focuses on how love is described as a *performance* within an existing social order.

A second purpose is to analyze how love constitutes the self in the transnational field. In their labor migration, Filipina entertainers come to explore their own sense of self as romantic, desirous, and sexual subjects through the language of romantic love. The discourse of romantic love naturalizes affective and erotic desires as reflections of, and their fulfilment as realizations of, the authentic self.[7] In this discourse the individual is an ahistorical and autonomous subject capable of developing spontaneous emotional attachment to "the one." The realization of the self is accomplished in an emotional relationship unencumbered by rational calculations and material concerns. Being the subject of love is proof of one's emotional capacity as a modern autonomous individual, while being the object of love is a validation of one's self as a unique, gendered individual. The pursuit of love sometimes becomes a code for individualistic desires and freedom from one's social obligations. The passionate drive of love is therefore antistructural, entailing a partial abandonment of normative values, made particularly pertinent in a migration site. Love in this analysis is referred to as an *authentication* of the autonomous self.

The third purpose of this chapter is to examine how love and its dilemma "serve as an idiom for communicating"[8] contending values about selfhood, intimacy, and family in processes of modernization and globalization. The uprooting experience of migration provides an opportunity for one to re-evaluate one's obligations to the family and to oneself and where one's emotional and sexual energies can be invested. For the Filipina, does one marry someone who can promise a secure future in the United States for oneself and one's family in the Philippines and all the accoutrement of modernity and cosmopolitan success, such as a concrete house on one's own lot, with an air-conditioner, water heater, and bright tiles? Or does one marry one's "true love," who offers none of these but who promises emotional fulfillment for oneself? For the GI, is one a "loser" or a gentleman in proclaiming "true love" for a Filipina entertainer from a club? What does this emotion of love for the Other say about one's sense of self in relation to prevalent gender and sexual norms? These dilemmas about love, I would argue, epitomize some of the major contradictions that migratory experience engenders for women.

It is important to state up front that these are necessarily interconnected processes. While the distinction between the performativity of love (the "game") and the subjectivity of love (that is, "real love") is emically derived, it will be seen in the ethnography below that the line between play and nonplay is often blurry, and there is always the potential of "love" going beyond its intended performativity and having unpredictable emotional consequences for its players.

Deconstructing "GI"

In anti-American nationalist discourses in both South Korea and the Philippines, GIs are the embodiment of the foreign masculine thrust.[9] Academic analysis of military prostitution has largely focused on the voices of the women and identified their oppression and sufferings as the result of masculinist state projects and their prostituted bodies as symbols of the dominated nation.[10] This perspective gives a valid account of gendered structural oppression in the current political order. Yet how adequate is this perspective for understanding power relations and domination on the level of everyday practice when the GIs, the supposed "perpetrators" or embodiment of these women's oppression, are left out of the analysis?

It is necessary to take one step away from this essentialization. GIs are an ambiguous construction in American society and in American foreign policy.[11] They are both condemned as drunkards and sex-craved young lads who would be fighting in the streets if not for the army and hailed as patriots and freedom fighters who champion noble causes. *Time* magazine named the GI Man of the Year for 1950, the Person of the Year for 2003, and one of the "Heroes and Icons" of the twentieth century in 1999. "GI" commonly refers to enlisted men rather than officers, and GIs are seen as working-class men rather than college graduates—as ethnic minorities and underachieving white people who "did not make it" except for the army.

However, this idea may be more a middle-class American construction than a reflection of reality. Recent statistics from the Department of Defense on the educational attainment and ethnic makeup of active-duty personnel of the U.S. military, supplemented by some of the personal accounts that I have collected, show that though GIs may not be "the best," they are not the "rejects" of society either. Many enlistees join for the pay and benefits that surpass those of civilian jobs. Some enlist for the college funds provided by the GI Bill, and many immigrants join for the accelerated naturalization process the military offers. It is significant that when these "perks" shrank in the late 1970s, the quality of new recruits fell.[12] Joining the army may actually be the best option of many, rather than a "last resort."

Because the two Koreas are still technically at war, a GI's assignment to South Korea is considered a "hardship" tour, as no government sponsorship of family members is provided.[13] The tour of duty normally lasts one year. The short duration of this assignment seems to justify the absence of any program that might help the GIs to integrate into the host country—there are no language-skills training and no briefing sessions on the social and cultural makeup of the country. Commonly and unofficially the little the GIs have heard about South Korea before they arrive concerns the cheap sex available.

Most of the GIs I talked with believed they were in South Korea to prevent North Korean aggression. Though none of them considered patriotism a reason for enlisting, their identity as soldiers of the U.S. forces in Korea was important to their sense of masculinity as American males—the "GI Joe" identity. In addition, whatever their marginality in the United States, their identity as Americans was doubly confirmed on their posting to Korea by their racial identities and by their jobs as GIs; an African American GI said that in Korea he felt more American because he was immediately recognized as such.

In the clubs the popularity of a man is determined by the amount of hard cash he possesses, especially among privates. Higher-ranking GIs with handsome salaries can buy multiple drinks for an entertainer as well as her coworkers and are greeted most enthusiastically in the clubs. Those who refuse to buy the women drinks are often teased with the name "Cheap Charlie." This is a challenge to masculine pride that many young GIs find hard to deal with, and many Filipinas are familiar with the power of such tactics to get more out of the men.

Though virility is an important tenet of hegemonic masculinity, and particularly so in the military, one GI who fulfilled the stereotype and frequented the clubs for sex drew disapproval from his fellow soldiers. Carl, a twenty-year-old GI, talked about the "loser" in his company:

Carl: He was a virgin when he first came. When he first arrived, he said he would not go to those bars, that he won't be paying the girls or doing that. But in less than two weeks, he was going down there every night by himself. Usually people go in groups to have drinks, but going alone means it's something else you are looking for. I used to go alone. He spends all his money on the women, all he does is drink and get women, we all think that he is a loser, he doesn't do anything except going "downrange."
S: Does he do well in the army?
Carl: No, he doesn't. He is a real loser.

GIs refer to the strip of bars outside Camp Casey in Dongducheon as "downrange." The analogy with a military offensive may valorize masculine aggression in the clubs, and Carl's description of the "loser" may resemble popular portrayals of the bawdy GI.[14] However, according to Carl, the excessive and solitary indulgence in alcohol and women met with strong disapproval. Key to the designation of the "loser" is the loss of control (over sexuality, alcohol consumption, and money) and the ignoring of the group. A man's apparently successful and continuous indulgence in aggressive sexuality to the exclusion of other ideal masculine qualities, such as discipline and comradeship, may mark him as a "loser" in the military.

The Game of Love

S: Do you have boyfriends?
Anna: Yes, it's our job. . . . Sometimes the GIs, if he [*sic*] is not your boyfriend, he doesn't buy you a drink. He'd say, "Ok, I will buy you a drink, will you be my girlfriend?" [I'd say,] "Ok, Ok. Buy me a drink and you are my boyfriend." Like that.
Katie: Ha, ha, everyone of us has boyfriends—*boyfriend* boyfriends! Just in the club. But we have just one real boyfriend. We need boyfriends because we need regular customers.

Stepping off the base almost immediately brings a GI into a jungle of clubs with scantily clad Asian women eager to shower their attention on any man for the price of a drink. While some GIs go in groups to play pool or darts, a visitor walking alone sends a clear message that he needs a woman. As soon as he enters a club, an entertainer will greet him and take him to his table. The entertainer will provide him with company if he buys her ladies' drinks at ten dollars each (twenty dollars each since 2006)— much more expensive than the two-dollar beer the GI could get for himself. If the man desires continued company, he will have to buy more drinks. What the entertainer will do in exchange depends on the customer, the club, and the woman, as well as her need to fulfill any drinks quota that day. She might just sit next to him, perform a small dance, or dance provocatively, gyrating herself against the man's private parts, before requesting a drink.

Club owners' observations that GIs favor Filipinas over Korean women were confirmed by many of the GIs with whom I spoke.[15] As aliens in a foreign land and English speakers, GIs and Filipinas find it easier to identify with each other; also, as a result of a century of American colonialism and neocolonialism in the Philippines, they share more in terms of culture and values.

No GI visits a club in search of love. Love is the game GIs play in the clubs for fun and sex. The Filipinas' job is to play the game of love. This game of love is far more than a "romantic exercise."[16] Conversations constitute an important part of the interactions between GIs and the Filipinas, allowing the women to generate and participate in an illusion of intimacy, to pose as women who are both sexually available and vulnerable and persuade the faithful and continual patronage of the GIs. The lines between play and nonplay, however, often become blurred in the process. Self-representation and negotiations over money and sex converge in what entertainers and GIs refer to as "the game," with its participants as "players" and those "being played." The rules and logic of the game are culturally informed and contextually manipulated. Its players draw on the rhetoric and symbols of romantic love for often imperfect performances, as well as for the construction of their own experiences. In the words of Carl, the GI mentioned above, who spent the first six months of his time and salary in the clubs in search of a girlfriend before giving up: "You see, they either make you feel pity for them, or make you feel special, or make you think that you are going to get something." Carl's insight points to three common tropes used by women to gain their customers' patronage: their own powerlessness, their customers' individuality, and the prospect of sex. These might operate separately, but more frequently they are combined to structure the illusion of intimacy in *gijichon* clubs.

The personalization of relationships in *gijichon* clubs relies on creating the potential for a relationship beyond the mediation of money. To this end, altruistic ideals of both friendship and romantic love are mobilized. A concatenation of lies, truths, and partial truths permeates relationships between entertainers and their regulars. To maintain their appeal, Filipina entertainers lie about their age, their virginity, their boyfriends, their marital status, and the number of children they have.

In *gijichon* GIs often offer Filipinas gifts to usher a relationship from the commercial to the personal realm. Gifts range from such mundane objects as lotion, clothes, shampoo, medicine, phone cards, and fruit, snacks, and other food to luxury goods such as stereos and gold necklaces bought on base. When a GI invites a Filipina to lunch, she might bring two or three of her friends along. Such material and financial support is crucial to the well-being of the Filipinas. It is also important to recognize the affective dimension of these gifts. Much like the gifts Chinese cadres in Yunxiang Yan's (1996) study[17] bestowed on their clients to maintain their loyalty and support, these gifts and favors are also offered within the context of a power relationship that nonetheless recognizes the importance of affective engagement—in this instance the friendship of the Filipinas. It is a friendship between gendered "haves" and the "have-nots." Very often these gifts may also be "the props of a love affair," functioning as a means of legitimation.[18] Many Filipinas adorned their rooms with stuffed toys, baseball caps, flowers that had been hung to dry, and other gifts from their customers (see Figure 7). Like the pictures of family and friends they also put up, these were mementos of their identities beyond the "buy-and-sell" relationships in the clubs and of their connections with places and possibilities beyond *gijichon*.

This discourse of romantic love, imbricated with its material manifestations, allowed the women to deny or delay sex by calling for further demonstrations of love. "You would be my boyfriend, but we need to know each other. If you want me, you wait." Meanwhile, more gifts and drinks could be extracted. The successful entertainers were the "top drinkers" and usually the ones who managed to lead several men to believe that they were their "real" boyfriends.

The notion of romantic love constitutes mutuality and reciprocity between self and other. The romantic script also directs gender-appropriate "give-and-take" beyond the mutual exchange of the "I-love-you" utterance—the man protects and supports the woman materially, while the

Figure 7. Filipina entertainers in their room, decorated with gifts and photographs

woman offers herself sexually. Hence, what is being given and taken differs between men and women. While utterance itself becomes a kind of music,[19] the exchange of names in the utterance gives substance and maintains the discourse of romance, building links of obligation and emotional attachment in *gijichon* clubs—and sometimes beyond.

Bella: [Boyfriends] do your laundry [on base], they buy you phone cards, buy you food, take you out, buy you drinks and gifts. And they give you money!

S: Do you think you are "playing" the GIs?

Bella (adamantly): Yes. Because our owner is using us, so we are using them [the GIs] too. Our owner is making money with us, so we have to use them to make money too.

Among many of the Filipinas there was a poignant awareness that the club owners and managers were exploiting them. They were also keenly aware of the power differentials between their American male customers and themselves, and between the United States and the Philippines. They were the "have-nots" in each of these relations. Such awareness was the basis for their emotional manipulation of their GI customers and allowed them to see it as a compensation for their relative powerlessness.

James Scott coined the phrase "weapon of the weak" in his study of Malaysian peasants to describe how class struggle can take place on an everyday level and how the poor refuse to accept the terms of their subordination.[20] Erik Cohen argues that Thai women working in tourist-oriented bars are skilled in manipulating the ambiguity in their relationships with foreign men to assume a position of dominance, a capacity he calls "the power of the weak."[21] Filipina entertainers in *gijichon* often seek to trigger in their customers a sense of pity for their predicament. Regular customers usually learn of the women's woes, ranging from family breakdowns to the abuse they suffered at the hands of managers and club owners. In the sexualized context of the clubs, where all women are potential prostitutes, important means to gain control over one's sexuality are the claims of virginity and ignorance of the jobs in which they find themselves. The powerless and the pure thereby command the pity of the powerful, who subsequently feel obliged to extend their support and protection.

Love serves as a "weapon of the weak" for these Filipinas, who draw on the symbols and rhetoric of love as a moral framework to negotiate their subordination and pursue their aspirational projects. As migrant women who have no official channels of redress for the human-rights violations taking place daily in the clubs, they focus their energies on turning love into a source of power. In other words, where the state and the market fail them, love gives them hope.

The Power of Virginity

The power of the weak comes in the gendered (and also racialized) form of female virginity and its symbolic meaning as feminine purity, innocence, and virtue in need of masculine protection. The strength of the purity ideal also hinges on its association with romantic love and related ideas of loyalty and monogamy. It is therefore a common practice for Filipinas to deploy the feminine ideal of virginity and purity, which commands particular reverence among people with a strong Roman Catholic upbringing, to manage their sexuality. These ideas feature significantly in their interactions with their customer-boyfriends. My concern is not whether they are "real" virgins or not, but with their cultural creativity in deploying the virginity trope to establish benevolent power relations and achieve the mercy (*herak*) and obligation of their protectors.

Annabel was a twenty-six-year-old, never-married, single mother with an eight-year-old son. When she was low on her drinks count, her club owner put a lot of pressure on her to go into the VIP room with customers. Because of the pressure, one night she finally said yes to a black GI. As soon as she went into the room, she broke down crying and muttered between sobs, "I am a virgin. . . . I only came in because the club owner forced me to." When she retold the story to me, she suggested that she had picked a black GI because black GIs "have a good heart." She apparently found it amusing that the GI believed her story of virginity and also that he started to "hate" the club owner. She was even prouder to say, "The next night, he came back!" By capitalizing on the abuses of the club owner and her need for protection as a virgin, Annabel actively assumed and constructed an asymmetrical power relation with gendered values that obliged her customer not only to ally with but also to protect her.

Claims of virginity were important for women in managing their sexuality—in maintaining an image of female innocence that might be "given" to the right man while at the same time putting off sexual advances. It is interesting to note that notions of virginity were important to the Filipinas' GI customers, as demonstrated by the fact that the trope worked: not only did Annabel succeed in getting out of the VIP room without compromising herself, but she also gained a regular customer.

This trope of virginity was particularly useful within what had already become a "boyfriend-girlfriend" relationship. Roy (thirty-four) and Lilly (twenty-six) dated for two months but "never really did it," despite Roy's having paid for her bar fine twice. According to Roy, "We just didn't. I think it must be her convictions, or that she thinks it should only happen after marriage. . . . I don't know." In fact, Lilly was married with a son. She never told Roy, but Roy was ready to attribute the refusal of (penetrative) sex to Lilly's religious faith and to her status as a virgin. Drawing on the Americans' readiness to accept their conservative sexual norms as Asian women from a Catholic country, many of the Filipinas actively constructed and recycled their "virginity" with their customers.

The Moral Calculus of Love

The discourse of love is a chief driving force in the economics and interpersonal dynamics of *gijichon* clubs. A GI telling a woman "I love you" in an attempt to get her into bed is as much a part of the game as the woman saying the same thing in the hope of getting a share of his paycheck. Love serves as a moral discourse accounting for the give and take, and the gains and losses. That this is a game, however, does not mean there is no love—it is just a different type of love.

Defining different kinds of love delineates the obligations that different loving relationships entail. Justin and Roy both argued that the "love" Roy felt for Lilly did not oblige him to answer her plea for an air ticket back to the Philippines (Lilly, in fact, was using her request in a last attempt to get money from Roy, as her air ticket had already been paid for by her club owner):

Roy: There is a difference between loving somebody and being in love with somebody.
Justin: [Nodded.]
S: Loving someone is different from being in love with somebody? You have to explain this to me, I don't quite understand.
Roy: You see, the English language is not very good for expressing ideas of love. In some other languages they have more terms for it. But we just have "love." Loving someone means you care about her, you are concerned about her, but you come first. But being in love with someone means that you put the other person's welfare first. That's the difference.
Justin: It means [being] willing to sacrifice for someone.
Roy: Yes, so I love many people, but I come first before these people. I love Lilly, I am concerned about her, but I come first.
Justin: You love someone—you have good sex. You are in love with someone—you make love.

Justin's last statement sums up the two different forms of love and the kinds of sex that each entails. The distinction lies in the relative weight that the self and the other carry. It confirms that, even in *gijichon* clubs, "love" is always a part of sexual encounters.

The common knowledge that promises should not be taken seriously qualifies the interactions in a club as "play." Yet one important feature in this play of romantic love is that the ideal of faithfulness becomes built into the interactions and operates as a form of control, in particular on the GIs. For example, Winnie took a picture of Justin and showed it to other Filipinas, telling them he was her boyfriend—thus circumscribing his behavior in *gijichon* clubs. Others tried to spread such information by word of mouth, hoping to claim ownership over certain customers as boyfriends. While such ownership was generally respected, fights over customers-boyfriends were not uncommon.

Unfaithfulness was also common. GIs' confessions to their girlfriends usually followed the same narrative: after a fight with his girlfriend, the GI went drinking in another club and bar-fined another woman. Most of the women chose to show their magnanimity and forgiveness, tipping the balance of power toward themselves by manipulating the "guilt" of the men. Shirley said that she was hurt when she found out that her boyfriend had paid the bar fine for another woman. One of the first questions she asked him after learning of the betrayal was, "How much did you pay for her bar fine?" When he told her, three hundred dollars, she replied, "Three hundred dollars! You paid her three hundred dollars? Why did you do that to me?"

In a context where money is a proof of love—or where economic and emotional intimacies are interdependent—infidelity is compounded by the sex act and the transfer of money. Regardless of the woman's emotional devotion, the need to police unfaithfulness was significant for both her pride and her material well-being. While the Filipina "girlfriends" could often explain their behavior of intimacy with other men as part of their jobs—and the logic sometimes went, "If you give me more money, I need not be doing this"—the "boyfriends" had no similar excuse and were subject to the control by the ideal of "faithfulness."

However, love could also be earned by loyalty and gifts. A customer was sometimes so important to an entertainer for the drinks he bought and gifts he gave her that the woman agreed to "give herself" after his continual patronage.

Alan, a thirty-seven-year-old GI, had been Beverly's most important customer since her arrival in the Ace Club. He claimed that he loved her, bar-fined her at least once a week, gave her money to send home, and bought her all her daily necessities. Beverly did not love him—she did not like "old men." However, after declining to have sex with him on the first two bar fines, she agreed to comply the third time around, continuing to play the role of his girlfriend until his departure in order to reciprocate his patronage.

Thus both GIs and Filipinas adopted gendered discourses of emotion to negotiate their relationships, mitigating the stigma of prostitution. Sex without emotional involvement would qualify the woman as a "whore" and the man as a "punter," labels that would undermine their respective gender values and identities. If sex took place, it was at least based on "feelings" (of affection and gratitude, if not love), rather than financial and material exchange.

Not Just a Customer: GIs' Search for Authenticity in the Clubs

After the first six months of his stay in South Korea, Carl finally chose to become celibate, casting aside the struggle between insincere relationships with "drinkie girls" who were easily accessible and the (potentially) sincere relationship with the few women in the military, who were virtually inaccessible. This yearning for authenticity despite the availability of sex reveals a desire for recognition as a distinct individual—more than, in Carl's words, "just a customer." Such a yearning is not exclusive to inexperienced young GIs like Carl.

Both Justin and Roy were divorced and in their thirties. They enjoyed having fun and meeting the many women in the clubs. With the ladies' drinks they could afford to buy, they decided which women they talked to and for how long. In *gijichon* clubs each paid "to be the king of the night' and be free from "the fear of rejection." "Back in the States," Roy said, "when I go to a bar, I have to get up and go to a girl. Here, I just have to sit down and they come to me. And they are mostly very beautiful women." Roy said he disliked American women, particularly those in the army, because they were "not very feminine." He found Korean entertainers too materialistic and rather passive in bed: "Filipino women are less inhibited. Some are even more aggressive, I would say. Like this woman in M——— Club. It was my first time in there and as soon as I got in, she took my hand, found the most secluded corner there was, and she was on top of me before I knew it." Roy did not use a condom and was "sweating bullets" for the next few days after the encounter in fear of having contracted sexually transmitted diseases. Nonetheless, the reversal of gender dynamics in sex pleased him:

S: And you liked it?

Roy (rolling his eyes): Oh, yes. I did. It's good to have someone else take the initiative.

Justin: It's every man's dream.

Roy: Yes, because you don't have the fear of rejection. She is there doing it to you.

The relief from gaining a woman's approval and the pleasure of being "done to" instead of "doing it," thus inverting the behavioral structure of everyday life, have been cited as the common appeals of commercial sex to men. In this instance, the masculine ego of the man found an extra boost in the willing submission of the exotic Filipina whose femininity and erotic appeal outbid her American and Korean counterparts. Roy, who insisted that he was only into fun and not love, turned out to be concerned not only about the sex but also about how "special" he was to the woman: "She told me that she didn't do it to everyone—it's just because she likes me that she does it with me. Well, I don't know if that is true. But the other night, I did sit there and observe her, and she didn't do it with other customers." The woman's utterance about liking him was important to Roy. He was happy to confirm that she did not do the same thing to other men. Had Roy been concerned only about the sex, he would not have felt the need to verify the exclusiveness of his "privilege."[22] The affection that the woman declared for him, to his relish, marked his distinction from "everyone."

Justin, who had given such a lucid definition of "loving" someone and "being in love" with someone, crossed the line by "falling in love" and subsequently marrying a twenty-two-year-old Filipina entertainer whom he initially intended only to be part of his nightlife in *gijichon*:

> I did not expect it to happen either. . . . At first I made it very clear to her that there would be no commitment and I was there just for fun. But later, I started to see her more and we talked more, and in late February, I started to get more serious. She passed some of my little tests. I wouldn't be played. I told her, you don't have to go into the VIP rooms, it's not in your contract, and anything that happens in that room is what you want to happen. If you want to be with me, you decide what you let happen in there. I don't want to hear that when we are married, "See, that's Sergeant XX's wife. She used to work in a club and she used to do this and this with me." I said I don't want to hear anything like that if she becomes my wife. I told her that to help her get some control of her situation, to help her look into the future. And I think it helped her a lot. . . . She lost many customers because of me, because she refused to do what they asked her

to. And the customers would ask for their money back. Sometimes [when] a customer would pay her to go out, she would pretend to be sick, go home early, and then called me up. Then I would come and meet her. They [the guys] paid for me to go out with her. [He sounded very proud of that.]

Justin explained why he had fallen in love with Winnie: "She really opens up her innermost thoughts to me." The search for authenticity of experience that is "everywhere manifest in our society"[23] is all the more pronounced in a context where "love" could be mere performance for material ends.

Winnie's revelation of what Justin believed to be her most private thoughts marked a significant departure from the "game." In Erving Goffman's terminology,[24] it ushered Justin from the performative and therefore inauthentic "front" to the "back," where the intimate "truth" lies. This privileged status became the basis for intimacy and commitment. In this brief summary of his relationship with Winnie, Justin outlined the negotiation of gender identities as a process within the discourse of romantic love in *gijichon* clubs. His words are consistent with Katherine Frank's argument that a clear distinction between "real" and "faked" emotional involvement is difficult for women and men alike. Both parties participate in a performance of intimacy that involves self-representations in which "the phantasmatic and the real can be intricately intertwined."[25]

To illustrate the experiences of love and its dilemma in the transnational field, I present two "love" stories with distinct endings—one resulting in marriage and one ending in a fallout from marriage plans. They illuminate the tensions between individual desires and family obligations, gender ideals and realities, and the heart and the brain.

Annabel and Philip: Love Looks Past All Things

I met Philip, Annabel's fiancé, three days after she left for the Philippines, in a coffee shop in Uijeongbu. He was brought up in a very devout Christian family. Both of his parents and one of his sisters were in the military, and Philip enlisted at the age of seventeen, before he had finished high school. He believed that his life was in the hands of God and whatever happened was the will of God. He had never seen the ocean, having spent all his life in Kentucky before boarding a flight to South Korea, to Camp Casey in Dongducheon. For the first six and a half months in Korea he stayed on base most of the time and would not join his colleagues in going "down-range." He found the clubs morally unacceptable and did not understand why they were there: "I mean it's not only here [in Korea], it's everywhere with the military. I don't know why it's like that; if I can do something to change it I would certainly get rid of it."

He first visited a strip bar when he was still in basic training in the United States. Trusting that he would not get drunk, his sergeant asked him to drive a group to the bar. When he saw a strip show for the first time, he cried. Philip explained, "It's just so sad to see the women doing that. I just couldn't believe that it was happening."

However, on his twentieth birthday his sergeants took him out barhopping. He met Annabel at midnight, after hours of drinking. "Then there was just this [snapping his fingers], and love at first sight. It just happened. I told her, 'I want to bring you back to the States.'"

For the seven weeks that followed, before Annabel ran away from the club, Philip said he saw her at the club almost every night. He said it was "very difficult" when he saw her enter a VIP room with another GI for twenty minutes. However, Annabel cried when she assured him that "nothing happened." He paid her bar fine twice to take her out—once to walk around the vicinity of the clubs, after which she returned to the club before midnight, and once to watch a video in his room (where Annabel tried to seduce him). When he was just beginning to wonder if he had been spending too much money on Annabel, she ran away with the other Filipinas from the club. They met again two weeks later. He was personally against premarital sex and went to bed with her only after he had decided to marry her.

Philip had promised to visit and marry Annabel in the Philippines in two months. He could understand why she was worried, since he had seen other GIs back out of their promises of marriage to Filipinas, and he was eager to distinguish himself from the crowd. "I guess no more than 9 percent of the guys in the army are good. I am not saying that all of them are bad, but most of them. . . . So everybody is out there for sex, yes, sex again, as if sex is all there is to life." Lamenting the moral laxity of the majority of his peers, Philip thus portrayed himself as a distinctly moral and upstanding God-fearing young man who was committed to being a responsible and good man. He was one of the "9 percent" of good guys in the army. He would marry Annabel, as promised.

I asked if his parents knew that Annabel worked in a club. He had been reluctant to let them know at first, especially since his father had been in the air force in Korea and "ha[d] an idea what the place [wa]s like. . . . But now they know. . . . But it doesn't matter. Love looks past all things."

What was there for love to look past? Philip's narrative of his life and his character focused on his moral rectitude and goodness, casting sex strictly within the confines of marriage. Even though he was glad that they had met soon after Annabel arrived in the club, "so she couldn't have done much," it remained a fact that she was a woman who worked in a club, who had gone into the VIP room with other men for pay and who could have had sex for pay had they not met. As such, Annabel was always liable to suspicion for being a part of the system that violated his sense of moral propriety. Yet marrying Annabel would fulfill the magical qualities of love, not just because it was "love at first sight" but also because it would allow him to defy what was antithetical to his moral universe.

However, he had yet to figure out how to explain this nonnormative encounter with his wife-to-be to his future family. He told me, "But I don't know what I would tell my kids when they ask how we met . . . 'I met your mother while she was working in a club . . . ' ha ha ha [embarrassed laughter]. I mean, I asked where my parents met, they met in the air force." For Philip, there was certainly a world of difference between meeting in the military and meeting in a military club.

I did not meet Philip again after that meeting, which took place in September 1999. Annabel got suspicious when I made an appointment with Philip to have dinner one Friday evening—a "date evening" in the club scheme of things. He never showed up. Annabel sent me an accusing e-mail the next day, highlighting that I would be stealing the father of her child, with whom she was two months pregnant. I replied immediately, explaining that my sole intention was to talk to him before he visited her in the Philippines and that, for the sake of her peace of mind, I would not contact him again. She replied with thanks and said that she was waiting for him to arrive.

However, an e-mail from Annabel arrived in December saying that she needed to talk about her pain. Alarmed, I gave her a call and found out that Philip did not go to the Philippines, claiming that he had had to take some training for his promotion. Then he told Annabel that he was confused. He seemed to have met another woman in one of the clubs. His friends were asking him to think about how different married life would be. Annabel was desperate and lost—she was four-months pregnant, and preparations for the wedding were well under way. Her family started to blame her. I could only comfort her by asking her to be strong and have faith.

News of their wedding reached me in August 2000: Philip had gone to the Philippines to marry Annabel in February, and their child was born in May. When we last spoke, in February 2001, Annabel was in the Philippines waiting for her papers to be processed so that she could move with her two children to the States and live as a family with Philip. She had hired a helper and devoted all her energies to looking after her children. Philip had been sending money to support them. She said that she would never forget the difficult days in Korea, and she did not want to go back ever again, but she considered it a blessing from God that she had gone there, met Philip, and then had run away in time. "If I stayed there for a year, I don't think Philip would like me anymore. I might meet other GIs. I might have done other things. Things might change."

Annabel had not gone to college before going to Korea, but she took pride in having had "a good job at an office, as a representative," unlike some other women in South Korea who had "worked in a club before." She had supplemented her income with a sideline business selling car accessories, but this was not enough to get her relatives' recognition: "I had problems with my relatives. I was not making a lot of money. I was a single mom. They kept on saying that I could not have more. They were pushing me down, rather than giving me more support. I ignored it. So I decided to work [overseas]." Annabel was aware of the fortuitous nature of her success during her tumultuous two months in South Korea. She had wanted to make more money and prove herself to her family, who had successfully opposed her marrying the father of the child.

On the day of her departure, Annabel showed me a picture of her and her then-fiancé, Philip. Her excitement about the impending marriage was obvious. Her marriage to an American man would prove her a "success" to her family. They could no longer bring her down. Then, interestingly, in the middle of this elated account of her marriage plans, Annabel said, pouting, "I don't like Americans, I like Filipino men, but I don't know." This was not an excited proclamation of love, nor was it a denial of her affection for Philip. She was merely raising a question about her "heart," which interrupted what she knew in her "head" to be a narrative of a migration "success."

Ira: Learning to Love, Dying for Love

Ira was a twenty-eight-year-old single parent who had left her three children in the care of her mother in the Philippines. She had run away from her violent husband and had worked as an entertainer in a club until she became pregnant with her fourth child by one of her regular clients. In April 1999 she went to South Korea. In May we met and began to talk on the telephone regularly. When she returned home in May 2000, I met her and her family at the airport in Manila and spent the next eight days with her.

At our first meeting, in Dongducheon, Ira had told me about her "boy-friends," and I had asked whether she wanted to marry a GI. She did not know, she said, but any uncertainty that existed then had been dispelled completely by the end of a year in South Korea. During that time Ira had come to recognize the many benefits that marrying an American GI could bring to her and her family. Thus, she did not fail to leave South Korea without securing a fiancé, who was to visit her family in the Philippines three weeks later.

At one of my first meetings with her, Ira told me about the three men she was seeing in South Korea: one was her "real boyfriend"; the other two were "just boyfriends." "But," she said, "I am still a virgin in Korea." Seized by my fascination with her sudden utterance of the word "virgin," I missed the subtle play Ira was engaged in by qualifying her use of it with the phrase "in Korea." I had completely forgotten that she was already a mother. I asked naively, "Really?" She responded, "In Korea, yes! I haven't slept with anyone yet!" Seeing my bewilderment, she added, "I have a kid, re-member?"[26]

Instead of deploying virginity to command respect, as previously dis-cussed, Ira called herself "a virgin in Korea" to produce a comic, ironical effect that implied subversive intentions, while at the same time asserting her subscription to the ideal of virginity. Virginity thus becomes renewable in migration.

Ira told me that her one and only true love was a nineteen-year-old black GI named Jamie, who was the only one with whom she had had sex ("I just want to have sex with one man; I want to be faithful"). Copulation set the boundary for faithfulness for most of the entertainers. Being physi-cally intimate with other men, calling them "boyfriends," flirting with them, and even going into a VIP room with a man for twenty minutes were behaviors that fit inside that boundary. This redefinition of codes of inti-macy often became a bone of contention between the women and their boyfriends, contributing partly to the volatility of relationships in *gijichon*.

"It's a new GI. We are finished. It hurts," Ira told me on the phone one day in January 2000, referring to the "GI girlfriend" Jamie said he had met in the army. I visited her the next day. In the room she shared with Jenny at the back of the club, Ira and I sat on her bed as she told me, crying, what had happened. Lou, Bella, and Bella's GI boyfriend were also there, all of them throwing in an occasional comment without offering much consolation. Then Ira proceeded to tear down from the wall the sketches scripted "Love you 4 ever" and a picture of her with Jamie, and she kicked off the bed her entire collection of stuffed toys, including the one that Jamie had given her when they first met. She picked up the big stuffed seal, threw it onto the floor, and kicked it while wailing and yelling, "I love him. I still love him." She took out a box containing all the notes and letters and photos from Jamie. She showed me a letter that said they had been together for three weeks, that he was serious, and that he did not want any more games and asked Ira to be serious too. On a small piece of paper was written "MARRY ME?" In fact, Jamie had given Ira an engagement ring three months into their relationship. He had further suggested that he would help her three children, her brother, and her parents to immigrate to the United States. Back then Ira had agreed to my suggestion that it would be "a dream come true."

The relationship had lasted for more than seven months, and Ira could think of only one reason for the breakup: "Maybe it's because I have a small mouth, maybe that woman has a big mouth. I can only take in a little bit [of his penis]. I can still hold his dick with my hand. But I want to give him satisfaction. . . . I really want to. I was so nice to him. I cook for him. I lost customers because of him. He gave me everything I wanted. He supported me. One hundred dollars, sometimes two hundred dollars a month."

Ira rarely initiated talk about sex except to joke, but this was no joke. Whether or not Jamie's sexual dissatisfaction was the true reason for their breakup, Ira's words reveal how intent she was on satisfying him. She never insisted that Jamie use a condom and started to take oral contraceptives only when I offered to accompany her to the pharmacy. Not only had she tried to uphold the romantic ideal of faithfulness to Jamie (which she believed women GIs, or "GI girls" in the parlance of Filipina entertainers, were incapable of), but she was eager to demonstrate her capacity to satisfy him domestically and sexually.

About a month later Ira called to say she was outside the U.S. Embassy in Seoul and wanted to meet me. I went and learned about Ira's decision to marry Larry, a twenty-three-year-old GI of Italian descent. She had come with Larry so that he could get the necessary papers for marriage. I was surprised at the news because Ira had never talked much about Larry except to say that there was "a white guy" who had been very nice to her even when Jamie had left her.

S: Do you love him?
Ira: No. [She sniggered, as if I just said something silly.]
S: Ha? So why are you marrying him? [I laughed.]
Ira: Because he gives me what I want.
S: And that is . . . ?
Ira: Money.
S: And . . . ?
Ira: [The opportunity] to go to the States.

Ira had decided to marry Larry while she was secretly seeing Jamie, unbeknownst to Larry. She had decided that it was not possible to marry Jamie, in spite of her love for him. Her family had never liked Jamie because he was black. Furthermore, Jamie was getting into a lot of trouble with the army. He was soon discharged for misconduct and returned to the United States, where he remained unemployed.

Ira had repeated that she could not have sex with someone she did not love. Through another skillful play on ideas about female purity, romantic love, and the ideal of sex within marriage, Ira had managed to refuse sex with Larry while she continued to lay claim to his financial support as a fiancé.

Ira: He even asked if I have slept with Jamie. And I said yes. I said yes, I gave myself to him.
S: And he doesn't mind?
Ira: Maybe he doesn't, but he accepts [it].
S: Why did you tell him?
Ira: Because he asked.
S: You could have said no.
Ira: I just wanted to tell the truth. I said I did.
S: And he accepts that you are not sleeping with him now?
Ira: Hmm, yes. Because I said, you know, OK, no more. I can't sleep with you before we are married. After what [has] happened between me and Jamie, I don't want to do it again. . . . Even though you have spent a lot of money on me, I couldn't sleep with you.
S: Has he slept with another Filipina?
Ira: No.

S: So he has never had sex after coming to South Korea?
Ira: He told me no. I think he is a virgin again.
S: A virgin?
Ira: Yes, again.
S: A virgin in Korea?
Ira: Yes.

I have to marvel at Ira's flexibility in kneading cultural and gender ideals to fit her scheme of things. By portraying herself as a selfless romantic who had "given herself" to a man she truly loved, who had abandoned her, she assumed the image of a woman who had been disillusioned by love. She used this "trauma of love" to justify her refusal of sex with Larry. Ira's portrayal of herself also put Larry in the position of a suspect who might inflict further trauma, possibly calling for further demonstrations of his "true love." Reminding Larry that the financial assistance she needed from him was not a sufficient reason for him to demand sex from her, Ira reiterated that sex was not for sale, despite her job. It was equivalent to saying that she had learned her lesson with men, and now sex was, in Ira's delaying tactic with Larry, only to be sanctioned by the marital contract.

Like many other Filipinas, Ira used the image of the Philippines as a religious and conservative country to back up her claims that she would not have sex again before getting married. Portraying herself as the forsaken heroine of a tragic love tale, she succeeded in representing herself as a victim of both economic and emotional woes, yet one who would not compromise her moral values. How much appeal did that have on the male ego of a young American GI to further pledge his love and support? Ira explained to me more than once that her plan to marry Larry was tied to her plans for her family. She wanted to marry a man who could help bring good fortune to them. She would get her three children and her seventeen-year-old brother to the United States once she was married. Ira wanted her brother to join the U.S. Army—to be a GI—so that they could both help with the family in the Philippines. She said that she could divorce him after she received her U.S. citizenship—but maybe not if he were nice.

During a telephone conversation following our meeting in front of the U.S. Embassy, I asked whether Larry had given her an engagement ring. Ira said indifferently, "Yes, he said he would. But I don't care. I can live without a ring." I was thinking of how Ira had put family interest and preference before her own when she suddenly said, "I am sorry I am just using my brain now. . . . I mean I am sorry for my attitude now, that I am only using my brain."

S: Oh, using your brain, and not your heart?
Ira: Not my heart. Yes. Not my heart.
S: What would you do if you were using your heart?
Ira: [Giggled for a while.] Maybe I am gonna kill myself? Ha ha ha.
S: Why?
Ira: 'Cuz it's hard for me. [She sounded as though she were sobbing but also laughed out loud.]

In our communications, from 1998 to 2008, it was typical of Ira to laugh while voicing her woes. She would also make a clear distinction between her "heart" and her "brain." She was aware that her scheming was "bad" or morally regrettable and yet had all been dictated by the "brain." The "brain" had come to stand for her family responsibilities, hard work, and calculations; the "heart" for her desires for love, romance, and freedom. A sobbing laugh or laughing sob becomes comprehensible in the context of such tensions between the heart and the brain.

Back in the Philippines in the presence of her family, I heard her continue to exchange pledges of love and longing on the telephone with Larry, repeating "I love you" or "I miss you" with a clear expression of weariness, preceded and followed by urgent requests for money. Her loathing for Larry seemed to grow with the vehemence of her complaints about him in front of her family, who had rejected Jamie but who approved of this marriage. Ira made no attempt to hide the fact that she was marrying Larry as a sacrifice for the family.

"I don't know. Maybe *I will learn to love him*. I will try," she said (emphasis added). This was probably the most positive statement Ira made about her marriage plans with Larry. I was intrigued by Ira's idea of "learning" to love, which contrasted sharply with her belief in romantic love— such as the love she had had for Jamie, which could not be explained. Listening together to Bryan Adams's "(Everything I do) I do it for you" in a karaoke in Olongapo, out of a compelling skepticism about romantic love rather than any urge to persuade, I had a conversation with Ira, while her eyes were transfixed on the screen:

S: Don't believe this.
Ira: What?

S: That someone would die for you because of love.

Ira: Why?

S: Do you think someone would really do that?

Ira (removing her gaze from the screen and turning to me): Yes. I will!
[Pauses, relaxing her straightened back and collapsing against the sofa, her gaze returning to the screen as the song was coming to an end.] But I don't know if Jamie will.

Fenella Cannell has found this distinction between "true love" and "learnt love" among the lowland Filipinas in Bicol.[27] The phrase "only learnt love" is used to emphasize one's reservations about being joined with a spouse and one's reluctant obedience to the family. This "narrative of reluctance" constructs the value and power of the woman over her family and her spouse, as she can turn herself into a "forced gift": "However great the degree of compulsion, and however powerful the notion that children owe obedience to their parents, the acts of obedience themselves obligate others, compelling recognition, a kind of return gift."[28] Ira's marriage plan should thus not be considered merely an act of female self-abnegation for the family. She was operating within a system of reciprocity in which she recognized her opportunities and constraints as a woman and was proceeding to construct her value as such, incurring debts from others that would have to be repaid in the future. As Ira clearly articulated to me on more than one occasion, she wanted to help her younger brother and sister go abroad so that they would help take care of her children when Ira got old.

Larry did visit Ira in the Philippines and stayed with her family for twenty days in May 2000. He left and continued to apply for Ira to join him in South Korea as a fiancée. However, after five months he stopped sending her money, having learned from other Filipinas that Ira had cheated on him. Ira was suddenly flung into despondence. Her last words to Larry were, "I never loved you. I just wanted your money. And you've given me so much money, but I never slept with you. So who's the loser, eh?"

The narrative of reluctance with Larry over sex, together with this ultimate denial of love, allowed Ira to claim her triumph over him when the marriage plan fell through. She refused to be the victim. This did not mean, however, that her conditions of subordination were altered. Prospects for alleviating her family burden were smashed along with the wedding bells.

*   *   *

As has been discussed in Chapter 3 and in this chapter, the *gijichon* club regime structures men's entertainment around accessibility to women's company and bodies for money. This idea is built into the R & R industry in the Asia Pacific, where the masculine desires of American soldiers are catered to by Asian women. On the level of the erotic economy underlying this commercial exchange is the mutual participation in the romantic parable of discovery and conquest by the American (white) explorer who is rewarded with an alien lover, submissive and devoted. The projection of Western men's erotic and romantic fantasies onto the Asian women reached a peak with the stationing of U.S. troops in the Pacific.[29] The sexy docility of Asian women in the Western imagination is further reproduced through sex tourism publicity and "mail-order bride" brochures and Web sites.[30]

Gamitin mo ang ulo (utak), wag ang puso (Use your head [brain], not your heart) is a common utterance among Filipina entertainers in talking about their work, their customers, their boyfriends, and their futures. Many Filipinas promise themselves that they will not get emotionally involved in South Korea—they go to make money and as such should use their brains and not their hearts. Yet almost all of them leave South Korea with tales of forsaken love. Most GIs have heard about the cheap sex available in South Korea before they arrive, but many of them spend months of time and salary looking for "love" in the clubs.

The commodification of intimacy and sexuality in the clubs threatens to undermine the personhood and individuality of both the Filipinas and the GIs. As the ethnographic discussions in this chapter illustrate, "love" and "marriage" become platforms for individuals' search for assurances and stability at a site strongly marked by the stigma of prostitution and personal vulnerability. "Love" personalizes the commercial exchange in the clubs with its claims of "authenticity," making it more acceptable to the parties involved, but it also impacts on the subjective experiences of the individuals.

"They are after just one thing," GIs and Filipinas frequently say about each other. To the men, the women are interested only in money and marrying an American man; to the women, the men want only sex. Yet human desires are rarely as simple and straightforward as this. Through their common desires for recognition, affection, and intimacy, Filipinas and GIs negotiate their own aspirations and longing with and through each other. Anna Tsing reminds us: "The kiss crosses cultures, proving mutual recognition. Yet mutual is not symmetrical."[31] This asymmetry, however, does not prevent the Dayak women whom Tsing studied from claiming control, knowledge, and status in their stories of "alien romance" with foreigners. These stories serve as a critical commentary on gender and regional hierarchies. Read in the larger political economy, they challenge the feminization of Asia and the exoticization of Asian women that have been part of conventional Western knowledge.[32]

As James Clifford suggests, "Diaspora women are caught between patriarchies, ambiguous pasts, and future. They connect and disconnect, forget and remember, in complex, strategic ways. The lived experiences of diasporic women thus involve painful difficulty in mediating discrepant worlds."[33] Love serves as an idiom to communicate their struggles to negotiate the discrepancies between their gendered obligations and gendered desires that come to light in the borderland of migration. For the Filipinas, *gijichon* is the "borderland" between the Philippines and the United States, between the past and the future, between familial responsibilities and personal freedom, between uncertainty and security, and between accepting one's weakness and transforming it within the current order of things. Their agency must be recognized without neglecting the constraints of power and knowledge. Their creative projects of self-definition in their "labor of love" are but expressions of their awareness of the multiple possibilities in this liminal space and time.

This chapter has identified the centrality of "love" for Filipinas and GIs in making relationships and lives meaningful. This would not be such a dramatic claim had the site of their interactions not been the *gijichon* club—a site known for the commodification of female sexuality for the U.S. military. In most discourses that readily associate GI clubs with various forms of violence against women, the power differentials and the capitalist logic are highlighted to render all interactions therein empty of intimacy, authenticity, and romance. My analysis echoes Elizabeth Bernstein's argument about the ways that transformations in postindustrial economic and cultural life reconfigure sexual subjectivities and sexual expressions. By paying careful attention to structural factors and the social locations of the men and women who participate in these labor and consumptive practices, alternative forms of intimacy in the shifting geographies of sexual commerce and its regulation emerge.[34] Concepts of "self" and "sexuality" are intimately embedded in each other and are entwined with larger social structures. Without dismissing the structures that generate abusive employment conditions and discriminatory practices, and the political economy that has perpetuated global inequalities, this ethnography hopes to remind analysts that the individual actors studied here are "persons"—rather than externally imposed institutional identities such as "punters," "GIs," "prostitutes," and "trafficked women." Love is important because it is the understood arena in which they engage in social interactions and cultural productions as feeling, thinking persons in search of opportunities to transform their lives in a transnational field.

PART IV

Home Is Where One Is Not

Disparate Paths: The Migrant Woman and the NGO

In November 1999 the Coalition against the Trafficking in Women (CATW) held a press conference in Manila, announcing and condemning the trafficking of Filipina entertainers as forced prostitutes into U.S. military camp towns in South Korea.

On May 9, 2000, at around 11:20 P.M., I waited with the crowd held back by railings in front of Centennial Airport in Manila. Ira and Bella were supposed to arrive soon. I kept trying to identify their families, but the sea of people made it impossible—a flight was arriving from Hong Kong slightly before that from Seoul. Fifteen minutes past midnight Ira and Bella, both dressed in black sleeveless vests and blue jeans, came through customs with their big black bags like those commonly used by U.S. servicemen. Ira was holding a big stuffed toy that was to be a gift for her eight-year-old daughter. Much flamboyant excitement and many eager embraces followed. I greeted both families and went away with Ira's, after agreeing to visit Bella in Laguna a week later. On our way to the van, after introducing me to her mother and father, her three children, her sisters, her nieces and nephews, and a boyfriend of her sister, Ira excitedly began to tell me about her newest sweetheart, a white GI named Conrad, with whom she had gone into the VIP room "just to kiss." She also talked about Candy, who had run away just before she was supposed to return to the Philippines, and Daddy, who wanted her and Bella to stay for another month, until he found replacements. She was still very absorbed in her life in Korea, in spite of her physical return to the Philippines.

The van driver demanded extra payment from Ira for the overloading—actually, merely an excuse to extract money from returnees. Ira took out a five-dollar note and thrust the money into the driver's hand with a frown. Almost fifteen of us jammed into the hired van for the three-hour drive back to Bataan. Ira and I were soon joined by her daughter in the front. I was treated like an honored guest and was embarrassed that her parents and families were packed like sardines in the back. Ira continued with her tales of South Korea.

We arrived at 3:00 A.M. A whirlwind of excitement erupted as her brothers, sisters, nephews, nieces, and in-laws ransacked her bags for gifts in the dimly lit living room. Chocolates were the first to go, then a few toys, and then shampoo, conditioner, and body lotion. Ira soon had to elbow her way through to get her own shampoo.

Ira and I were to share the only single bed in the only single room in the house, which was normally occupied by her nineteen-year-old brother. Before going to bed, Ira announced to me that she was broke but happy. It is interesting how she immediately associated her financial predicament with her familial bliss, as if her happiness came clearly with a price tag. She was aware that her family's excitement about her return involved much expectation of her to improve their lives. When I asked how she was going to spend the twenty-seven hundred dollars that she brought back with her, she started the list—family debts, a new TV and washing machine, her father's Jeep's registration, installment payments for her brother's tricycle, and on and on. "And then?" I asked.

Swinging her right arm skyward, Ira replied, "I'll fly away!"

*   *   *

In 2000 the first antitrafficking law in the Philippines, the Anti-Trafficking Persons Act (H. No. 7199), was tabled in congress by the Committee on Women of the House of Representatives—a success for lobbying efforts by the CATW and other NGOs.

In the same year the United Nations adopted the Protocol for the Prevention, Protection, and Punishment of the Trafficking in Persons, Especially Women and Children. In addition, the U.S. Congress passed the Trafficking Victims Protection Act (TVPA).

*   *   *

In 2001 Ira tried to return to South Korea as an entertainer. However, a Korean manager was arrested for taking Filipinas out of the country illegally, and she heard immigration control was tightening for travel to South Korea. In March 2001 she "flew away" and left to work in a club in Kuching, Malaysia.

Chapter 6
At Home in Exile

In late 1998 Annabel was making five thousand pesos a month working at Chow King (a fast-food chain) and selling accessories on the side in Manila. As the contract with Chow King was finishing, a friend introduced her to a Filipino recruiter. Annabel wanted to work as an entertainer in Japan. Going overseas was a chance for her to make money, to "have more," and to gain respect from her family.

Problems with her entertainer visa for Japan kept delaying her departure. Meanwhile, Annabel heard from her friend that some Filipinas made more money in South Korea than in Japan. She asked to audition with a Korean recruiter. Even though her Filipino recruiter warned her that she might have to do "this and that" in South Korea and she had to audition in shorts and a bra, she decided to go. In June 1999 she left for South Korea via Hong Kong, where an E-6 visa was stamped into her passport, and then arrived at the Angel Club. In early August 1999 Annabel and six other Filipina entertainers ran away from the club. In late August they returned to the Philippines.

In February 2000 Philip, a GI customer whom Annabel had met in the Angel Club, came to the Philippines to marry Annabel. Within a year Annabel was transformed from a never-married single mother to an icon of success in her neighborhood, with a family and a future waiting for her in the United States. With stable financial support from Philip, Annabel moved to a bigger house after giving birth to Philip's child. She hired a maid to help look after the baby. She went to the Internet café often to chat with her friends, including Winnie, who was already married and living in Fort Lauderdale, Florida, and also with her mother-in-law in Kentucky. She was already living a transnational life while waiting eagerly for her immigration papers to be processed for her and her two children. Without worries about her livelihood, she devoted her time to raising her children and spending time with her family.

I asked Annabel in one of our conversations in January 2001 if her relatives were treating her better.

Annabel: My real family, yes, the same as before. Some of my aunts, I didn't talk to them until now. But when they looked [*sic*] at me now, they don't say anything.

S: You feel that you have proved yourself?

Annabel: Yes, very much. Philip knows about that. I am happy about running away, about going to Korea.

Secure about her status in the neighborhood and her future, Annabel expressed incomprehension at the choice of two of her coworkers from the Angel Club who had gone abroad again as entertainers: "I don't know why. When we ran away, everyone said they didn't want to go back. Maybe because Kitty doesn't want to stay here [in the Philippines]. Beverly wants to go back because she has to, she is the only breadwinner for the family. She wants to find someone the same as Philip. She wants to settle [down]. But she can't find anyone."

Annabel marked her new sense of selfhood as a respectable married woman who had sympathies for others who wanted to be like her. She seemed to have forgotten that, back in late 1999 when Philip expressed doubts about their marriage, she had been fearful of the shame that she would suffer in the eyes of her family and kin if she failed to wed the father of her second unborn child. She had then immediately contacted her manager to arrange for work as an entertainer in Japan. Had her own marriage plan fallen through, Annabel probably would have embarked on another journey abroad as an entertainer—to avoid shame and to pursue her aspiration for success.

*   *   *

Migration as an entertainer, given its association with prostitution, is always a transgressive act for Filipino women, who risk their feminine respectability. This risk, however, is compensated for by the life-transforming opportunities that migration offers and the "success" one could come to embody. Annabel had come back pregnant and with little money, but her eventual wedding with an American man made her happy that she had taken her chance.

As discussed in Chapter 2, migrant Filipinas invest much hope in the possibility of transformation—of themselves as well as their families—as a result of their migration. Overseas migration is thus a seminal chapter in the migrants' projects of self-making. Cecilia Tacoli found that young, single Filipino migrants, both men and women, see migration "as a 'rite of passage' to adulthood and as a positive experience in terms of personal growth."[1] Filomeno V. Aguilar, Jr., used the template of spiritual pilgrimage to understand labor out-migration from the Philippines: both the religious pilgrim and the labor migrant go on "journeys of achievement" that involve isolation, suffering, and sacrifice, but which, upon their "success" and return home, eventuate in the transformation of their personhood.[2] While the success of a migrant is normatively assessed according to the material contribution she can make to family and kin, the journey is also subjectively an experience of independence and growth, as well as a pursuit of modernity in which the individual feels transformed by economic power and exposure overseas. Migrants' aspirations are shaped by various conflicting regimes of value, including, but not exclusively, economic empowerment. Migration for the Filipina entertainers is often considered an opportunity to negotiate the gender, family, and class constraints experienced at home. Their transnational subjectivities are shaped within the flows of money, goods, media images, and affective exchanges across borders. These processes of subjectification do not stop upon the migrants' arrival home— migrants continue to forge new desires, aspirations, and pursuits of mobility. The personal goals of migration constitute important premises for considering migration success and failure from the migrants' perspectives.

Upon returning home, migrants face two important tasks: subjecting their achievements to the evaluation of others; and projecting their achievements into the future. Failure in either task may subject them to shaming. The return home is therefore a critical juncture in migrants' self-making. Going home, whether as a success or a failure, does not mean that one will spontaneously feel "at home." This takes some explaining in relation to re-emplacement at home, especially given the romanticized notions of home as a haven of comfort, support, and belonging.

Ambivalence commonly marks migrants' return. Having found in exile "a source of independence, new pleasures, and [a] new sense of personhood,"[3] Filipina domestic workers in Hong Kong communicated with reluctance to Nicole Constable their ambivalence about returning to the Philippines. The reluctance stems from the overriding ideology that migration is supposed to be about self-sacrifice and suffering, not about finding pleasure, freedom, and social support in an alien land. Embedded in their narratives are conflicted feelings about familial obligations, gendered expectations, and troubled relationships. Underlying these emotional conflicts is the fear of unmooring oneself from the globally oriented "modernity" and returning to parochial "traditions."[4] Their awareness and development of a transnational habitus mediate their sense of belonging at home, instilling a sense of alienation. Deirdre McKay understands this ambivalence in terms of "structure of feeling"—attending to the interplay between economic relations and affective experience. The lack of opportunities, development, modern conveniences, and consumerist lifestyle in their home villages is often experienced as frustration, disillusion, and shame. McKay discusses how returnees deal with these negative emotions of reemplacement by reinterpreting home "as a landscape of sensual and aesthetic value, rather than a site of 'underdevelopment.'" To appreciate the sights, sounds, and tastes of home becomes a way to domesticate the migrant women's migration detour. McKay's point is important for understanding how migrant women exercise their cultural agency in negotiating their transnational subjectivity with their local reality, actively overcoming their sense of alienation at home. But how complete is this process? What happens to the excess affects that refuse to be domesticated?

Women's migration often leads to changes in gender and family roles, as well as economic and family relations. Repeat migration is often perceived as a necessity for sustaining improvements in a household's situation and the woman's own position in the family. Michele Ruth Gamburd analyzes the multiple negotiations that Sri Lankan migrant domestic workers face in their home villages as they struggle over the redistribution of remittances in the family, the systems of prestige they subscribe to within a society divided by caste and class, and the struggles with men over responsibilities and control in the household.[5] "Migrant mothering," a term Gamburd coined to describe the fragmentation of the mother's role among women who leave their children behind in the care of other women and the "redefining [of] a mother's role in terms of money and materials," points to changing cultural and social understanding of family responsibility, gender roles, and the meanings of love, work, and care.[6] This widening of acceptable ways to "mother" does not come automatically but only after a great deal of negotiation, assertion, and demand on the women's part.

As major reorganization of the family economy may accompany a woman's migration, migrant women who gain authority as a result of establishing their breadwinner roles have high stakes in maintaining their families' well-being and their own status after their migration. Very often the obvious way to do this is to go abroad again.

In addition, the stigma associated with migrant "entertainers" operates in two related ways to sustain and expand this outflow of migrant women. On the one hand, the fear of stigma marginalizes these returnees socially and compels their continual transnational existence. On the other hand, because of their vested interest in sustaining the myth of successful migration, returnees often remain silent about their negative experiences overseas—even though they may introduce their managers to other women interested in following in their footsteps.

This chapter discusses how migrant women's reintegration at home is often incomplete and fraught with tensions, generating momentum for repeat migration as a continuation of self-actualization. Their transnational subjectivity refuses domestication in a context in which "home" is understood as the antithesis of "abroad"[7]—a place that is exciting and beautiful, where jobs and money are readily available and there is the possibility of marriage to look forward to. The following stories of Filipina entertainers immediately before and after their return home from South Korea provide insights into this critical juncture of their self-making as migrants and the continuation of their vitality of hope on the margins of the transnational field.

"I Don't Want to Go Home": An Allegory of Ambivalent Return

Lilly has gone "crazy," according to the other Filipinas in the Mermaid Club. She had arrived from the Philippines in April 1999 with Ira and Candy. They were sent together to the O Club, where they had had to dance topless, although they had refused to "go all the way [naked]," much to the club owner's displeasure. In late June the three of them were transferred to the Highland Club, where Daddy was much less demanding, and they had few complaints about working there. According to Bella, Lilly began to behave weirdly in mid-July. One Saturday night in late July 1999 she tried to hit the Korean woman bartender and threatened GIs in the club with a pool cue. Daddy decided to send her back to the Philippines.

Lilly struck me as particularly sentimental when I first met her on June 17, 1999, with Candy, Ira, and Janet, all of whom were working in the O Club. My coresearcher and I bought them fried chicken meals at a burger joint. Over Coca-Cola and chicken bones, we discussed their motives for coming to Korea.

At the age of twenty-three, in an act of defiance, Lilly had left her husband and son behind in the Philippines. Neither her parents nor her husband had agreed to her seeking a job overseas: "My husband didn't give me permission to leave. But I want to come. . . . But if he asks me to go back, I will. Maybe after three or six months."

In Lilly's understanding, going overseas was a rebellion and a struggle for autonomy, particularly from her husband's control. Huge teardrops started falling as she talked in a muffled voice about her two-year-old son as a "mama's boy." Candy and Ira did not look as sympathetic as I had expected they would. Lilly did not smile once during our meeting, although Ira joked about getting a boyfriend as part of her job and Candy about her tears running dry from missing her children. I got the impression that Lilly missed home most among her coworkers, but I did not foresee the emotional crisis that was to follow.

I went to visit Lilly and tried to talk with her on July 28, 1999, three days before her departure from South Korea—a plan she had kept secret. Ira invited her over to the room that she shared with Candy. Lilly came in without looking at any of us and sat quietly on Ira's bed, leaning against the wall, legs curled up on the side, eyes cast downward. Most of the time her big round eyes were filled with tears. She answered only intermittently the questions we posed, mostly staring into empty space or looking down. I asked about her son, as this was one of the more engaging topics with the Filipinas. She said that her son was still in the Philippines and that he was probably OK. I asked if she had a picture of him. She said that she had it in her bag but would not show me. She seemed to be in deep melancholy.

"Do you want to go home?" I asked, expecting her to say "yes." Continuing in her almost inaudible voice, she answered "no" and said that she wanted to stay and work hard. She had a few bruises on her arms and a big one on the inside of her calves. She would not tell anyone how she got these bruises but said only which ones hurt and which ones did not. Her coworkers did not seem to think that she had suffered any sexual or physical violence. She had no stable boyfriend and had not been bar-fined. She looked dazed and unfocused, in sharp contrast with the way she looked in pictures taken in the clubs just weeks previously, now pinned up on the wall in Ira's room. The radiance was gone. The sight of Lilly was truly worrying. I feared that she would gradually sink into an abyss of depression. Her coworkers told me that her transformation had been a gradual process over the previous two weeks. Many questions ran through my head: What could have happened to her if she had not been bar-fined? What would happen to her in the Philippines when she went home? How would her family treat her—in particular, her husband? Would she recover at home? As we sat next to each other looking at Lilly with utter helplessness, Ira sighed, "I feel sorry for her." Just when I was about to agree with her, she continued, "She is going to go home with no money."

Indeed, Lilly would not be receiving any salary, since the first three months of the Filipinas' salaries were deducted as expenses for getting them to South Korea. However, in my middle-class sensibility, my concerns were about her mental well-being rather than her financial state, and her future in the long run rather than the immediate prospect of her returning home penniless. The disappointment, scorn, and criticism in the Philippines of families and friends, who would expect money and gifts, failed to register until Ira voiced her concern that Lilly would be a failure not so much because of her apparent mental instability as because of her empty-handed return. For many Filipinas, the shame of returning home without money was a strong deterrent against leaving prematurely. Bella offered her observations and opinions on Lilly's behavior:

> I think she is not normal. Like, she laughed by herself, she is always jump-ing, like a kid. Then she sits on men, I don't know. We all have our prob-lems, but you don't need to be like that. . . . She always says like, "I want to fuck, I want to have money and if that's the only way. . . ." She would cry and talk. . . . I know one reason why she became like that. Because Candy and Ira always have dates, they are outside. Always Lilly was alone, even though she had a phone, no one would call her. That's why she got jealous—why Ira and Candy have a lot of dates, and calls, and she got jealous of everything. Like somebody gave Ira a ring, she said, "Why me don't have ring [sic]?" . . . She always says that she wants to marry GI. We ask her, "Do you want to go back to the Philippines?" "No, I want to stay here." She always says that she doesn't want to go home.

I suggest that Bella's account be read, rather than as *the* truth, as her interpretation of Lilly's condition in terms of issues pertinent to Filipina entertainers in *gijichon* in general. Taken together with Lilly's broken articu-lation and Ira's lament, these utterances constitute a joint discourse of Fili-pinas' struggles in *gijichon* over money, sexuality, freedom, and romantic yearnings, as well as their ambivalent feelings for home.

Sexual politics and violence in the Philippines have been significant "push" factors in the outward migration of many Filipinas.[8] Lilly dearly missed her son, but migration was a chance for her to renegotiate the power dynamics at home—as she waited for her husband to ask for her return. Before he did so, it was all the more important for Lilly to prove herself a success. To say that she would have sex for money "if that's the only way" highlighted her determination. Ira had made similar assertions in a fit of anger after Jamie broke up with her: "Find me someone who will pay for sex. I will do it once before I go, do you know anyone? Yes, I will do it, just once! To make the money." Such outbursts epitomize the dilemma that Filipinas live with on a daily basis in *gijichon*—whether one should sacrifice one's respectability for money or remain a "good woman," all the while wondering if marriage with a GI and life in America were possibilities. None of these considerations is purely economic or practical, as each is invested with particular gendered values about female sexuality, love, and marriage, as well as one's sense of self.

From her coworkers' perspective, Lilly was failing financially, socially, and emotionally in *gijichon*. Their evaluations can be interpreted collectively as an expression of the Filipinas' conditions and anxieties in *gijichon*, and Lilly's "craziness" as a radical protest.

Consistent with the primacy of the body as the site of resistance (see Chapter 4), Lilly's silence, aggression, and incoherent utterances make sense within the limited options for self-expression and protest in the Filipinas' displacement. Medical anthropologists have studied how "somatized illness" is a weapon of the weak. "In somatization the body is called upon to produce an explosion of chaotic symptoms—fictive, factitious (i.e.[,] frankly deceptive), or psychosomatic—in attempts (most of them semiconscious) to demonstrate one's goodness through suffering to solicit help and/or sympathy, or to express one's secret indignation."[9] As such, illness is part of a "minor genre of resistance"[10] for these women situated between home and exile.

My focus here is not on the pathos of Lilly's story, which still troubles me, but in the ways it illuminates the dialectic relationship among experiences, identities, and desires in dislocation. Specifically, how do the experiences of Filipinas in *gijichon* serve as a rite of passage, ushering in a changed sense of self in this liminal space and time? Lilly's reiteration of "I don't want to go home" is a rare direct expression of unwillingness to return to the Philippines. On one hand, it may be read as a resistance to oppressive expectations at home that a migrant will return as a "success." On the other hand, it articulates the positive association of the migration site with self-actualization, otherwise inaccessible at home. Nicole Constable found that

Filipina domestic workers in Hong Kong were extremely reluctant to talk about the ambivalence they had about going home, as they were constrained by the gendered ideology that women's migration overseas was about self-sacrifice rather than personal pleasures. Similarly, going home does not by default evoke the excitement of homecoming for these Filipina entertainers that conventional wisdom has us believe (see Chapter 2). My suggestion is not that Filipina entertainers do not want to go home but that we should attend to the ambivalence that they feel between home and exile—a sentiment that Lilly exhibited publicly and vehemently.

No one knows what happened to Lilly upon her return home. None of her coworkers had her address or telephone number. They could not even remember where she came from, only "somewhere very far away, in the province." Lilly came and left almost without leaving a trace, but she clearly returned home a different person.

This ambivalence that Lilly embodied extends into the time and space of the Filipinas' return to the Philippines. The two following stories of return and subsequent migration allow a textured understanding of how the migratory experiences of Filipina entertainers impinge on their sense of self in relation to their families and the transnational field of possibilities for labor, love, and money. Together they permit an in-depth understanding of these changes at the microlevel, particularly concerning the migrant women's assertions of power and autonomy, the impact of their return on the emplaced, and the challenges that they pose to social institutions such as gender and class, as well as the projection of their desires to the world beyond for the maintenance and/or expansion of their powers.

"I'll Fly Away": The Making of an Absent Breadwinner

We have seen that Ira was planning to "fly away" again on the first night of her return. Like many migrants, Ira had clearly identified her role in the family as that of provider—but one that could provide only from a faraway land.

Having become the main breadwinner, Ira was bold and daring in her comments and behavior. Smoking in the front yard of the family house facing the main road was a daring behavior that few Filipino daughters would engage in. Talking about her "scheme" to marry Larry drew expressions of awe and incomprehension, although not of disapproval—her parents, sisters, and in-laws just shook their heads and shrugged with a laugh. I asked if her parents knew about her job in South Korea. Ira replied, "No. I don't think they want to know." Instead of asking about her overseas experience, Ira's family focused on the financial help she could give the family and her possible marriage to the American man.

Ira was the fourth of six children. Her family was from Bataan Province in central Luzon. All except her younger brother and sister (ages nineteen and sixteen) were married. She was the only one who had had to leave her marriage.

After finishing high school Ira had worked at a restaurant. She married at eighteen and then started working at her husband's family's fish stall in the market. Her husband was violent. Ira gave birth to her daughter, Dana, when she was twenty and to her son, Donald, when she was twenty-three. In late 1995 her husband's violence grew worse, and at the age of twenty-six she ran away with her two children, leaving them in her mother's care and going to work in a karaoke club in Bulacan, a place chosen because it was away from any place she knew. A forty-year-old married policeman became her regular customer. Her husband came and demanded she return home with him; she refused, and he raped her. She was soon pregnant but unsure who had fathered the child, the policeman or her husband. She decided to tell the policeman that he was the father, and he gave her some money to leave her job and later sent money to support her during her pregnancy. She gave birth to Jeannie in Bulacan in May 1998 and then returned home to Bataan, telling her family that her estranged husband had fathered the baby girl—the truth was too shameful. Eleven months after Jeannie was born, Ira left for South Korea, telling her parents that she would be working as a "GRO (Guest Relations Officer)."

Although she had repeatedly been a disappointing daughter before going to South Korea, Ira returned as a *panalo* (winner) and came to be looked up to in the family. Her remittances from South Korea, which had averaged two hundred to three hundred dollars a month, had helped maintain the family finances, keep her youngest sister at school, pay for a land telephone line at home, and hire a maid. The money also helped pay the first installment on her younger brother's motorbike, which he used for work immediately after finishing high school, and for the endless repairs to her father's decrepit Jeep. Ira thus commanded the respect of her family. The first two days of her return confirmed her importance. A significant outflow of cash for various consumer products and groceries generated much excitement within the family. At least ten family members and friends rode her father's Jeep to different marts and shops to enjoy the spending spree. Ira also went with her brother to the pawnshop to claim back the gold necklace that her sister had pawned after her husband had committed suicide. Ira's father approached her quietly at least twice to ask for spending money (from two hundred to one thousand pesos). In my field diary entry on May 11, 2000, I wrote, "It's amazing how this single woman is supposed to solve all household problems immediately after she came back. Her father's Jeep's registration $100, her mother's debt $100, the phone bill was 1,800 pesos, the TV set, the washing machine, the fan, and the grocery. She is now the boss in a way. The smoking [in front of the family], the ordering around, the yelling."

In South Korea, Ira had been adamant that she would purge her club-girl demeanor when she returned to the Philippines. This did not happen. In addition to the heavy makeup, the smoking on the front porch, and the wearing of shorts (although she was careful not to wear her shortest pair), Ira had had her left nostril and tongue pierced in South Korea together with her GI boyfriend, Jamie. Body piercing had become part of the youth culture among GIs and Filipinas (although not so much among the Koreans) in *gijichon*. Ira thus gained membership in this global urban youth culture. A tongue ring was even more "cool" than the American slang, baseball caps, and basketball jerseys that many of the Filipinas adopted from GIs, who were the purveyors of American culture in *gijichon*. Ira's piercings were also a ritual of love. Through merging in the pain and blood flow from the manual piercings with Jamie, Ira acquired embodied experiences and mementos of love that she had longed for. However, this was a radical violation of the feminine ideal. Ira grew into a habit of sticking her tongue out and rolling the pearl at the tip of her tongue stud against her lips repeatedly. I asked what her father thought of her piercing.

Ira: My father asked me, "Can you take off your tongue ring or nose-piercing?" I said, "Hell, no!" Why should I? He can't make me do that now.
S: Why?
Ira: Because I am the one who gives them money! [Laughs.]

Ira soon took over command of family affairs. As soon as Ira came back, her sister asked for her assistance to go to South Korea. She wanted to look for a factory job, as her husband's suicide a month earlier had left her a single parent with two children, ages nine and ten. Ira negotiated various deals for her, and when she backed out Ira was furious. She had always tried to help her sister, she said, and was let down every time. She was also astonished that her sister, who had been unemployed for months, decided to let Ira continue supporting her children. Ira then announced to her parents that her sister would not be allowed in the house again. "I asked them to choose. It was either her or me." The choice was obvious. The fact that Ira could demand this choice of her parents was remarkable.

Migration reconfigures the role of migrant mothers, reconstituting gender roles and the gendered boundaries of home and family in the process.[11] It is fundamental to understand motherhood as a social and cultural construction with historically and culturally diverse expressions, rather than assuming a universal "maternal instinct."[12] Ira had left her two children in the care of her mother when she started working in Bulacan in 1996 and so had not been taking care of them on a daily basis even before leaving for South Korea. However, upon her return, Ira's two older children, Dana (ten) and Donald (seven), demonstrated their attachment to their mother by hugging her and trying to stay close to her. Dana was an articulate girl who liked to perform in front of her mother by imitating pop singers; Donald jumped, yelled, and made faces excitedly in front of Ira and me. However, Jeannie, who was almost two years old when Ira returned from South Korea, called Ira's mother "*nanay* [mother]" and refused to let Ira come close to her for the first five days. Only after Ira had given her a lot of chocolate and her lipstick to play with did Jeannie finally let Ira hold her. She slept with Ira's mother or sister but not with Ira (my presence might have been a reason for this, but at any rate there appeared to be no strong physical bond between the two when I was staying with them). She was still refusing to call Ira *nanay* when I left the Philippines, eight days after Ira's return. Ira was irritated but not particularly saddened to see this, convinced that Jeannie would learn to address her properly with time. She was most excited about Dana doing well at school. "I don't want my children to grow up like me," she said. Motherhood for Ira was performed and demonstrated not by a doting everyday presence but by sending her children to private school; providing the new clothes, toys, and food that they enjoyed; and by envisioning for them a better life different from her own.

If Ira seemed weighed down with responsibilities at home, she was particularly vivacious when she spent time with her old friends. As relations based on choice, friendships are important to the project of self-making, and visiting friends offered some respite from the frenzy of familial demands. Ira, her brother, and I went on a trip to visit her "best friend," who had worked in the same club with her in Bulacan. Her nineteen-year-old friend was married and pregnant. We stayed for a night at their concrete house, which stood out in a row of wooden stilt houses on muddy ground. It had whitewashed walls, a matching garden table and chairs in a tiled veranda, tiled floors, three big rooms, and a modern kitchen and bathroom with all modern electrical appliances. Ira came back from the bathroom excited. "Sealing, take a shower. They have hot water here!" An electric water heater was a luxury that few could afford in the provinces. I soon found that the elder sister of Ira's friend was married to a Japanese man. The house and its modern luxuries stood as a monument to the success of a *Japayuki* (Japan-bound entertainer). "When will I get a house like this?" Ira asked.

That night Ira threw a long drinking party for her friends, her ex–club owner, and the probable father of Jeannie, declaring at the outset that she wanted to get drunk. Her brother was clearly uncomfortable to see the flirtation and intimacy between Ira and the men, which broke all codes of female modesty. He whispered repeatedly into my ears, "Ira is crazy," apparently to express his embarrassment. Ira paid for all the liquor (the Spanish whiskey Fundador) and food and left two thousand pesos poorer. Her brother was incensed, putting his head in his hands and trying to control his scream: "Ira spent two thousand pesos in one night! Two thousand pesos! She is crazy!" The disbelief of this nineteen-year-old was understandable—two thousand pesos could pay the whole family's expenses for a week. For Ira, though, this seemingly irrational spending made sense as an attempt to display her success, to recapture old friendships and therefore the social life she once had in the Philippines.

Yet a whole year of overseas experience was difficult to communicate to her friends, who had also undergone significant changes during the same period. In addition, the physical distance between their homes made it all the more difficult to resume the intimacy of a bygone era. After the night of revelry Ira sat in bed the next morning with a serious hangover, while her pregnant friend was chopping vegetables for the soup outside in the kitchen. On our long bus ride from Bulacan, Ira said that she did not approve of her friend's husband nor of her pregnancy. She lamented that she and her best friend no longer shared the understanding they had once had of each other.

S: Who understands you most?
(Long pause)
Ira: Maybe you [laughs]. Because my family, they know about my past. But

they don't know what happened to me in Korea. My friends too. But you know.

Underlining this evaluation is the significance that Ira attributed to her first overseas experience in constituting herself as distinct from her family and friends. My knowledge of this important period of her life, together with tiny fragments of her past, had made me appear to be someone who understood her best at this particular moment of her life. Her laugh punctuated the irony of this. To consider that a foreigner who had known her for only half a year understood her better than her family or long-term friends poignantly exemplified how Ira had been uprooted from home.

Social relations ordered through mobility are different from those structured around emplacement.[13] Friendships Ira made in South Korea constituted an important support network as she tried to deal with the stress and anxieties of a returnee. Rather than any expectation of utilitarian reciprocity, central to these relationships are the "affective dimensions of friendship; a sense of connection deriving from shared values and times together."[14] Ira depended particularly on Lou, her coworker at the Mermaid Club, for support in the year following her return from South Korea. In exchanging news about the latest family expenses they had to pay, Ira and Lou commiserated on the phone, exclaiming the familiar Korean phrase "*Ton-obso* [No Money]," which evoked their common migratory experiences and reinforced their bonding through a language inaccessible to others.

After her marriage plans with Larry broke down in October 2000, Ira was cut off from her only stable source of financial support. She had no means to fulfill her responsibilities and maintain her breadwinner status. Neighborhood rumors about her working overseas as a prostitute became more audible. Ira found comfort by fleeing from her family and going to stay on various occasions with Lou, who had failed to find a job in the Philippines. Lou's home telephone had been cut off—an event I came to learn was the first sign of financial difficulties in a Filipina's home. When I talked to Ira at Lou's in mid-November, she said that she could not go home: her phone line too would soon be cut off, the bills were piling up, and her mother was always calling her mobile phone. Over the next few months Lou and Ira went to Lou's manager, and in November they were recruited to return to South Korea. As it turned out that they would have to wait too long before going, due to extra vigilance in Philippine immigration control caused by the arrest of the Korean manager, Ira went to Malaysia instead, in March 2001, on a faked passport. Lou, however, went to South Korea two weeks later. They were thus back on their trajectories of overseas migration within a year of their return from South Korea.

In the subsequent years, during which I traced Ira's migratory trajectory across the continents, she was emphatic that her time in South Korea had changed her life in many ways, and her Filipina coworkers from the Mermaid Club continued to be her "best friends." By keeping in touch with each other in their subsequent migratory journeys by phone, text messages, e-mails, and Internet chats, these Filipinas established their own transnational network of sociality, defying the traditional spatially bound definition of community and solidarity.

"I Wish I Didn't Come Back": Failed Ambitions of an Aspiring Migrant

Katie once explained that migration was a decision to assert her independence from her mother, since she was "old enough" to support herself and her son. Going to South Korea was thus an act of rebellion. "My mom, she wanted me to go to Japan. I am hard-headed . . . I can go wherever I wanted to."

Katie, a single mother with an eight-year-old son, said that she had been the "black sheep" in the family. She was the fourth child in a family with eight children. Her uncle had raped her since she was eight, stopping only when she turned twelve. She never told anyone in the family about the rape, but she began to behave "strangely" and did poorly at school. Though all her other siblings finished high school or college, her parents did not let her finish high school. Katie felt bitter about this—she had wanted to go to college. She left her home in Pampanga to work in a factory in Manila when she was eighteen and gave birth to her son at the age of twenty-two. Since the man who impregnated her was a drug addict, her father did not let Katie marry him. Returning to Pampanga, Katie helped look after the mom-and-pop family store and took over the management when her father died in 1996. In January 1998, after meeting a club manager through a friend, she left for South Korea as an entertainer.

Katie's mother had been the first migrant in the family. Her migration was followed by that of two of her daughters, both of whom married U.S. military personnel. Her mother had been the breadwinner and had worked overseas after losing her job at Clark Air Base when the U.S. military withdrew from the Philippines in 1992. She had first worked for two years in

Kuwait as a domestic helper. Then, with the help of Katie's sister and her husband in the U.S. Air Force, her mother went to Okinawa in Japan and worked at a fast-food shop on base, staying with her sister, whose husband was stationed there. After Katie left in 1998 to work as an entertainer in South Korea, her younger sister left to work in Japan as an entertainer in order to get away from her abusive husband. Unlike Ira, who was the first of many in her family to work overseas, Katie's family was already acquainted with transnational existence. Before Katie made her decision, her mother shared her own experience of bad employers and an attempted rape, in addition to that of the hard work overseas, but still Katie "wanted to have the experience."

In July 1998, after seven months in a *gijichon* club, Katie ran away with Anna, her eighteen-year-old coworker. Katie then fell in love with a married Filipino friend who worked in a factory and asked Anna to become the girlfriend of one of his friends so that she could have a place to stay in the same compound. She found a stable factory job in June 1999 and worked there for the next six months. Though she was making good money and was in love with her boyfriend, she decided that she needed to exit South Korea—both to leave a relationship that had no future and to take care of her deteriorating health. In January 2000, during an amnesty period for illegal migrant workers, she returned to the Philippines. Though exempted from penalties, she was blacklisted as an illegal migrant and was not to return to South Korea in the following three years. She did not care—she would live on her savings until she could find a job in the Philippines. She had no wish to return to South Korea then.

When I visited her in May 2000, just four months after her return home, however, Katie was hoping to return to South Korea as an entertainer. She had "borrowed a friend's name and her birth certificate" in order to get a new passport. She could not find a job at home, and her savings were running out. At the age of thirty-two and without a high-school diploma, even a factory job was out of reach, and her attempt at being an Avon distributor did not work out. She was ashamed to stay in the house, supported by her mother, and felt the need to make money for her son. In addition, she missed her boyfriend in South Korea, realizing that she did not love her boyfriend in the Philippines even though he wanted to marry her. Katie joined a recruitment agency for entertainers because of the cheap agency fee (about twelve thousand pesos)—considerably less than that for factory workers to Taiwan or South Korea (more than seventy thousand pesos). She thought that she could always run away, just as she had before, and become a factory worker in South Korea again.

Events took an unexpected turn, however. I learned from Ira that Katie had gone to Japan in November. When I called Katie in Japan, she was in no condition to work, she said. She had jumped at the opportunity of going to work in the Japanese club where her sister was working, with no agency fee upfront and a passport that belonged to a Filipina who had married a Japanese. The morning before they left for the airport, according to Katie, the club owner had attempted to rape her. Though Katie fought him off, she was seized by her childhood trauma of rape. When she arrived in the club in Japan, she was still in shock, and she grew increasingly weak. She demanded to be sent back home. The club owner said that she would have to pay four thousand dollars to cover all the expenses she had incurred in coming to Japan. Her sisters and her mother tried to convince her to start working again. When Katie insisted that she was mentally and physically unfit to work, they warned her not to try running away, which might endanger the safety of her sister who worked in the same club, as everyone believed that the club owner was a *yakuza* (Japanese gang) member. In spite of my attempt to solicit the help of the International Organization for Migration, which offered Katie counseling and her possible options, she dared not move. For the next five months Katie was essentially under house arrest and lived in constant fear of rape, sleeping with a knife under her pillow every night until her sister paid the club owner the four thousand dollars. The price for this freedom was being cast out of the family. Her mother would not allow her to stay in the house again. Not only was Katie a failure as a migrant, but she also became too great a liability to the family and was therefore cut off.

Upon her return on March 7, 2001, Katie had to depend on her boyfriend in the Philippines to rent a room. She visited her son daily at her family's house. Although she was the oldest child remaining in the Philippines, her cousin had taken charge of the house in her place. Her boyfriend soon became physically violent: Katie had secretly been taking contraceptive pills, while her boyfriend was trying to get her pregnant. She knew that her boyfriend's parents disliked her—all their children had gone to college, and they disapproved of her work as an entertainer. Marriage became an increasingly unlikely option both because of his domineering behavior and because he no longer talked about marrying her.

Stranded in the Philippines with a four-thousand-dollar debt, family rejection, violence from her boyfriend, and financial need, Katie's only hope was to leave the Philippines. Without her boyfriend's knowledge, Katie successfully auditioned in early June as an entertainer in South Korea. Her plan was to save enough money to start her own business in the Philippines. Unfortunately, tightened immigration control prevented her departure. In July 2001, still stuck in the Philippines, Katie sounded depressed and lifeless on the phone. In light of her increasingly miserable experiences since her return, Katie realized that her time in South Korea after running away had been "the best time" in her life,[15] as she had had relative independence, a job, and a life with a man she loved. She said, "I wish I didn't come back." Underlying her nostalgic lamentation was a keen perception of "abroad" (South Korea, in this case) as the antinomy of "home" and all its despair, stagnation, and powerlessness.

The Meanings of "Abroad" at Home

"To move is to travel. To be moved is to open one's heart."[16] Travel opens one's heart and changes one's sense of self. It also changes one's relationship to home. The above stories of homecoming capture the struggles of individual women who tried to find their place at home *through* exile. Annabel, Lilly, Ira, and Katie set out on their migration journeys with dreams of respectability, autonomy, and wealth upon their return, mediating their gendered subordination in the family and Philippine society. While they achieved it to varying degrees, they all returned with transnational modern subjectivities predicated on mobility, autonomy, and access to financial and cultural capital that could be neither fulfilled nor sustained in the Philippines. This eventuated in an aggravated sense of alienation that propelled repeat migration. Having found "no place back home,"[17] "abroad" became *the* place for these Filipinas to pursue their dreams of modernity. In spite of their knowledge and experience of the pitfalls of employment overseas as entertainers, they were eager to recapture the potentials for empowerment and self-actualization that they had already tasted. They could more easily have found hope in journeying among the risks of the transnational field than in staying at home, which itself was far from risk-free.

Gender-related violence, both on the interpersonal (direct violence) and systemic (the indirect and subtle forms of coercion that sustain relations of domination and subordination) levels, had been a propelling force in these women's return migrations.[18] As Nobue Suzuki argues in her study of Filipina migrants to Japan, gendered surveillance and sexual politics are important push factors in the continual flow of female migrants overseas.[19] These are intimately tied to larger political and economic structures, not least of which are problems of unemployment and underemployment for women in the Philippines.[20] These migrants identify the Philippine government more as an obstacle to be overcome than an arbiter of social and economic justice. The government is largely mentioned by the Filipina entertainers in discussions about the channels and costs of getting false documents, such as passports and certificates of marital status (as single), and in bribing immigration officers to enable their smooth passage.[21] It is a matter of course for these women to rely only on themselves and their recruiters for their futures.

For entertainer returnees, migration proves a liberation from the shackles of their controlling partners, the disgrace of single motherhood, the stigma of working as an entertainer, and the lack of employment opportunities at home. The difficulties that they face abroad remain more negotiable and transient than the relatively permanent problems at home. Being abroad physically removes them from these oppressive conditions and facilitates access to financial, social, and romantic possibilities unavailable at home. These are crucial for women like Ira who have become breadwinners by virtue of their migration overseas and for those like Katie who believe that they have learned the ropes of working overseas and could better benefit from it during a second time around. For these women, well beyond the ideal marriageable age (the average age of first marriage for women in the Philippines is twenty years)[22] and with children to raise, family to support, and little job prospects in a country with decreasing employment opportunities, migration offers hope for transforming their lives and approximating their imagined selves. Modernity exists no longer as mere images and commodities but as embodied knowledge.

For the emplaced, who have had only limited participation in modernity through the cultural consumption of mass media, the remittances, gifts, experiences, and networks of returnees come to feed their imaginations of realizing their own global self-making potentials as migrants. Whether the returnees' evocations of their experiences are accurate representations of their time spent abroad is not necessarily the most important consideration—migrants are important agents in the global flows that spur imagination of possible lives in a faraway world. The cumulative causation of migration operates through the returnees by readying more hearts to be moved.

Flows in the Global Circuit of Desires

According to Arjun Appadurai, imagination has become "a part of the quotidian mental work of ordinary people in many societies,"[23] entering into the logic of everyday life through the twin forces of modernity: mass migration and mass mediation. The global capitalist system generates an economy of symbols encoding status and identity in commodities. The desire for mass-market commodities and entertainment becomes a way to express one's modern identity. The acquisition of this knowledge and these goods and experiences is incorporated as one's cultural capital and functions as a symbolic confirmation of one's membership in a global community of shared aesthetic and cultural values. For these Filipina entertainers and their kin, consumption is a way to live the "fantasy of identity"—becoming "the kind of person one would like to be and the sort of person one would like to be seen to be by others."[24] The Filipinas and their families are "the desiring" in the global system of consumer and popular cultures, but they are also aware of their commodity value as "the desired" and plot their own imagined selves onto the global map of migration accordingly.

Migrant Filipinas consider it crucial to bring home luxury goods that mark their membership in the class of global consumers. In 2000 PlayStation 2, stereo systems, and Nike sneakers, in addition to the more conventional items such as television sets and gold jewelry, were default objects of desire for the young. I visited Milla in her one-hundred-square-foot room, which was lit by one dim lightbulb. She had shared this place with her father, brother, and sister for ten years in a squatter area on the outskirts of Manila. After showing me the only bed in the room, which she shared with her sister, and the floor space where her brother and father slept, Milla pointed out to me where she wanted to place the new TV set, the PlayStation 2, and the new stereo that she had purchased and which were being shipped from South Korea. Her father smiled and proudly said that they were going to renovate the room. Milla protested, saying that her fiancé would buy them a new house when he arrived. For Milla, a house of one's own, with all the accoutrement of modernity, was the full-package ideal—as it was for many migrant Filipinas.

The consumption of modern cultural forms brings the world beyond into migrant households, making it a part of everyday life and reconstituting the perspective and habitus of its residents in an interplay between local reality and global culture. When I was in the Philippines in 2000, the pop song "Sex Bomb" by Tom Jones was an immense hit featured frequently on the radio and TV. Behind the closed doors of her room Ira played the song and performed the dance gyrations she had learned in South Korea in front of her younger brother and me one afternoon, much to the former's embarrassed amusement. On a different occasion, and to the great amusement of other children and me, her nine-year-old niece and ten-year-old nephew danced excitedly to the same tune, with sexualized body movements such as clutching their genital areas, which they had picked up from TV. In both performances there was a nervous exposure and simultaneous concealment of the performers' sexuality with giggles. None of these "Sex Bomb" performances was made in the presence of people older than the performers, except for me, the foreigner. These were displays of affinity, not only with Western pop culture but also with the erotic code that was part of it—something "modern" and "out there," transgressive and desirable at the same time. Embedded in these consumption practices were ideas about gender, love, and sexuality that represented a break from tradition and locality.

For those in rural homes who have been embracing dreams of urban modernity beamed in through the satellite dish, the returnees are the bridge to fulfilling them. Advertisements for consumer products not only boost individual choice but also generate an insistence about what are desirable forms of modernity. One afternoon in Bataan, Ira took her whole extended family to a resort-like, amoeba-shaped swimming pool with colorful slides and fountains at the center and sunbathing chairs on the side, which cost four hundred pesos per person (about one dollar). No one knew how to swim, and all the adults had to help hold the smaller children while they kicked and splashed, but everyone had a good time.

On our way back home in Ira's father's Jeep, Ira's sixteen-year-old sister, Amy, and her seventeen-year-old maid eagerly asked if I wanted to go bowling—a way of having me ask Ira to take them. Ira's sister had been bowling once before in Manila, while the maid had never been. I complied, in view of their bright-eyed enthusiasm, in spite of my lack of interest in the sport. After dinner we set off on a tricycle and went to the nearest bowling center. None of them had been there before. We were dropped off outside what looked like an old school hall of mostly wooden construction. When we went in, there was no electronic display or any brightly illuminated lanes. It was so quiet that it became embarrassing. Three boys in their early teens came running out of a door next to the counter and to the back of the lanes. They started setting the pins and rolling some small wooden balls down the tracks toward us. After everything was set, the boys crouched in the cramped space above the ends of the lanes, putting their heads through a window so that they could see the pins falling and hop down to reset them when needed. I had never seen anything like this before and was flabbergasted. Ira decided that we would try one game. Amy and the maid, however, refused even to touch the ball. Only then did I realize that the attraction they had was for bowling as a modern entertainment—the bright lights, the music, the electronic automation, and the young crowd that one commonly saw on TV—rather than the act itself. The two young women's enthusiasm died out completely upon seeing the unsophisticated setting.

When Amy and I first met in 2000, she was still in high school. She told me she wanted to study fashion design but that she also wanted to go abroad "to see the world." When she graduated in 2002, she wanted to leave for Malaysia as an entertainer, as Ira had in 2001. Ira strongly advised against this because of her terrible experience in Malaysia, but when Ira left the Philippines to work as a domestic for a diplomat in Belgium in 2002, Amy immediately left for Malaysia.

Individual assertions of autonomy and personal goals, rather than considerations of a "household strategy" and planning with the interest of the family as a collective unit, were important in making Ira's household a transnational family.[25] Ira's stable income from Belgium allowed other members of the family to consider leaving for overseas employment, as they could pay the agency fees with Ira's remittances. Ira's elder sister was unhappy with her marriage and had been trying to leave since 2000. Her first attempt to leave for Germany through family connections failed. Then she was rejected as an entertainer for South Korea by Ira's recruiter, on the grounds that she looked too old. She left for Iraq in 2006 as a manual worker, with Ira paying her agency fee.

Ira had intended that migration of her elder sister would help relieve her burden as breadwinner, but Ira's sister never sent more than one thousand pesos back home in the year she was in Iraq. Rumors of her returning with her Egyptian coworker boyfriend surprised the distant breadwinner. Ira continued to pay for her sister's two children's educations and living expenses while they stayed with her mother. Likewise, the financial support that Amy received from her "boyfriends" in Malaysia did not become an important part of the household economy. Significantly, when Ira's father began to experience kidney failure in 2007, all her siblings decided that dialysis would only exhaust their savings and so refused to contribute to the cost of treatment. Ira was shocked, but she was also aware that her father had alienated himself from the family in many ways. She went into debt for close to one thousand euros for her father's treatment before, finally, deciding to let go.

Other family members continued to let Ira be the breadwinner, much to her dismay: "I have been working for so many years, and I have nothing for myself." Thus, while migration may operate as a household strategy, individuals may also prioritize their own needs and desires over those of the family, amplifying intrafamilial differences and conflicts at home.[26]

Filipinas with migratory ambitions are well aware of themselves as particularly gendered and sexualized objects in the global "ethnoscape." Nicole Constable has discussed how Chinese and Filipino women represent themselves on Internet matchmaking Web sites according to particular perceptions of feminine qualities attractive to Western men. This allows them to deploy such images for their own projects of marriage and mobility.[27]

The Filipinas were well aware of *where* their sexual appeal and labor could be best applied in the global market. Ira and Katie never really stopped asking me to find them men in England, where I was doing graduate studies, though they always did so jokingly. Katie's friend Terry ran a store-cum-restaurant and lived with her two children. She had started the store with money she got from a Chinese-Filipino businessman who had been her lover after she left her abusive husband. I complimented her on her cooking one day in her kitchen, and she responded by asking me to find her a job in South Korea so that she could cook and make money. I asked if she thought Katie made good money in Korea. Instead of answering my question, she immediately turned to propose her gendered labor within a different regime of value:

Terry: So, find me a boyfriend in England, a very good, nice, and rich [man].
S: What about Hong Kong?
Terry: Fine. Find me a job, for my two kids.

No one ever made the reverse request—for a husband in Hong Kong or a job in England. The distinction between Hong Kong and England as places for jobs and marriage, respectively, indicated the women's awareness of how their labor value in certain places was shaped by the political economy of globalization in Asia, and specifically by the white, masculinist gaze that looks upon them as racial and sexual commodities[28] formed in the political economy of the Philippines by, particularly, the colonial and postcolonial influence of the United States and the Philippine government's promotion of sex tourism. In making the request for English boyfriends, even in jest, they demonstrated their readiness to make use of their commodity value to improve their lives.

Dreams, Home, and Cultural Change

"The other night, I had a dream. We live in one place, a native hut. I live there with my friends. All girls. Just one guy—my son. My son was sleeping in bed, wearing just a blanket. And I woke up. I was talking to him. I woke him up. He said, 'Your friends are outside.'" Katie shared this dream with me just before she was about to return to the Philippines in early 2000. To have a house and lot for one's family is a dream for many of the Filipina entertainers who do not stop hoping to go abroad again. Ira's dream in 2000, independent of her marriage plans, was to have a house of her own where she could live with her three children. In 2007, seven years and two more countries of migration later, she owned a lot in an area near her parents' home in Bataan. The building of the house, however, would have to wait until she had saved enough, working as an undocumented domestic worker in Belgium. However, things were uncertain in 2008, as her appeal for legal status had been turned down.

In spite of such obstacles—and this is the core argument of this chapter—the outside world has continued to operate both symbolically and practically as a hopeful site for these Filipinas to transform their lives. They are not disillusioned with the idea of home—just at the realities of home. These women's transnational desires contrast with their dreams for a "native hut," but they are not contradictory aspirations when one sees the social, cultural, and economic logics for these women to leave home in order to be comfortable at home. The title of this chapter, "At Home in Exile," thus has a double meaning: that of their sense of alienation at home and of their hope for self-actualization in exile. These stories of homecoming unsettle assumptions of home as a haven for safety, comfort, and belonging as opposed to overseas migration sites as those of risk, distress, and alienation.

In their pursuit of aspirations abroad, migrant Filipinas acquire a transnational subjectivity that changes their relationship with home. Curran and Saguy have argued that women, because of the greater constraints on them than on men at home, feel the impact of relative deprivation more intensely than men do and therefore find migration more appealing than do their male counterparts.[29] Women who return home experience in poignant ways their transformed identities and relationships with home. They have acquired an expansive orientation of self in the world. The corollary is their more intense rejection of their gendered boundedness at home. As seen in the stories of homecoming in this chapter, it was their "routes" upward in a global system marked by inequalities, rather than their "roots,"[30] that these Filipinas found empowering. The multiple sources of gendered and class subordination in the Philippines faced by these Filipinas became more poignantly felt after their experiences overseas. "Abroad"—encoded in Katie's dream as "outside"—became confirmed as the space for finding one's autonomy and friends, for self-actualization, and for making life meaningful. The conclusion to her dream, "Your friends are outside," foreshadowed the conundrum that Katie and others faced upon their return.

Filipina returnees contest cultural ideas about gender, family, generation, and class. Migrant Filipinas negotiate their roles as mothers in the family, reinscribing their responsibilities in terms of financial and material support, as well as in the vision they have for their children to go beyond what their parents have become. With their financial resources, they struggle to realign power and to fend for their independence and status in the family.

The cumulative effects of such migration magnify gender inequalities at times while diminishing them at others.[31] The effects of migration are unpredictable, but we have to recognize migrant Filipinas as an important source of social and cultural transformation in the Philippines. In addition to the enticing images generated by the mass media, the material and social achievements of "successful" returnees have fed the imaginations of many with "possible" lives. The gifts, clothes, electronic appliances, computer games, and new houses circulate as concrete objects and also as visions. They generate a momentum for movement: to move and to be moved. In these ways imagination in social life foretells a shift in the global cultural order.

These stories of return highlight the dynamism of individual women and their dreams in the making of global flows and networks, as well as in the remaking of locality. Their overseas experiences are crucial for expanding the transnational practices and outlooks for both themselves and those at home. For the returnees, the muddled, contradictory, and ongoing struggles for emancipation in diaspora—the mediation between "discrepant worlds"[32]—do not end with the return home. The returnees continue to evaluate their everyday experiences, the past, and the future with a transnational perspective "garnered from transnational links and a transnational conception of self."[33] Even though the Filipinas I met liked to use the refrain "It's God's will" when I questioned them about the uncertainties of their jobs and lives in general, they hardly left everything in the hands of God. Their ambitions to go beyond what they had been given by what social scientists call "social structure" brought them into the global structures of inequalities and mobility—they negotiated their fates at home by taking on the world, so to speak. The stories presented in this chapter reiterate the call for recognition of the activity and agency of Filipinas in the production of their own destiny. The accounts of Filipina entertainers who come to realize the impossibility of their return reveal the social, cultural, and economic logics behind their apparently ill-advised decisions to work overseas through illicit channels. The basis for this recognition of agency comes from a dynamic understanding of identity, movement, and culture but without privileging the static and territorially bounded view of cultural and social formations such as gender, class, ethnicity, and nation.[34]

It may be appropriate to return to Annabel and her incomprehension that her fellow Angel Club Filipinas took off as entertainers yet again. Having proven herself a success, respectably married to an American man, sitting in the comfort of her own home with no financial worries and a secure future for her nuclear family in the United States, Annabel spoke from a very different gender and class position than did women such as Ira and Katie. In the certainty of her new identity, Annabel's incomprehension marked her distance from the others, whose uncertainties in life propelled their hopeful migrations to challenge their gender and class constraints. This discursive distanciation inadvertently contributes to the shaming of migrant women who leave as entertainers, as Annabel had done not long ago, and reinforces the idea that their choices are irrational and immoral. In many ways Annabel had become more akin to the middle-class activists who clamor against the out-migration of Filipinas as entertainers. The dissonance between these women's capacity and willingness to act against their social and cultural constraints and the seemingly sympathetic attempt of nongovernmental organizations to stop these women from leaving home in the name of "anti-trafficking" campaigns has to be understood within the conflicting positionality and views of culture. The next chapter explores this in detail.

Chapter 7
"Giving Value to the Voices"

After the negotiations with the Lees, the seven Angel Club Filipinas and I were standing in a circle in the middle of the busy street in central Seoul waiting for Mr. Lee to return with photocopies of the agreement that they had all just signed. They were talking animatedly in English and Tagalog, attracting quite a few glances from passersby. They thanked me and seemed happy with the amount of compensation. The women decided that they wanted to go straight back to the club area in TDC that evening with the club owners rather than return to the shelter where they had spent the last week. Annabel, who had been the chief liaison with Father Glenn and the center since before running away, called the Filipino Center to inform people there of this decision, while the others continued to chatter excitedly. Frowning, Annabel suddenly snapped shut the cell phone and reported that the woman who had answered the call, upon hearing that they would be returning to TDC, had asked her, "Why are you women like that? Father Glenn worked so hard for you and you do this to him. Why?"

The questions were an accusation of betrayal couched in terms of incomprehension and indignation. A foregone conclusion had been made about these Filipinas, and it was not necessary to listen further. Having plotted the binary "good/bad women" onto shelter/club, there was the expectation that the women, who had left the club and stayed in the shelter, should leave their disreputable past behind and turn over new leaves. The shelter was not just a temporary residence for those in need; it was also a transition point for women such as the Angel Club Filipinas to become "good" again. The hard work of Father Glenn and others was all for this goal. The female staff member interpreted the women's voluntary return to *gijichon* as a betrayal, expressed in the nonquestion question, "Why?"

Annabel immediately picked up the implication that they were "bad" women and turned to me. "Why did she say that? Maybe Father Glenn said something about us in front of her." I calmed her down, saying that I did not think Father Glenn would do that and that the woman probably did not understand their situation.

Having said this, however, I was aware that a distinction between "worthy" and "less worthy" victims might well be embedded in the organizational mentality of the Filipino Center. That very morning, before becoming embroiled in the negotiations concerning the Angel Club, I had been in a meeting with two well-known Korean activists who were working for women in prostitution. The meeting had been called to brief Father Glenn and a visiting priest from the Philippines, Father Marco, about service provision and government support for women in prostitution in South Korea. The priests were concerned about the number of Filipinas in prostitution around U.S. military camp towns. The tenor of the activists' presentations concerned the lack of government support for women in prostitution in South Korea and what this might mean for migrant entertainers. Knowing that my research was specifically about the Filipina entertainers in *gijichon*, Father Glenn turned to me, with genuine puzzlement, "Sealing, there is something I want to ask you—do the women enjoy their work?"

Surprised, and sensing the danger that a simple answer might qualify the women as "happy hookers," I asked, "What do you mean by 'enjoy'?" He was taken aback. After a pause he explained that he had seen a lot of Filipinas laughing when he walked the streets in the GI club area of Songtan. The seeming assumption of his question—that if the women were laughing, they must be enjoying their job and therefore could not be victims of any kind—struck me as insensitive and unimaginative. I restrained myself and tried to be polite: "They have to be happy. They can't sulk away all day now that they are here." I could have done better to bring out the complexity of the Filipinas' situation—my suggestion that the women tried to make their lives better in spite of their suboptimal conditions did not seem to register, and the "happy hooker" phantom continued to saturate the air.

Father Marco said, "We know that some of them came knowing that they would be doing this kind of work, but it's just their employers' treatment they have a problem with."

"Yes, but that is also a problem that needs to be dealt with."

Father Marco immediately responded, "Yes, yes."

*   *   *

Preoccupation with the sexual labor of entertainers is prevalent in anti-trafficking discourses. The assumptions are (1) that migrant entertainers are prostitutes; (2) that women are by default suffering from these sexual-economic exchanges and are therefore "victims" who could not possibly "enjoy" their job; and (3) that employers' maltreatment and other labor practices are extraneous circumstances to this genuine female victimhood. This hierarchy of victimhood is prevalent in a great deal of anti-trafficking discourse that, as will be argued below, reproduces a hierarchy of female virtues and sexuality that ultimately disempowers women entertainers and sex workers by reproducing their marginality.

In contrast to the vitality of hope and the multiplicity of goals that migrant Filipinas embrace, activists and scholars discursively contain them within the singular identity of "victim," highlighting innocence, misery, and powerlessness as their defining traits. This, in turn, justifies interventions to restore gender and sexual propriety, often in negation of the women's projects of transformative self-making. The ethnography in previous chapters demonstrates how Annabel's and other Angel Club Filipinas' decisions to return to TDC were part and parcel of their material and romantic pursuits in their displacement in South Korea. In spite of their structural vulnerabilities as migrant women in *gijichon*, they cannot be flattened into a singular identity as either "victims" or "agents." Any other meanings remain opaque to the very people who try to help, who often remain fastened to the binary understanding of "good" women who deserve to be saved and "bad" women who, to say the least, are less deserving. This is partly because they cannot see women consenting to any form of sexual-economic exchange. I argue that this obscuration is a product not so much of a lack of facts as of an ideological investment in particular gender and sexual orders that foreclose alternatives.

This chapter departs from a focus on how Filipina entertainers perceive and experience their migration; it examines the people who proclaim to know them and help them. Through ethnography, I examine how activists interact with the women, how they produce knowledge about them, what they do with this knowledge, and ultimately, how their work affects the lives of the women. I situate anti-trafficking activists and their work in national and transnational contexts and examine the knowledge production concerning victims of trafficking. In relation to the parlance of nongovernmental organization (NGO) activists and scholars, we need to critically study the concept of "giving voice" to the disenfranchised, not just in published reports but also in the arena of policy-making.

In her study of the "vernacularization" of human rights in local responses to gender violence, Sally Merry has identified the salient role that activists play as intermediaries between different sets of understandings of gender, violence, and human rights.[1] "Trafficking in persons" has become an international phrase that NGOs translate into images, symbols, and narratives that are meaningful to local audiences. With such translations NGOs play critical roles in constructing the subject of "victims of trafficking" in both national and transnational arenas, as they publish reports, rouse public awareness, hold the state accountable for the human-rights violations exposed in their findings, and demand policy and legal reforms to address such violations. Advocates, in the role of spokespersons, use the language of human rights to include the disenfranchised and demand due recognition from states and supranational bodies. They are thus important intermediaries between individuals as claimants of rights, states as protectors (and violators) of rights, and international agreements as guarantors of a universal framework for the protection of rights.

An international network of women-focused nongovernmental organizations has come to apply the language of "trafficking" in identifying the conditions of Filipina entertainers in *gijichon*, whom they identify as victims of prostitution ("prostituted women") and of trafficking. This formulation assumes a strong linkage, if not an equation, between prostitution and trafficking, so that both constitute violations of women's human rights. According to this logic, prostitution is no longer a matter of local jurisdiction but one of global import for nation-states and transnational activist networks. In 2000 a global anti-trafficking campaign gathered momentum with the adoption of the United Nations Protocol to Prevent, Suppress, and Punish Trafficking in Persons, Especially Women and Children and the U.S. Victims of Trafficking and Violence Protection Act (also known as Trafficking Victims Protection Act),[2] and a concomitant rise in media attention and funding opportunities opened up a political space for NGOs to engage the state in shaping relevant national legislation. The production of testimonials became an important part of NGO representations of the urgency of their cause.

Issues of legitimacy and accountability in NGO production of testimonies are rarely discussed. These are understandably thorny issues for NGOs that represent stigmatized and migratory groups who are difficult to access and who rarely participate directly in political action. Advocacy for "victims of trafficking" constitutes one such problematic category. The problem of accessibility justifies the generalization of a few (often the most tragic) testimonials as representative of hundreds of thousands of cases that appear as no more than statistical estimates. This gives NGOs disproportionate power to speak for a largely invisible group. How is such knowledge obtained? How do activists meet and interact with their "clients"? How do they establish their legitimacy and accountability—in both domestic and transnational contexts? These questions are particularly important for NGOs representing stigmatized, criminalized, or migratory groups.

Recent feminist studies of the politics of representation in rights claims help us question the ways knowledge is produced in human-rights discourses. In transnational feminism, scholars and activists have pointed to the important role that cultural advocacy plays in shaping women's activism and policy. Uncritical uses of women's experiences and calls for women's human rights could revictimize women in different social and global locations and be deployed for repressive political ends.[3]

Delving into the world of activists, Laura Agustín's *Sex at the Margins* is a powerful critique of "the social sector."[4] Agustín argues that "those declaring themselves to be helpers actively reproduce the marginalization they condemn." Using ethnographic material and poignant quotes from migrants, Agustín looks at how anti-trafficking discourses impose the victim identity and deny the agency of Third World women. Through archival material she shows how this helping culture emerged in the context of the Enlightenment, when a newly empowered bourgeoisie set out to define how society ought to be constituted and how citizens should live. In this process, "our contemporary understanding of 'prostitution' was fashioned and philanthropy was carved out as a women's sphere of work."[5] Bourgeois women in Britain and France set out to rescue "prostitutes" and restore family and social order, in the process opening legitimate channels for their own participation in the public sphere and getting respectable jobs. Agustín shows that in the twenty-first century most of the social programming to combat the trafficking of women and to eradicate prostitution that proliferates in Europe has contributed to the policing of migrant women and persons of deviant sexuality, as well as to an isolationist immigration policy. Warning against buttressing governmental ambitions, Agustín argues that "reflexivity is in order" for those who try to help.

Elizabeth Bernstein helps point out the possible direction of this reflexivity. Her poignant analysis of contemporary U.S.-based evangelical and secular feminist anti-trafficking efforts and their pro-business social remedies exposes the neoliberal underpinnings of both. Bernstein discusses how these efforts promote a "corporate ideal of freedom and carceral paradigms of justice." Their "rescue and restore" model aims at removing women and children from brothels and training them to become good workers in sewing workshops and factories, while incarcerating the evil traffickers and brothel owners. The harms of trafficking thus become located in the actions of evil individuals and criminals outside the institutions of corporate capitalism and the state apparatus. "In this way, the masculinist institutions of big business, the state, and the police are reconfigured as allies and saviors, rather than enemies of unskilled migrant workers."[6] This echoes a growing body of critiques of anti-trafficking legislations in different national contexts that lead to strengthening law enforcement and border control and fortifying anti-immigrant policies and antiprostitution agendas, thereby diverting attention from problems of unsafe migration and the exploitation of unfree labor in the current neoliberal economy.[7]

Advocates' interpretative frameworks—informed by their preexisting political ideals, ideological commitments, and strategic considerations—become the primary lens through which testimonials are produced and labeled. Interrogating "the mediations involved in the discovery and presentation of testimony,"[8] I argue that the preoccupation with sexual harm and victimization narratives silences many anti-sex trafficking activists and erases the agency and personhood of individuals. This focus on powerlessness and misery merely reproduces a version of the autonomous individual enshrined in civil and political rights, marginalizing discussion of economic, social, and cultural rights that importantly shape women's vulnerabilities.[9] With all their good intentions, those with an ideological anchorage in prostitution as inherently a form of violence against women impose a universalizing framework that prohibits alternative experiences and readings. As such, women in prostitution become individuals whose rights are important in their violation but not in their assertion.

Through this lens, all experiences in the sex trade are evidence of victimhood—even if the women concerned do not think so or resist such categorization. If oppressed women such as migrant Filipina entertainers have to speak through anti-trafficking NGOs, what kind of voice comes through? "Giving voice" to women through advocacy may reproduce the social, moral, and global divide between Western, middle-class women advocates and the passive and sexless "Third World women" whose cause they advocate—as a number of critical analyses of anti-trafficking discourses targeting the elimination of prostitution have shown.[10] Such efforts may collude with state projects in maintaining particular sexual hierarchies and border control.[11] Instead of asking what the women *want*, victimizing discourses focus on what the women *are* and what activists have decided they *need,* and these discourses demand protective legislation that ultimately reproduces the paternal authority of the state.

"Trafficking"—Defining a Global Issue in a Local Context

Concerns about trafficking in the global arena gave rise to changing political opportunity structures for transnational women's activism in the 1990s.[12] Different international funding agencies began to support projects for research, discussion forums, and service provision around the subject of "trafficking." While the U.N. protocol definition was introduced in 2000, the concept of trafficking had been taken in diverse directions in the decade before that, and this contributed to the contested meanings in the U.N. protocol in Palermo.[13]

"Trafficking"—Contested Global Definitions

International advocacy and legal instruments on "trafficking" began in the early twentieth century with the concern to protect women—as wives and mothers who belonged to the domestic sphere—from the evils of prostitution. This protective approach has fostered "the view that women are unable to take full responsibility for themselves and, therefore, that they need State (male) protection, including supervision of their performance as wives and mothers and restrictions placed on their participation in areas of public activity."[14] The powerful grip of this protective narrative has continued to haunt contemporary anti-trafficking initiatives, some of which address the women-specific nature of trafficking into forced prostitution, while others tackle the broader phenomenon of forced labor in the context of global migration, irrespective of gender. Activists, states, and supranational agencies that address issues of trafficking in persons all play roles in the contested definition of the term in the twenty-first century.

The connection between trafficking and prostitution began with the panic over "white slavery"—a term that came to describe women in prostitution at the end of the nineteenth century. Following the abolition of slavery in Britain and the United States, concerns about women engaging in prostitution in conditions akin to bondage incited the "new abolitionism" movement. There were protests in the United Kingdom against the Contagious Diseases Act, which regulated prostitutes for public health, and urgent calls to halt the trafficking of white European women to work in brothels in Latin American countries, allegedly by Jewish immigrant men.[15] Thus state regulation of prostitution was replaced by criminalization, as sexual labor came to embody a new form of slavery. Though historians have shown that these were largely unfounded allegations against the immigrant Other and that most of the women were of the working class and were traveling overseas for better livelihoods, these allegations resulted in the 1904 International Agreement for the Suppression of White Slave Traffic to identify and repatriate women in this "criminal traffic."[16] The United Nations adopted the 1949 Convention for the Suppression of the Traffic in Persons and Exploitation of Prostitution of Others. The convention declared that "prostitution and the accompanying evil of the traffic in persons for the purpose of prostitution are incompatible with the dignity and worth of the human person." Trafficking—the enticing, procuring, or leading away of a person for the purposes of prostitution—was prosecutable "even with the consent of the person [Article 1]." This convention confirmed the view that any form of prostitution is a human-rights violation and that all prostitution is coerced.

Beginning in the late 1980s, transnational activism for "women's human rights" was facilitated by the broad spectrum of rights issues that could be addressed under the rubric of "violence against women." This shared platform gave rise to the growth of transnational feminist networks and advocacy, but also to intense disagreements and divisions. Within this context, questions about whether prostitution was a form of violence against women or whether it could be a legitimate form of labor ("sex work"), as well as its relationship to trafficking, became more heated.

Broadly speaking, three different "camps" of NGOs can be delineated in this trafficking debate, according to their divergent understandings of the connection between trafficking and prostitution. The abolitionists advocate an end to all forms of prostitution. Prostitution, in this perspective, is either a form of bondage or an institutionalization of sexual violence and therefore categorically violates women's human rights. Consent is impossible in this understanding. The Coalition against Trafficking in Women (CATW) is the main body in the abolitionist lobby.[17] A second tendency makes a distinction between those who have been coerced into prostitution and those who have voluntarily entered into prostitution or who have migrated overseas to engage in sex work. According to this perspective, prostitution is not inherently harmful, but coercion into prostitution must be stopped.

The Global Alliance against the Traffic in Women (GAATW) is a representative of this second camp.[18] A third camp proposes a broad human rights framework to understand the harms of trafficking, arguing that the "voluntary/forced" dichotomy in understanding prostitution is untenable because it serves to reproduce the "whore/Madonna" distinction. In this view, the "harms" of prostitution are caused by moral attitudes and criminalization, both of which continue to stigmatize people engaged in sex work. Groups belonging to this camp call for the decriminalization of prostitution and the adoption of a migrant- and labor-rights framework for dealing with trafficking into forced prostitution. The Network of Sex Work Projects is the key organization in this last camp.[19]

The above differences came out at the deliberations for the U.N. protocol on trafficking in 1999. As a result of advocates who lobbied for a definition of trafficking in persons "via three internationally recognized and legally translatable elements (forced labor, slavery and servitude) rather than by reference to the kind of work migrants might perform," the final document was a significant departure from previous conventions, recognizing trafficking into sites other than prostitution.[20] In the 2000 United Nations Protocol to Prevent, Suppress, and Punish Trafficking in Persons, Especially Women and Children,

> "Trafficking in persons" [means] the recruitment, transportation, transfer, harboring or receipt of persons, by means of the threat or use of force or other forms of coercion, of abduction, of fraud, of deception, of the abuse of power or of a position of vulnerability or of the giving or receiving of payments or benefits to achieve the consent of a person having control over another person, for the purpose of exploitation.
>
> Exploitation shall include, at a minimum, the exploitation of the prostitution of others or other forms of sexual exploitation, forced labor or services, slavery or practices similar to slavery, servitude or the removal of organs.[21]

In other words, trafficking in persons can take place at a range of labor sites, including but not exclusively those of prostitution. Women and men, adults and children, girls and boys can all be trafficking victims. This is one of three optional protocols under the Convention for the Prevention of Transnational Organized Crime—in other words, it is primarily an instrument for criminal justice, not a human-rights instrument, and is therefore limited in its potential for developing rights-empowerment mechanisms. Its definition of trafficking is "an unusual mix of compromises" between lobbying groups with distinct ideas about the relationship between prostitution and trafficking, according to the anthropologist Penelope Saunders, who participated as a lobbyist in drafting the protocol.[22] First of all, even though this definition includes "forced labor" and "slavery," making it applicable to all forms of labor, it singles out prostitution as a distinct form of exploitation. Second, the protocol leaves undefined the concept of the "exploitation of the prostitution of others" to allow for adaptation in what constitutes prostitution in national laws. Therefore, although the protocol departs from equating trafficking with prostitution and includes the important notion of "coercion,"[23] it nonetheless resonates with a historical conflation of trafficking, prostitution, and violence that has been circulating since the "white slave trade" panic of the late nineteenth century.[24] In effect, while the U.N. protocol sets the parameters within which "trafficking" can be understood, it also allows NGOs and states to deploy customary meanings and prevalent anxieties in shaping its local understandings.

Since 2000 the U.S. government has been shaping the global anti-trafficking discourse toward a definition of trafficking as a special form of abuse distinct from migration or labor issues,[25] with prostitution as the main raison d'être of trafficking and women and children as primary victims. Far from empirical "truths," these are normative claims without empirical bases[26] that have been repeatedly expressed in U.S. legal and diplomatic instruments. The Trafficking Victims Protection Act (TVPA) of 2000 separates "sex trafficking" as a distinct category under the definition of "severe forms of trafficking in persons," privileging "the recruitment, harbouring, transportation, provision, or obtaining of a person for the purpose of a commercial sex act" as inherently exploitative regardless of the absence of abuse or coercion. This isolates "sex trafficking" from other forms of trafficking and isolates trafficking from the discourse of migration. The U.S. government, therefore, not only gives currency—through published reports, fact sheets, and funding initiatives—to normative claims about prostitution as inherently conducive to trafficking but also further deploys such information and initiatives in diplomatic maneuvers to globalize this particular definition of trafficking and its recommended solutions.[27]

The U.S. Department of State publishes an annual trafficking in persons (TIP) report ranking and evaluating countries according to their efforts to combat trafficking. The 2001 report gave South Korea the lowest possible "Tier 3" ranking, along with countries such as Burma, Sudan, and Albania, for failing to fulfill minimum standards in combating trafficking. This was embarrassing both because it placed modern industrialized South

Korea in the same category as some of the least developed countries and because it openly challenged the South Korean government of President Kim Dae-jung, which prioritized human rights and gender equality. It was important in instigating the government to take up the issue of trafficking, defined solely as a problem of prostitution. The U.S. Department of State endorsed this narrow focus with enthusiasm: South Korea became a "Tier 1" country in 2002 and a country of International Best Practices in combating trafficking in the 2005 TIP report.[28]

The customary and legal definitions of human trafficking and prostitution in the Korean language allow for much conflation between trafficking and prostitution. As explained in the 2002 International Organization for Migration (IOM)'s *Review of Data on Trafficking in Korea, insinmaemae* and *seong maemae* in Korean literally mean "sale of human bodies, slave trade" and "sale of sex, prostitution," respectively, but "both of the above terms can be understood to mean 'trafficking' depending on the context of use."[29] The report further explains that "trafficking" refers to the trade in women and minors and "is not necessarily seen in conjunction with migration or irregular migration. Instead, due mainly to the ways in which the problem has been portrayed in the Korean media, South Koreans view trafficking within the context of the sex industry and human rights violations."[30] This IOM report thus notes, but leaves unchallenged, this conflation of trafficking and prostitution. This means that all anti-trafficking efforts in South Korea continue to be concerned only with prostitution, despite being a party to the U.N. protocol. It is notable that no migrant organizations in South Korea have made any claims about "trafficking in persons" for purposes other than prostitution, in spite of the multitude of reports about migrants' abuse and human-rights violations.

With the upsurge of state and private funding initiatives and media attention, "trafficking" has been actively embraced by antiprostitution organizations to highlight the global and timely significance of their work. As Laura Agustín argues, such conflation of "prostitution" with "trafficking" conceptually relocates women migrants who sell sex from the category of migrants to that of "victims," causing "the disappearing of a migration category" and the erasure of their agency.[31] In other words, this framework allows activists to apply the blanket label of "victims" to all women suspected to be migrants in the sex trade, while making little connections to restrictive border controls, migrants' rights, or labor rights. The following sections examine how these ideas are manifested in the actual practices of NGOs.

The Global-Local Process: The Making of "International Trafficking" in South Korea

I arrived in South Korea in 1998, when local NGOs were actively seeking support and solidarity from international partners to build transnational networks in general and to address the issue of migrant entertainers in the country in particular. A new language of "international trafficking" (*geuk-jae insinmaemae*), referring to foreign women's entry, was making its way into local activist awareness, and local reports on the presence and conditions of foreign women in *gijichon* built a body of data on the "international trafficking of women" into South Korea.

From August 1998 to April 2000, while completing my fieldwork, I volunteered for Saewoomtuh, a community-based NGO in the *gijichon* in Dongducheon. I chiefly helped translate their material (for example, speeches at international conferences, reports, public statements, pamphlets) from Korean into English. I also suggested the name "Sprouting Land" as their English name (which they used between 1999 and 2001).[32] Thus, I became part of Saewoomtuh's drive to build a public space between the global and the local for its advocacy work. I also collaborated on a number of occasions assisting Filipina entertainers, some of which I will discuss below.

It needs to be said at the outset that, in spite of my critical analysis of Saewoomtuh, I had a cordial working relationship with the organization, and I am grateful for the generous support it gave me, especially at the beginning of my fieldwork.[33] I would like to emphasize that the criticisms laid out below are not targeted at Saewoomtuh per se but at the broader historical, institutional, and political environment that constrains the scope and effectiveness of Saewoomtuh and similar organizations in alleviating the hardships of migrant entertainers, "trafficked" or otherwise.

The analysis below draws predominantly on my interactions with NGOs that took place during the main body of my fieldwork between August 1998 and April 2000. While I initially relied on local NGOs for orientation in the field, I soon became acquainted with a growing number of Filipina entertainers whom the NGOs wanted to access. Thus, from being a complete outsider who was dependent on NGOs to learn about the Filipinas in *gijichon* to becoming an intermediary between various NGOs and the Filipinas, and also through translating many of the organizations' documents for an international audience, I became part of the process of the globalization of the subject of trafficking women in and out of South Korea.

Because of the burgeoning interest in the subject, local activists seized new opportunities to build their work and profiles, facilitating opportunities for me to observe how NGOs approached the Filipinas and how they represented their positions regarding them, especially internationally. It was through these processes that my critical reflections regarding anti-trafficking advocacies developed.

Saewoomtuh—A Politics of Powerlessness and Misery

"Oh, I am so sorry you live in a place like this. It's so dark in here. And there is no window. . . . With the high humidity, you will get sick easily. . . . How could someone live in this kind of house?" When the Korean activist from Saewoomtuh started to repeat this chain of laments for the third time in front of the two Filipina runaways, I stopped interpreting for the Filipinas. In any case, the activist's exasperated looks and the pitch of her voice communicated not only her assessment of their humble abode but also her overwhelming sense of pity. Katie, the more diplomatic of the two, responded twice by saying, "It's OK. We are used to it." May just gave an embarrassed smile. I caught myself with burning ears, mortified to be speaking those words and annoyed by the condescending emotional outflow from this guest I had brought to their house. The tin-roofed building was small, but Katie and May had been living in it for over seven months with their Filipino boyfriends. Each couple had a double bed in their own room, with their own TV, and they shared a small kitchen with a single stove. The electric wiring was obviously illegal and ran loosely along the ceiling and out one of the windows. It was, however, by no means a picture of human misery.

The above incident occurred in April 1999. The Saewoomtuh representative was meeting these two Filipinas for the first time. My coresearcher and I had brought her there at the request of the executive director of Saewoomtuh, who wanted to offer help to Filipinas. Even though the organization was based in *gijichon* and could easily have provided help to migrant entertainers, the staff members had neither conducted research nor provided organized assistance to Filipinas. Language was only part of the problem—until then Saewoomtuh has been an organization for *gijichon* women, and *gijichon* women have historically been Korean. The Korean women in *gijichon*, however, considered Filipinas competitors for business and livelihood and had considerable biases against them. In order not to alienate their primary "clients" while trying to address the needs of these new arrivals, Saewoomtuh wanted to meet runaway Filipinas who lived far away from *gijichon*.

Katie and May were both unemployed at the time of the above anecdote and were living with their Filipino boyfriends, who were undocumented factory workers. Saewoomtuh offered the women paper-flower making as a means of generating income. This flower making was soon dropped by both the women and Saewoomtuh, the former having lost interest because of the monotony and the low income,[34] the latter having become too busy to pick up the finished products regularly. In subsequent months Saewoomtuh staff took Katie to see a doctor when she complained of chronic heartaches and headaches, and when she wanted to return to the Philippines in January 2000, they assisted her in going through the necessary procedures at Immigration. However, Saewoomtuh had no organized outreach program catering to the needs of Filipina entertainers who were working and living in *gijichon*.

Despite the lack of research and the limited outreach, Saewoomtuh had campaigned openly and vigorously since 1998 for migrant entertainers in *gijichon* to be considered as "trafficked women" in the international arena. Saewoomtuh first spoke of Filipina entertainers as "women who have been trafficked" in October 1998 at an international conference in Washington, D.C., organized by the East Asia–U.S. Women's Network against Militarism.[35] Saewoomtuh's director at that time, Kim Hyun-sun, drew on media reports and anecdotal information from Korean women in *gijichon* to protest the ill treatment of Filipinas by the Korea Special Tourism Association (KSTA) and implied government involvement in the international trafficking of women. According to this report, Filipinas

> are being dragged into the military bases and forced into prostitution. However, they are placed at an even more miserable position than their Korean counterparts in terms of human rights. . . .
> The scene of three to eight women living in the same room is a miserable sight. Not yet acquired a taste for Korean food, these women survive on around two meals a day made up only of milk and ham coming from the U.S. bases. It is incomprehensible how they can put up with a life living on these foods.[36]

However, Kim speculates later in the report that "the monthly salary that they receive in Korea is even higher than a senior civil servant in the Philippines. Since they have been coerced into a situation where they could not break their contracts, these Filipino women decide that they might as well just make the money and thus follow their clubowners' orders."

The language of powerlessness and misery prevails, and the tone echoes the Saewoomtuh representative's overwhelming compassion at Katie and May's house. The incomprehension expressed in each account stresses the speaker's sympathy and the innocent Other's misery, as well as the distance between the two.

· *   *   *

At its inception in 1996 Saewoomtuh was a community-based organization for women prostitutes and their mixed-race children in *gijichon*. It identified these women and children as victims of U.S. militarism and the unequal relations between the United States and South Korea, as well as of the patriarchal nationalism that relegates both *gijichon* and *gijichon* women to the fringe of the nation. The founders of Saewoomtuh were former student activists who had been involved in *gijichon* issues since the 1980s.[37] The political sentiments of Saewoomtuh thus took root during the peak of the anti-American and antigovernment democratization movement that toppled the authoritarian President Roh Tae-woo in 1987. Saewoomtuh's basic objectives, according to a 1999 pamphlet that I helped translate, included "to eradicate war, militarism, and prostitution." The work of Saewoomtuh involves both advocacy and service-provision (counseling, social activities, child care and education, collective meals, and alternative income generation activities such as paper-flower making).

From its inception, Saewoomtuh had a very narrow political space in South Korea, given the stigma against prostitutes—in particular, *gijichon* prostitutes. Saewoomtuh tried to align *gijichon* women with "comfort women," arguing that both groups' loss of innocence was due to national weakness and foreign domination. Yet comfort-women leaders and other members emphasized that they had been sex slaves who were systematically "kidnapped" and "enslaved" by the Japanese military[38] and did not want to be linked to "willing whores" in U.S. military camp towns, where there had been no comparable system of enslavement.[39] Apart from the occasional tragedy of a *gijichon* woman's death, neither Saewoomtuh nor *gijichon* women gained much national attention. When it came to migrant entertainers, Saewoomtuh faced even greater obstacles in gaining support or sympathy, especially during the post-1997 Asian economic crisis period.

However, Saewoomtuh found a ready audience in international activist circles concerned with militarism, violence against women, and (more recently) "international trafficking in women."[40] Its international pursuits took shape within the rise of the global anti-trafficking drive.[41] In reporting on migrant women "trafficked" into *gijichon*, Saewoomtuh was not only "naming and shaming" the South Korean government for condoning such violence but was also actively building its international network.

Saewoomtuh's international orientation was clearly stated in a 1999 pamphlet that incorporated the language of "international trafficking" (*geukjae insinmaemae*): "On the international level, we bring to international attention crimes and human rights violation committed by US military in Korea. We also make efforts to stop further oppression caused by militarism and capitalism suffered by women and children, in particular we hope to join hands with other international organizations in stopping international human trafficking."[42]

This new internationalist orientation needs to be understood within the fundamental shift in the political economy of *gijichon*. With the declining numbers of Korean women and Amerasian children in the late 1990s,[43] the basis for Saewoomtuh's operations began to erode. This coincided with the entry of foreign entertainers into *gijichon* and the rise of transnational activism over the issue of trafficking women into prostitution. Given Saewoomtuh's limited political leverage in the domestic arena, successful entry into transnational activist networks allowed the organization to take advantage of the boomerang pattern of influence.[44]

However, these efforts for migrant women were not sustained. Saewoomtuh came to take a leadership role in an antiprostitution movement in South Korea, incorporating the discourse of "sex trafficking" with a focus predominantly on Korean women. In this process, migrant women's concerns were marginalized as Saewoomtuh moved its concerns out of *gijichon*—where migrant women were gradually becoming the majority of entertainers in GI clubs—and back onto the Korean nation.

In 2001 Saewoomtuh began to focus its advocacy efforts in the domestic arena and actively lobbied for a new law against prostitution in South Korea. It recast itself as an organization for "women victimized by prostitution" (rather than for "women and children in *gijichon*"), shifting from a *gijichon*-based organization to one with a national constituency.[45] Kim Hyun-sun became an active spokesperson in a new national women's movement against "sex trafficking." The Act on the Punishment of Procuring Prostitution and Associated Acts (Punishment Act) and the Act on the Prevention of Prostitution and Protection of Victims Thereof (Protection

Act) were passed by the National Assembly in March 2004 to replace the Prevention of Prostitution Act passed in 1961.[46]

In what ways do the new antiprostitution laws protect the human rights of migrant entertainers? Only one provision refers specifically to them. Article 11 of the Punishment Act, "Special Provisions for Foreign Women," stipulates that those who file reports or are being investigated as victims of trafficking into forced prostitution are temporarily exempted from deportation in order to file suits and claim damages, but they must leave Korea eventually, usually within three months. No service provision (other than two shelters for foreign women), allowance, or work permit is provided. Thus, even if a woman is being investigated as a victim, she has no means to make a living during the period of investigation or trial. Even women who win favorable verdicts may not get damages from club owners since they are required to leave the country. It is doubtful how such migrant victims may benefit from prosecution, as the new, "successful" laws fail to generate empowering conditions for migrant women to report abuses. Instead, the laws turn them into disposable instruments of investigation and prosecution, ensuring their speedy repatriation when the prosecution no longer needs them.

*　*　*

Saewoomtuh's brief encounter with Katie and May offers a preview of its circumscribed advocacy for migrant entertainers as "trafficked women." Saewoomtuh's compassionate members believe that migrant women need help. Yet they have neither the knowledge nor the resources to provide more than limited and short-term assistance. Helping Katie and May leave the country was the most that Saewoomtuh could do. Unlike other advocacy or service organizations in South Korea, Saewoomtuh's various proposals for these foreign women make no reference to their rights as migrants or workers.[47] In presumptions of the victimhood of prostitution and Third World poverty, Katie and May appeared only as violated women who needed to be repatriated, rehabilitated, and restored to their home country. Protecting women is often a far cry from protecting women's human rights.

By conflating prostitution with trafficking in persons through the language of "sex trafficking," Saewoomtuh thus has contributed to the delinking of trafficking from issues of migration. Even though South Korea is a signatory to the U.N. protocol, the majority of migrant workers in the nonsex sector continue to be excluded from any anti-trafficking initiatives that, as the U.N. protocol suggests, address issues of forced labor, slavery, and servitude. This tendency is not exclusive to Saewoomtuh or its partner organizations or to Korea, but it sometimes appears to characterize entirely the aims of international anti-trafficking NGOs such as the Coalition against Trafficking in Women.

The Coalition against Trafficking in Women–Asia Pacific (CATW-AP): A Drive for Victimhood

"In Korea, our women are once again subjected to the same brutality [around U.S. military bases]. The same experiences continue to haunt our women. In Korea, the Philippines and elsewhere, the women are viewed as commodities to be bought, and being Asians, they are certainly perceived as less than human."[48] Jean Enriquez, a representative of the CATW-AP from the Philippines, made the preceding statement during her first visit to South Korea in November 1999 in a speech entitled "Filipinas in Prostitution around U.S. Military Bases in Korea: A Recurring Nightmare." She had been invited by the Korea Church Women United (KCWU) to speak at the press conference for the release of the first field research report on Filipina entertainers around U.S. military camp towns in South Korea.[49]

Even though Enriquez had not had a chance to meet any Filipina entertainers who had worked in South Korea or conduct any research on the subject there, she spoke with conviction about the exploitation of Filipina entertainers in U.S. military camp towns. Speaking to her South Korean audience, Enriquez invoked an anticolonial and anti-American rhetoric, causally linking what she identified as women's objectification in general and the dehumanization of Asian women in particular with both the Philippines' and South Korea's experiences of U.S. militarism and imperialism. The verdict was out: Asian women are victims of U.S. military brutality, and Filipina and South Korean women activists now had to unite in a common struggle against their colonizers.

It should be noted that a tendency to assume a common fate, as "Asians," of dehumanization by a common oppressor misses the multiple and contradictory dynamics of power within the present-day Asia-Pacific region.[50] By relying on the rhetoric of a dichotomous model of domination—men from the First World (in this case, the United States) as exploiters of women in the Third World (here, Filipinas)—Enriquez was able to bypass the complicated network of the actual participants in the "trafficking" of Filipinas into South Korea, highlighting a form of violence that is foreign, masculine, and sexual.

*   *   *

CATW was founded in 1988 by Kathleen Barry, who is renowned for her book *Female Sexual Slavery*. CATW, according to its online statements, is an organization that "promotes women's human rights" and "works internationally to combat sexual exploitation in all its forms, especially prostitution and trafficking in women and children, in particular girls." Its philosophy is that "all prostitution exploits women, regardless of women's consent" and its vision for women and girls is that they "have the right to sexual integrity and autonomy." It further states that "[p]rostitution affects all women, justifies the sale of any woman, and reduces all women to sex"[51] and that "[s]ex trafficking involves the transport, sale and purchase of women and girls for prostitution, bonded labor and sexual enslavement within the country or abroad."[52]

CATW obtained Category II Consultative Status with the United Nations Economic and Social Council in 1989. CATW and its regional branches have been the recipients of significant private and governmental funding for research, law-enforcement training, and awareness-raising programs on "human trafficking, especially sex trafficking of women and girls."[53]

The themes and delineations summarized above are contradictory. First, prostitution is seen as inherently a form of sexual exploitation, and the link is established between prostitution and trafficking. Second, all women, not just women who become prostitutes, are considered to be victims of prostitution. Third, CATW draws a parallel between women and girls that dismisses any differential degree of autonomy between these groups. Fourth, CATW's vision of women's human rights and the achievement of sexual integrity and autonomy does not recognize a woman's ability to consent to commercial sex. In other words, this perspective discursively constructs women as "innocent victims" and, hence, mitigates against reading social agency into their entrance into the sex trade.

The construction of "trafficked women" as young, innocent, poor, and ignorant is central to Enriquez's description of women's victimization: "Profiles of women trafficked show that they are mostly young, with high school or less education, coming from the rural areas and from poor families."[54] Uneducated, poor, rural women have come to symbolize the vulnerability of the nation and culture, and hence the fears and anxieties of the dominated. Enriquez told the press that airport officials in the Philippines allegedly received "at least $25,000" from a Korean recruiter for each departing young woman. When questioned about this large amount, Enriquez unconvincingly explained that the girls chosen to be trafficked "were 'young and innocent.'" This explanation—rather than answering the question—further highlighted the virginal innocence of the alleged victims. This exaggeration (my research showed that immigration officials at the airport were paid three hundred to four hundred dollars for each woman) fits in well with the general victimization formula of the abolitionist camp analyzed by Alison Murray—"if any money is offered to the women or their parents it should be as pitiful as possible, whereas the profits being made from their sexual labor should be as enormous as possible"[55]—and I would add that the victims need to be as "pure" and as irreproachable as possible.

In her CATW newsletter article "Meeting My Sisters in Korea," Enriquez called on "sisters in Asia and other parts of the globe" to engage in a feminist struggle against "the West." She highlighted the importance of personal testimonials for the crusade, stating that "what would be most important in winning cases . . . is *giving value to the voices* of prostitutes in the courts and other arenas of battle" (my emphasis). In the ethnography below, I extend this concern and ask, "Giving *what* value to the voices of the women?"

*   *   *

My encounter with CATW-AP took place within the context of my collaboration with KCWU to produce the "Fieldwork Report on Trafficked Women in Korea" in 1999.[56] Working as a researcher for KCWU, I met Jean Enriquez, who was invited to Seoul for two days by KCWU to attend the press conference for the release of the report. I briefed her on the situation of Filipinas in *gijichon* as she did not visit the sites herself. When she found out that I was visiting the Philippines in May 2000 to meet with some Filipina returnees, she asked me to introduce some of them to CATW-AP, as staff members had not managed to talk successfully with any of these women. Supposing that meeting the women might give CATW-AP a greater understanding of the phenomenon of women in the sex trade, I went with Katie (whose story is detailed in Chapter 6) and Milla (mentioned in Chapter 4) to CATW-AP's Manila office one afternoon.

The following conversation is transcribed from the videotape I took of the meeting between Katie, Milla, Enriquez, and me at CATW-AP in May 2000:[57]

(Milla arrives after the meeting has begun.)

Enriquez (turning to speak to Milla): We are just talking about, as an organization, what we can do to help you. Because we come up with an idea of what happen [*sic*] to women in Korea, what some of you may have gone through, what others have gone through, that's the purpose [*sic*] why women, you included, escape. Did you also escape?

Milla: No. I met a guy there. He is now my fiancé.

Enriquez: A Filipino?

Milla: Black American.

Enriquez: GI?

Milla: Yes, GI air force. He had to buy the contract. . . .

Enriquez: But you didn't receive a penny. . . .

Milla: No. I received my six months' salary, but he had to pay twenty-five hundred dollars to buy my contract. And I just received like seven hundred or eight hundred dollars.

Enriquez (turning away from Milla and speaking to the group): So going back. We were thinking about how to help.

Enriquez's attempt to find an ideal victim in Milla's story failed at every instance in this short exchange, with Milla's straightforward denial of each of Enriquez's assumptions: Milla did not escape; she received her pay; and her fiancé who helped her out of the club was not a Filipino but an American—and a black GI—who was supposed to embody foreigners' sexual exploitation in CATW-AP's discourse.

Finding that Milla did not fit into her paradigm of victimhood, Enriquez went back to her own agenda and reasserted her position as a helper, thereby asserting an epistemological hierarchy allowing her to read Milla as a victim. The rhetoric of help was repeated throughout the meeting:[58]

> So, basically, the thing that we were saying was that these are the things that we do, and wonder how we can help each other, and how we can help you. So to begin with, if you can tell us your stories. For confidentiality, absolute confidentiality . . . OK. So we can talk about this. . . . [Slowing down and softening her voice] There may be some *sad stories* you have to go back [*sic*]. (My emphasis)[59]

It is interesting to note that Enriquez mentioned "helping each other" and in particular "how we can help you" but never "how you can help us."

Giving a nod to the mutuality of their "sisterhood," without acknowledging their need for victims' stories, Enriquez also made clear the hierarchical relationship between the helper and the helped. In her turning away from Milla, one could observe what Shih Shu-Mei calls a "politics of selective recognition"—in this case, outside of the mode of victimization ("sad stories") within which these women were readily recognized, there is a lack of desire to know the Other.[60]

* * *

CATW-AP contacted Katie, not Milla, for two interviews, one in Pampanga, near Katie's hometown, and one in Manila, a three-hour bus ride from Katie's home. The second interview was, according to Katie, conducted by staff from the Women's Education, Development, Productivity and Research Organization, Inc. (WEDPRO). Below is the transcript of my first phone conversation with Katie after her interview in Manila in August 2000:

> All the worst things. Like if they hit me, or how they treat us. . . . They asked about other girls. I told them everything. . . . They said they will have my story in a book and then they will give me one. It's a book on all Asian girls, I think. They are kind. I cried. They made me tell all . . . things since I was a child. . . . It's kind of difficult to tell. The woman who interviewed me said, "You have something in your heart that you can't tell. . . . It seems that you have a real problem."

Upon this prompting in a prolonged interview by an apparently skillful interviewer in search of "sad stories," Katie revealed that she had been repeatedly raped by her uncle since she was eight. After getting this sensational piece of personal history, the interviewer said to Katie, "You need a doctor" and left it at that.

Excavating the childhood experiences of sexual abuse in a "victim of (sex) trafficking" may not make immediate sense to the reader, except for the obvious "sexual" connection. Indeed, one needs to see this framing of trafficking as an issue of "violence against women" in its own right. Including childhood sexual abuse in the profile of victims of trafficking highlights the sexual vulnerability of women. By illustrating the extensiveness of violence (that one woman can be the victim of multiple acts of violence) and implicitly suggesting that one form of exploitation leads to the other, this framework reinforces the connection of womanhood with victimhood.

Katie went home from the interview with only 460 pesos (1 USD = 43 pesos in August 2000) for bus fare and open wounds to heal. Apart from her sexual victimhood, the interviewers had not expressed any concern about her current needs, her livelihood, or her future. Neither CATW-AP nor WEDPRO communicated with Katie again, nor did they send her "the book" with her story as promised or provide the "help" that was pledged in the first meeting. The question arises: What was the value of Katie to CATW-AP after she had given them her "voice"? Only her heartrending past, not her present or her goals for the future, had value in her configuration as a "trafficked victim."

What was the value of the interviews to Katie? Did Katie see CATW-AP as an organization she could seek help from—in view of Enriquez's alleged commitment to help? Apparently she did not. As discussed in Chapter 5, Katie left for a job in Japan in November 2000 and ran into worse abuses, eleven months after returning from South Korea and three months after her interviews with CATW-AP. Upon her return from Japan, I suggested that she might benefit from visiting the CATW-AP office since Enriquez had promised to help her, but Katie did not see the point: "You know some people just telling [*sic*] that. They just tell that."

When Enriquez went to Seoul in 1999, CATW-AP had been advocating an anti-trafficking bill in the Philippines for four years. The proposed bill was soon tabled in May 2000 in both the Philippine Senate and the House of Representatives, making CATW-AP's visit to Seoul an opportune moment to highlight its views of the plight of these "trafficked Filipinas" and augment the legitimacy of its cause. In 2003 the Philippine Anti-Trafficking in Persons Act[61] was passed. Hailed as a success by CATW-AP and its allies, the act increases the range of prosecutable acts and penalties for trafficking and also provides stricter regulation and protection of women who intend to leave as overseas performing artists. Although the legislation adopts the U.N. protocol's definition of trafficking, the preoccupation of NGOs and media rests predominantly with cases of trafficking into prostitution. The first conviction under the law was in 2005 for the trafficking of a Filipina woman from Zamboanga City in the southern Philippines to Malaysia by boat for what she thought was a job at a restaurant but turned out to be forced prostitution.[62]

CATW-AP was successful in lobbying for the 2003 anti-trafficking bill which institutionalized greater vigilance in monitoring women's out-migration. Yet it in no way addressed the needs, desires, and conditions of working-class women like Katie who continued to feel compelled to go overseas.

In fact, such anti-trafficking measures made it more difficult and dangerous for these women to leave.

* * *

Giving voice to the voiceless is the mission of many NGOs. Activists labor to produce victims' stories as testimonials in order to convince the public, the media, and policy-makers of the urgency of their cause. Stories of misery and pain are supposed to incite action. The analysis above captures some of the processes through which NGOs identify, interact with, and represent Filipina entertainers as trafficked victims to the global anti-trafficking community. It is indisputable that the Filipina entertainers in *gijichon* are being subjected to exploitation and abuse. In Chapter 3 I discussed how a victimizing discourse focused on sexual violence silences general assessments of migrants' vulnerabilities, working conditions for entertainers, and labor rights. This chapter invites readers to think critically about NGOs' production of knowledge about "trafficked women."

Anti-trafficking NGOs, in spite of their pledged commitment to (women's) human rights and social justice, are not exempt from the usual political proclivities of any organization. As we see above, they may have their own ideological commitments, needs, and agendas formulated *independently* of the women they try to help. Invoking nationalistic sentiments—in particular anti-American and anti-imperialist—reinscribes women's bodies as symbols of the nation. As a result, learning about the needs, aspirations, and dreams of the people on whose behalf they seek to speak becomes secondary to eliciting victims' stories. This selective recognition flattens the complexity of women's lives and desires and unwittingly revictimizes the women by ignoring the agency and desires invested in their migratory journeys. In other words, it is precisely the lack of an independent political voice of migrant women that allows anti-trafficking activists to project their own readings onto them. Giving voice to others only on one's own terms is a form of silencing and can be an aggressive act.

One may argue that NGOs have good reasons to emphasize the powerlessness of victims and even better reasons to expose the evil individuals, crime syndicates, and corrupt officials who are responsible for their plights. Reality is too messy, and describing things other than suffering and villainy would dilute the clarity required for claims-making and retribution. The production of convincing victimization narratives is a necessary and strategic step in communications with governments, funders, the media, and other non-state agents. As we know from fairy tales and the mass media, stories that sell best are those that have clearly identified villains and inno- cent victims—stories that are simple, unambiguous, and emotionally ap- pealing. To these objections, I pose the following questions: Who decides what the main story, and what the "complications," should be? What kinds of voices are being silenced? What critical perspectives are we erasing to- gether with the complications? What status quo are we buttressing when we reduce the lives and aspirations of the disenfranchised into uncomplicated stories of poverty and abuse by traffickers?

In the anti-trafficking discourses examined above, the abject victim— encapsulating women's passivity, powerlessness, and incapacity to decide or consent—continues to be the only subject position from which rights claims can be made for women. Sexual violations are extracted and con- structed as core and specific to women's victimhood. Using CATW's lan- guage, women are thereby "reduced to sex."

This victim subject circumscribes the paradigm for women's human rights in two major ways. First, prioritizing bodily harm gives rise to a set of remedies that offers "protection for women" rather than "protection for women's rights."[63] The female subject that emerges in these anti-trafficking discourses is marked by passivity, vulnerability, and dependency and is therefore in need of protection by the masculine state. This protective ap- proach reproduces the binary gender understanding in which women be- long to the domestic sphere and men are their defenders. The protected female subject reinforces the notion that "women primarily need rights that support them as mothers and wives, which endorses the protective dis- course that links women's enjoying of 'rights' to their association with pro- tecting men."[64]

Second, the preoccupation with sexual harm in the globalization of anti-trafficking initiatives effectively constitutes a new global knowledge/ power regime around sex and women's rights, creating female "victims of trafficking" as subjects in need of state protection and justifying greater state regulation of mobile populations and sexuality. This reading of the U.N. protocol perpetuates what Diane Otto calls the "glaring" blind spot in the pursuit of women's equality in international agreements—the failure to promote rights associated with women's physical integrity and sexual au- tonomy.[65]

Despite the rhetoric of human rights, anti-trafficking discourse in this vein constructs women's migration as a suspicious form of globalization. As a result, we are witnessing the development of a global network of NGOs collaborating with states to intensify the policing of mobile subjects while simultaneously engendering the benevolent state. By capitalizing on the unequivocal moral repugnance that "sexual harm" commands, the laws, policies, and high-profile arrests to combat "sex trafficking" and protect its victims confer moral authority upon the state, leaving relatively untouched the structures that have generated gendered disadvantages, capitalist exploitation of migrant labor, restrictive immigration policies, lack of intergovernment collaboration for the protection of human rights, and global economic and political disparities. To cordon off migrant entertainers' experiences of injustices from their general vulnerabilities as women laborers in a developing country with an unstable postcolonial regime and huge international debts is to insert an artificial rupture in these women's lived realities.

This echoes Wendy Brown's warning of the limited transformative potential of the "injured identity."[66] Injuries provide the moral authority to demand protection from the state, without questioning the structures that generate the "injuries" in the first place. Missing in the picture are such issues of social justice as gender, class, and ethnic inequalities in the economic, educational, and political arenas and a conservative gender and sexuality regime that emphasizes feminine purity and masculine valor, all of which intersect to generate the multiple vulnerabilities of women and men in different locations. These are also the structural conditions that make violence against women possible in the first place.[67]

Efforts to introduce anti-trafficking laws, the indictment of traffickers, and intergovernmental cooperation are often expressions of middle-class morality imposed on the working classes for the promotion of an ideal that is necessarily reactionary. Against the grain of this discourse of sexual victimhood, this ethnography, particularly Chapters 3 and 4, documents the agency and experiences of mobile women at the intersection of multiple disciplinary regimes. Ratna Kapur powerfully argues that the focus on a unitary victim subject in the international women's rights movement reinforces gender and cultural essentialism, neglecting the multiplicity of women's subjectivities.[68] I wish to contribute to an emancipatory politics for women by disrupting the naturalness of the authentic victim subject by attending to the power eruptions on the margins.

This brings us to the larger context of the revival of a global trafficking panic at the turn of the twenty-first century. Concerns about trafficking have arisen in the context of burgeoning migration—both legal and illegal—across borders. This climate has given rise to critical questions: What are the political implications of an anti-trafficking discourse that frequently conflates trafficking with prostitution and with violence against women? What are the unintended consequences of state powers over migration and sexuality?

Are anti-trafficking advocates unwittingly facilitating the aggrandizement of state powers and reproducing a particular gender order? The formation of a transnational activist network that pools together perspectives, experiences, and strategies at different locations can be a critical force in social transformation on a global scale. However, if this transnational network operates to impose a particular sexual morality, feminist ideology, and nationalist ideal on the poor and working classes, it is obliterating the voices and visions of the individuals it claims to serve. Whatever their successes on the stage of international politics, anti-trafficking activists risk creating yet another disciplinary regime with which individuals have to contend in pursuit of alternative possibilities and dreams.

Chapter 8
Hop, Leap, and Swerve—or Hope in Motion

I started this ethnography with the story of the Angel Club Filipinas, all of whom left South Korea that summer of 1999. I would like to end it with the stories of Filipinas who arrived earlier that summer—all first-time migrants—and with whom I have kept in touch since then. Lou, Candy, Bella, and Jessie all worked together with Ira for at least one year, in 1999–2000, at the Mermaid Club in TDC. For all but one of them, this first trip overseas launched their transnational careers.

Lou—our heroine who told her club owner that she was going to "fuck" in the Philippines—returned to South Korea in March 2001. She found her new employers unfair and unkind, as they did not pay their employees their drink money on time and pressured them to go out with customers. Lou resorted to alcohol to cope with her stress and was planning to run away when I visited her in June 2001. She subsequently worked in a factory for a few months and then moved in with her twenty-four-year-old GI boyfriend, George, who said he would divorce his wife and marry her. When we met again in June 2003, Lou was in her fourteenth month of waiting for George's divorce papers to come through so that they could be married. She was then living in a small apartment that George had rented for them in an area behind the military base. She had managed to work only for a few months as a salesperson in a phone-card shop before complying with George's wish for her to stay home. Without a job or a social circle and in an alien mountain town, her daily routine involved sleeping, watching TV and videos, and doing household chores. George's purchase of a puppy did not seem to make her any happier. However, in November 2003 they registered their marriage at the U.S. Embassy in South Korea, although Lou still had to return to the Philippines to wait for her spousal visa to the United States to come through. This took more than two years—a common fate for spouses of U.S. citizens from developing countries. Lou landed in a suburban town in North Carolina to live with George and his parents in January 2006, after having been separated from her husband for almost three years.

"Crazy" Candy, who flaunted the power of her vaginal muscles by opening a beer bottle with them onstage, ran away from the Mermaid Club in 2000 to be with her boyfriend, whom she eventually married and with whom she had a son. I last saw her in Lou and George's apartment in June 2003. She was living in South Korea legally, as the spouse of a U.S. military person. As boisterous as ever, Candy spoke and gestured excitedly about her upcoming week-long family vacation in Hawaii and their $150-a-night hotel room. By 2006 Candy and her family had relocated to the United States.

Jessie returned to the Philippines and worked as a hostess in the Filipino karaoke club owned by her cousin, who had worked in Japan as an entertainer. She was soon courted by a high-ranking Filipino police officer, who offered to support her, her three daughters, and her parents. Jessie accepted his assistance but also decided to pursue opportunities abroad, wanting to be self-reliant rather than dependent. Her cousin helped her get an entertainer visa to work in Japan. Over the next five years Jessie was in circular migration between Japan and the Philippines. Her family lived in a well-furnished modern apartment in Olongapo, with air-conditioning and a hot-water boiler and stocked with brand-name shampoo, conditioner, and skin-care products from Japan. She had two cell phones, one for communication in the Philippines and one specifically for receiving long-distance calls from her many regular customers in Japan. However, in 2006 the Japanese government announced that it was cutting eight thousand entertainer visas issued to Filipinas as part of its anti-trafficking effort, in response to U.S. government pressure. To maintain her transnational life, Jessie had to pay a Japanese man about five thousand dollars for faked marriage papers in order to gain residence in Japan. She moved to Japan in 2007 and has continued to work as an entertainer.

Bella, the seventeen-year-old who delighted in scaring young GIs with her gothic makeup while dancing naked, returned to the Philippines with Ira in 2000. She soon became pregnant and married her high-school sweetheart. In July 2003 Ira and I visited her and her family in one of the slum areas on the fringe of Manila City. Bella had gained much weight, exaggerated by her loose-fitting T-shirt and cropped leggings. Ira did not contain her surprise that Bella was "not beautiful" anymore. As the godmother of

Bella's daughter, Ira brought gifts and bought daily supplies such as shampoo, soap, cooking oil, crackers, and noodles for Bella's family in a supermarket nearby. Bella's husband was running a small computer-game store for local kids and making a very modest income for the family. Both Ira and I asked Bella if she wanted to go abroad again. She smiled and shook her head, saying, "No. I want to be with my family." She looked genuinely happy. She showed us her photo album from South Korea—pictures of herself in the club posing with other Filipinas with heavy makeup and sexy dresses, in the national park, on the snow-covered streets, and on a set in a television studio where she and Ira had given an interview—an event I had helped to arrange. The only photos Bella had thrown out were those of her with her GI boyfriend, whom she had considered marrying at one point (see Chapter 3). Bella was happy to have had the experience of going to South Korea and to have made friends there, but she had now chosen to stay close to her family in the Philippines.

These stories of "after Korea" not only mark how migrating as an entertainer to South Korea opened up a transnational field for these Filipinas but also speak volumes about the agency of these women in negotiating the possibilities and constraints that globalization processes offer. Their diverse trajectories also illustrate how their migrancy was determined—not by structural inequalities alone but also by their aspirations.

As Filipina migrant entertainers working in GI clubs in South Korea, these women had mobility and participation in a sexual economy of *giji-chon* that has been structured by histories of uneven economic development, militarism, colonialism, and the gendered pattern of migration in the Asia-Pacific region. From the perspective of global capital, they are cheap labor; from the perspective of the South Korean state, they are aliens who need to be kept on the margins; together, the market and the state maintain the flow of documented and undocumented migrant workers in accordance with the neoliberal principle of "flexible labor." From the perspective of the U.S. military, these women provide the entertainment that the "boys" need. Throughout all these regimes, the regulation of migrant women's sexuality and labor is geared toward other people's pleasures and gains, and the women appear as little more than numbers on a spreadsheet. Ironically, from the perspective of anti-trafficking activists who are committed to women's human rights and to addressing problems of migrant abuses, they are reduced to little more than their victim testimonies, which further the agendas of NGOs.

In this ethnography my goal has been to throw into relief the vitality of hope that propels these women's transnational movements and the agility they exercise to make their lives meaningful on their own terms. They are complex beings with multiple subjectivities grappling with the contradictions between imagined worlds and lived realities. Unless we want to concur with the perspectives of capital, state, and patriarchy, we must not be remiss about these women's dreams, desires, and aspirations. Considering their agency in tandem with their structural vulnerabilities illuminates all the more their energies and resilience and compels us to consider the contradictions of globalization processes.

I have discussed how migrant Filipina entertainers in *gijichon* experience migration as a process of self-making. They embark on their migratory journeys hoping that they will come back different persons—hoping for the better but realizing it may be for the worse, a possibility they prefer not to think about, leaving it to "God's will." They dream of the personal and material rewards of migration success, they imagine the adventures of life abroad, and they yearn to participate in the modernity that overseas employment promises. Migration therefore opens up a space for exploring their aspirations and imagining what they could become. Yet migration is also an experience saturated with uncertainty, full of questions about what, who, where, when, and how. The romance of migration overlaps with the romance of cross-cultural encounters, both experientially and analytically. Both involve crossing boundaries; both embody acute hopefulness and profound uncertainty; both animate conflicts among individual desires, social obligations, and historical forces; and both open up spaces for transformation.[1] Migrant Filipina entertainers in *gijichon*, whose job is to perform and reciprocate heterosexual romantic and erotic desires and whose gendered subjectivity (structures of feelings) is heavily invested in romance and marriage, poignantly experience these tensions.

I refer to their multiple tactics and strategies, as well as the ever-changing visions of themselves enabled by migration and its prospects, as their "vitality of hope," echoing the sense of what Hirokazu Miyazaki calls a "method of hope."[2] Miyazaki follows the philosopher Ernst Bloch in understanding agency as a manifestation of human hope, illustrating hope in the way Fijians consistently introduced a "prospective momentum that propelled their pursuit of self-knowledge."[3] In his ethnographic examination Miyazaki identifies indeterminacy as a condition of the possibility of hope and explores the ways Fijians achieve such a condition. Migration, in this light, embraces the condition of indeterminacy over that of familiarity and certainty at home, making one open to new ideas and challenges, and to possible transformation. Migration is therefore a source of existential mobility: "Better the uncertainty, which also means the possibility of mobility, than the perceived certainty of immobility."[4] It is also a manner of questioning the status quo. For the migrant entertainers discussed in this book, their seemingly benign ambition to "see the world" takes shape among the effects of the global capital regime that engenders this cosmopolitan desire. These effects include the global and social inequalities that make its fulfillment so difficult. These women's migrations thus challenge gendered opportunities and constraints, class hierarchies, national borders, and citizenship regimes in an active pursuit of self-knowledge through travel. Migration is a method of setting hope in motion.

I do not wish to romanticize migrant women's agency or heroism but to situate their hopeful pursuits squarely in the sliver of space they forge between the disciplinary regimes of state, capital, patriarchy, and (to an extent) NGOs. A major goal of this book is thus to destabilize homogenizing tendencies in the attempt to understand migrant women who work in the sex trade. No single label—be it "entertainers," "sex workers," or "victims of trafficking"—can capture the multiple subjectivities and experiences of these women, just as no single structure of power can explain their vulnerabilities. The myriad intersections of power and difference—according to gender, ethnicity, sexuality, capital, and state regulation—generate contradictory identities and desires. The transnational social field allows creativity in the identity and cultural politics of cross-cultural encounters. By presenting themselves variously as poor Filipinas, obedient daughters, innocent virgins, loving girlfriends, devoted fiancées, and exploited employees, Filipino migrant entertainers not only challenge any attempt to contain them within a single identity but also further position themselves to question the legitimacy of their subordination. As shown in Chapters 4 and 5, they consistently exceed their sexualized roles as "entertainers" by deploying idioms of family, friendship, and romantic love. Through such cultural and social maneuvers they weave multiple webs of resistance, accommodation, and openings to negotiate what would otherwise be their powerlessness. It is a keen awareness of their subordination *as well as* their agency that generates these tactics and strategies.

However, resistance, in spite of its oppositional character, often has the unintended effect of reproducing one's own oppression. The migrant Filipina entertainers in *gijichon* embody what Anna Tsing calls the "friction" of globalization and its productive power. In the "zone of awkward engagement" in *gijichon*, we see both the hegemonic inscriptions of power, identity, and desire and the limits of hegemony—between which lie the "gaps" in which the creativity and versatility of individuals become manifest. This ethnography thus aims to provide a textured understanding of everyday practices as forged beneath multiple oppressions and also an understanding of the openings for transformation offered within the transnational social field. In their struggles *against* the disciplinary regimes of capital, state, and family—predicated on their identities as women, migrants, wage laborers, and stigmatized "entertainers"—they also struggle *for* respect, autonomy, and the chance for the self-actualization promised by modernity. Acquiring new subjectivities as well as embodying the practices of cosmopolitan consumers, romantic lovers, and skillful seductresses, these migrant women not only follow and create transnational trajectories but also usher in new challenges to the global, national, gender, and sexual orders that seek to deploy and regulate their bodies and their sexuality.

However, the multivalence of migrant women's agency is silenced by a seemingly benevolent discourse of victimhood that, in effect, flattens their experiences and reproduces their marginality. In the discursively and politically intersecting sectors of the media, NGOs, and policy-makers, migrant women's sexualized labor is readily associated with violence against women, trafficking in persons, and slavery. Consistently represented as powerless and innocent victims, these migrant women come to embody the negation of freedom, as it is understood in neoliberal thought. Yet, as the analysis in Chapter 6 shows, this benevolence may operate as a smokescreen for a conservative sexual regime and a celebration of state power. Predicated on a heteronormative sexuality that reproduces binary understandings of women/men, public/private, and forced/voluntary, women in this discursive construction do not have the capacity to consent to sexualized labor. This discursive move and its extensions into the policy arena are appealing because of their anchors in a masculinist understanding of colonial history, nationalism, gender, and sexuality. However, they reinscribe women's proper roles as mothers and wives, so that women's sexuality and mobility appear legitimate only in the domestic realms of the family and the nation. In other words, the rhetoric of sexual victimhood forecloses sexuality as a site of female agency. In "Can the Subaltern Speak?" Gayatri Spivak laments that "the possibility of the collectivity itself is persistently foreclosed through the manipulation of female agency."[5] This foreclosure renders invisible the political, economic, and cultural structures that make women vulnerable in the first place, and thereby the common conditions of disempowerment and discrimination that they share with other migrants.

To go beyond a framework of sexual victimhood is to remove the blindfold and allow ourselves to see systemic violence. A preoccupation with sexual labor as exceptional and inherently harmful blinds us to the harms that a capitalist regime inflicts on all labor and an international state regime metes out to non-nationals. This ethnography has shown that subordination as foreign workers, rather than sexual violence, is central to the vulnerabilities of migrant entertainers in South Korea. It is important to see beyond the specter of individualized violence (evil traffickers, corrupt officials, sex-crazed clients, for example) and grapple with the complexity of the struggles of individuals—as women, migrants, wage laborers, and ethnic others. Their vulnerabilities need to be contextualized in a broader analysis of history, culture, and political economy. It is therefore important to examine the structural and symbolic violence that has produced masses of mobile populations engaging in unsafe migration and laboring in unjust conditions. Livelihood has always been precarious for wage laborers, who may toil away day and night and yet have no living wage due to the naturalized hierarchy of "skilled" and "unskilled" labor. Neoliberal economic policies further produce flexibility in a labor force that can be disposed of virtually overnight, without adequate adjustment programs for alternative livelihoods, under the banner of free trade.[6] Meanwhile, ethnonationalism and economic nationalism justify both the importation and the marginalization of migrant workers. We need to challenge the discourses that obliterate from view these forms of violence but implicate us by our participation in them. For example, the "smuggling" versus "trafficking" distinction, based on the idealization of the victimhood of a small number of "trafficking" victims, has allowed for the criminalization of a large body of migrants who are faulted for actively violating border controls. This discursive construction, translated into legal instruments, bolsters state powers and a carceral paradigm of justice that does little to address the problems faced by migrants. Conceptualizing the problems faced by migrant entertainers within these contending structures of oppression, rather than according to the concept of "trafficking" alone, opens the space for solidarity with movements for global justice, human rights, gender equality, peace, corporate responsibility, sustainable economics, and democratic governance.

*   *   *

As I wrote this in May 2008, I received a Skype call from Ira. She was calling from Brussels, where we have met every summer since 2004 and have often reminisced about South Korea. "Korea changed everything for me. The way I look, the way I think. Everything. EVERYTHING," Ira once declared. She has become convinced that migration was the only way to get what she wanted and what she could achieve for herself and her family. She has also acquired an expression of her sexuality that could be read as risqué, at the least, by other Filipina domestic workers in the Filipino community in Brussels: heavy makeup, revealing clothes, an effervescent demeanor, and more frequent visits to the club than to the church. She has also discerned a different ethics in the vast but differentiated Filipino community in Brussels. She once told me, "The [Filipino] people here only care about themselves. Not like us before in [South] Korea. We had boyfriends, but we still took care of each other." She still keeps in touch with Jessie and Lou but has lost touch with Bella, whose cell phone was broken. However, she has seen neither them nor her family for five years.

I clicked the "Answer" button and the screen opened automatically on my computer, immediately covering the document on which I had been laboring. There she was, with her long straight hair and bright smile, in an azure and white striped T-shirt and jeans, sitting on the lap of her blonde boyfriend from Switzerland. Ira told me that they had been together for five months, since meeting in a club in downtown Brussels. He had been traveling from Switzerland to visit her every month. He is eight years younger than she is and only gradually came to learn about her children, her dying (now dead) father, and her illegal status. This was the first time I talked with him and saw his pixelated face on the screen. They were two giddy lovers. Ira looked happy—even though her father had died two weeks earlier, her sixteen-year-old daughter was four months pregnant, and she was in debt and did not like cleaning other people's toilets.

After her return from South Korea in May 2000, Ira had gone to Malaysia as an entertainer in March 2001, when the wait for South Korea turned out to be too long for her. In Malaysia she worked in a club that made the entertainers work much longer hours and paid them less than those in South Korea had. In addition, she was pressured to go out with customers; she was raped by one of these customers but never reported it. An immigration crackdown sent her back to the Philippines in November 2001. When her savings ran out and she could not find an agent who could help her leave soon enough, her youngest sister, who had just graduated from high school, offered to leave the Philippines as an entertainer. Ira tried to stop her—she had wanted her sister to go to college. She asked me for help.

A diplomat friend of mine who was working in Brussels offered to use her diplomatic privilege to arrange for Ira to move to Brussels as a domestic worker. Ira could then find another diplomat to hire her. It was a very drastic move for Ira, who had never had to do much housework. She took a few days to consider the option and then agreed. By July 2002 she was in Brussels as a domestic worker. However, she was frustrated with her employer and ran away in August 2003, right after she had returned from her one-month annual leave in the Philippines. This move turned her immediately into an undocumented worker, and she lost all her privileges of returning home once a year. She had to look for part-time cleaning jobs on her own, rent her own apartment, and deal with all the sundries of living in Brussels as an undocumented migrant.

In early 2008 the Belgian government rejected her application, meaning that she would have to either live in constant fear of deportation or leave the country. She decided to appeal the decision, even though her lawyer advised that it would be difficult. She solicited the help of her aunt, who was married to a U.S. GI stationed in Germany, and asked her to adopt her two older children and bring them to Germany so that Ira could take them to Brussels with her. Ira supplied her aunt with documents to show that she had disappeared and effectively abandoned the children. If this plan works, official statistics will record another broken family caused by migration. However, this would allow Ira and her children to be reunited in Brussels. Then, maybe, her boyfriend would marry her.

When I pointed out that she had not annulled her marriage with her husband in the Philippines, Ira said that was okay, as she could pay ten thousand pesos to get "the paper" certifying that she was single. "Is that legal?" I asked her. (I have a habit of asking very naive questions of Ira; the last time I remember was about her "virginity in Korea.") Ira replied, "No, it's not legal, giving the money. But the paper, it's legal." (Ira enlightened me again on the contextual understanding of the term "legal.")

*   *   *

Marshall Berman, in *All That Is Solid Melts into Air*, his exposition of the contradictions of modernism on the streets, guides us through Charles Baudelaire's 1865 poem "The Loss of a Halo," about an encounter "between an isolated individual and social forces that are abstract yet concretely dangerous." As part of Napoleon's project to modernize France, the city of Paris saw its first boulevards. In Baudelaire's poem a poet loses his halo as he negotiates the "moving chaos" in the new urban landscape of boulevards and ends up in a sinister place, "probably a brothel," inappropriate for a man of his station (his "halo"); yet the poet feels triumphant, with a new sense of self-definition. In Berman's interpretation, modern traffic directed by the rationality of the boulevard is forced upon people, but it simultaneously permits new modes of freedom for those who find ways through the chaos, opening up new experiences and releasing creative energies.

The *mouvements brusques*, those sudden leaps and swerves so crucial for everyday survival in the city streets, turn out to be sources of creative power as well. In the century to come, these moves will become paradigmatic gestures of modernist art and thought.[7]

For Berman, the boulevards both reflect and symbolize the contradictions of modernity and capitalism—regulation and rationalization produce their own chaos and irrationality. The boulevards in Paris and other modern cities became the space for the masses to challenge, and sometimes to overthrow, those in power in moments of disruption that have given rise to "the people."

In the new cartography of globalization, migrant entertainers and other working-class migrants acquire the survival skills to leap, swerve, duck, and hop the loops of "scattered hegemonies" that seek to regulate their flows. They develop a kind of amoebic existence in the interstitial spaces of disciplinary regimes. Their prospective propelling force on the ground translates into instability in the very institutions that seek to tame their transgressive bodies. Their tactics, strategies, and challenges on different scales are at once part of the political processes and cultural project of modernity and globality.

Migrant entertainers seize the openings generated by globalization processes for their own projects of aspiration. They negotiate with regimes of state, capital, and sexuality "from below." They question the sanctity of ideal femininity and home and open themselves to new experiences of and opportunities for sex, love, and labor, releasing their creative energies into the transnational field as they forge new identities, connections, and possibilities.

Appendix I
Methodology

This book draws on research between 1998 and 2008. Apart from prolonged fieldwork in 1998–2000, return visits were made to *gijichon* in 2001, 2003, 2005, and 2006. During my first eighteen-month stay in South Korea between 1998 and 2000, I was affiliated with the Institute for Cross-Cultural Studies, College of Social Sciences, Seoul National University (SNU), as a researcher. This affiliation offered me the privileges of library access at SNU, and the prestige of Seoul National University was very helpful in offering me institutional protection and greater access to information, particularly at the institutional level, in status-conscious South Korea.

Selection of Informants

Access to the Filipinas was limited—both because of club owners' surveillance and because the women were suspicious of strangers interested in the details of their lives. It is therefore important to note that the narratives in this book are from women who could move freely outside of the clubs and from those who had run away. A small number of clubs did not allow their migrant workers to leave the clubs without escorts, and at least two clubs in Dongducheon prohibited the women's use of mobile phones (to prevent them from contacting customers outside the club). However, these are by no means the dominant pattern of control in *gijichon* clubs for Filipinas.

The help of GIs was essential to making initial contacts with Filipina entertainers, in particular in Dongducheon, which had a closer system of surveillance than Songtan did. Two Latino GI friends—Martin, a forty-five-year-old sergeant from Bolivia, and Juan, a twenty-three-year-old private from Mexico—agreed to help with our research. In December 1998 they accompanied us to two clubs in Tokkuri, the area famous for clubs with explicit shows and women easily available for sex. Our first attempt to talk to the Filipinas in a club with the help of our GI friends turned out to be a failure. Posing as female customers in a GI club raised only suspicions and distrust. A second attempt to meet Filipina entertainers through their GI boyfriends and friends was much more effective. The personal connection generated more trust and thus willingness to talk. From these contacts, we managed to snowball our contacts with Filipinas through their own networks.

I also made some successful contacts with a few Filipinas outside the club by initiating conversations with them on the streets or in restaurants they frequented. Through the Filipino Center based in Seoul, Ms. Back and I also were able to meet with a few Filipinas who had either run away or left the clubs. Regular visits, phone calls, and sometimes e-mails were the means we used to keep in touch with these women. Through these Filipinas, I also met more GIs who were customers/boyfriends, as well as three club owners.

Collaborative Research: December 1998–August 1999

Collaborative research with Ms. Back Jaehee, one of the founders of the first feminist research collective on issues of prostitution, Maemaechun haegyeul uihan yeonguhui (Study Group for the Solution of the Problem of Prostitution) formed by students and alums of Ewha Women's University, between December 1998 and early August 1999 contributed to this project. In November 1998 I met Ms. Back through the administrative director of Hansori (United Voice for the Eradication of Prostitution). Ms. Back had extensive voluntary experience working with women in *gijichon*. She wanted my help with English translation in meeting Filipina entertainers, and I needed her assistance with orientation in *gijichon*.

A GI acquaintance of mine helped arrange our visits to *gijichon* clubs and a meeting with a GI who was dating a Filipina entertainer. After meeting a few Filipinas who agreed to interviews, Ms. Back drafted a list of questions, and we went through the list together. I was responsible for the actual execution of the interviews and any follow-up questions. Ms. Back sometimes made suggestions in the process, and we would have discussions after each interview. I transcribed the interviews for Ms. Back and also made follow-up phone calls to the women after the interviews. Ms. Back stopped visiting *gijichon* with me in late August 1999. In early 2000 Ms. Back assisted me in my interviews with officials at the Ministry of Culture and Tourism, representatives of the Special Tourism Zone Committee and the Korea Special Tourism Association, a journalist, and a Korean manager.

Ms. Back and I agreed that both of us have the right to use the material we collected together. Although we were both interested in Filipina entertainers, our concerns lay in different manifestations and scopes of the phenomenon. Ms. Back's "A Study of Foreign Women Employed in the Korean Sex Industry" addressed the issue in terms of the exploitation of foreign women's sexuality in South Korea in the context of international women trafficking, and it drew on data collected between December 1998 and August 1999. I was interested less in interview material than in a more ethnographic account of the women's lives and changes during and after their migratory experience, which brought my research to a space spanning South Korea, the Philippines, and the women's subsequent destinations. Coincidentally, it was after August 1999—following my participation in the distribution of flood aid packages for Korea Church Women United, the runaway of the seven Filipinas, and the introduction of two Filipinas to speak on a Korean television documentary program—that more trust and rapport developed between some of the women and me.

Research Methods

Language

My knowledge of the Korean and English languages was essential to the research. Research with the Filipinas and GIs was conducted in English. Since the presence of Filipina entertainers was not foreseen, I was not equipped to speak Tagalog. However, since all Filipinas were working in GI clubs and since talk was the most important means of making money through drink sales, most Filipinas could express themselves reasonably well in English. Though I learned a small amount of Tagalog during my visit to the Philippines and tried my best to communicate with the women's families in a mixture of English, Tagalog, and body language, my experiences in the Philippines have chiefly been filtered through the Filipinas' interpretations.

Formal Interviews with the Filipinas

During the initial stage of research with Ms. Back, formal interviews with the Filipinas were conducted to gather information on the women's backgrounds, conditions of work, and the problems they faced. Many of these interviews took place in restaurants and coffee shops, and most of them were taped and transcribed. The formality of the method, however, maintained the distance between interviewer and interviewee, and these interactions lacked the smooth flow of a more spontaneous exchange and led to the reproduction of certain rhetoric in their answers. A typical answer to the question "Why did you come to Korea?" was "To make money for my family."

Information from these early formal interviews was more useful as a counterpoint to the women's subsequent articulations and actions than as the "truth." This is because the interviews were conducted at one specific point or stage of their lives in South Korea, while the women's ideas, aspirations, and working conditions might have changed significantly in the course of their stay.

Informal Methods with the Filipinas

Most of the material used in this book was collected through informal methods. I lived midway between Dongducheon in the north and Songtan in the south, in an area of Seoul two to three hours away from either *giji-chon*. I visited each *gijichon* one to two days a week on average. I started to meet the Filipinas around noon (the usual time for starting their daily activities) and spent time with them until around 7:00 p.m., when customers started to visit the clubs. In addition to four week-long visits with my core-searcher to Dongducheon, Songtan, Gunsan, and Busan as commissioned by the KCWU, on several other occasions thereafter I spent more time in the clubs and stayed overnight in a motel. In between visits I made phone calls to keep in touch.

This is very different from traditional ethnography in which the eth-nographer interacts with informants on a daily basis for a prolonged period of time. The relative infrequency of meetings was necessary to minimize the suspicion of club owners and Koreans working in the clubs, who certainly did not want any researchers around. This was particularly the case if the club owners saw me with the Filipinas and became necessarily curious about what a Hong Kong woman was doing in a *gijichon* club. I told all club owners that I was an anthropology student at Seoul National University. In Dongducheon, I explained my presence in the area by saying that I was a volunteer at Saewoomtuh's playroom for Amerasian children. My identity as a volunteer was confirmed when I helped distribute the flood aid from

KCWU to each of the clubs in August 1999. In Songtan, I told club owners that my Korean *onni* (older sister) lived in the area—if asked, I would explain that it was Ms. Kim Young-Ja, ex-*gijichon*-woman-turned-minister.

Having lunch or coffee with the Filipinas and sometimes their customers/boyfriends; window-shopping on the streets; spending time with them in their rooms, talking about their customers/boyfriends, club owners, families, and other Filipinas; and occasionally visiting them in the clubs and chatting on the phone with them not only allowed me to gain a better sense of their lives in *gijichon* but also revealed details of their lives in South Korea and in the Philippines. The informal atmosphere generated a greater sense of intimacy than formal interviews would have allowed.

Establishing trust with women whose class, national, ethnic, and sexual identities are so distinct from mine was a challenging task. I considered it a breakthrough in my relationship with Bella and Ira when over lunch one day in October 1999, five months after our first meeting, the two of them volunteered to tell me that they had lied to me—Bella was not nineteen years old but seventeen, and Ira had not one child but three. A few other women made similar confessions about the "truth" at later stages of our relationship. My rapport with some of the Filipinas developed significantly after I visited them in the Philippines and continued to keep in touch in the years afterward.

Visiting the four Filipinas in the Philippines allowed me to observe them in the capacity of daughter, mother, and sister rather than entertainer. Meeting the women's families and glimpsing their lives in the Philippines in their newly acquired role as breadwinners also gave substance to the awareness of differences between lives in South Korea and lives in the Philippines. The shift in physical, social, and cultural space not only offered insight into the negotiations of identity that women went through in their migratory experience but also gave meaning to the lives the women assumed in South Korea.

Interactions with Gijichon *Women and People in* Gijichon

Voluntary service and participation in Saewoomtuh's activities (for example, picnics) allowed me to interact with Korean *gijichon* women and gain a notion of their daily concerns and their views of foreign women in *gijichon*. I also regularly visited three Korean veteran *gijichon* women in Uijongbu—one of them was a madam in a club, and the other two had retired completely from the club business but continued to live in the area—and spent time with them. This gave me a sense of what life was like for the older generation of *gijichon* women who had spent a large part of their lives living, mostly alone, in this marginal space.

Two Korean *gijichon* women whom I befriended in Saewoomtuh agreed to talk about their life stories with me toward the end of my fieldwork. In Gunsan, Ms. Back and I befriended two Korean women who agreed to talk to us about the entry of Filipino entertainers. With these connections, I returned and conducted more interviews with other Korean women.

Chitchat with shopkeepers, food-stall *ajummas*, and taxi drivers was also an important source of information and anecdotes. These people were at the same time witnesses to *and* participants in the change that foreign entertainers brought with them.

Interactions with GIs

Except for formal interviews with four GIs whose Filipina girlfriends worked at the Angel Club, I learned about life in *gijichon* from the GIs' perspectives through informal conversation. I met with five GIs, and sometimes their friends, on a regular basis during their posting in South Korea. I also talked to the boyfriends of the Filipinas; during these conversations I had to protect the interests of my Filipina informants by aligning my "stories" with those of the women (for example, that the GI was her only "boyfriend"). I was sometimes turned into a mediator between a GI and a Filipina and had to offer "counsel" to both at times of conflict. There were some rare moments when I found it emotionally demanding to deal with the discriminatory and callous comments a few GIs made about the Filipinas. Except for chance encounters, the GIs were aware of my research purpose and my interest in their lives in South Korea.

Interactions with Club Owners, Government Officials, and the KSTA

While representations from club owners, government officials, and the Korea Special Tourism Association (KSTA) are important discourses of policy, management, and economics that shape the conditions of life and experiences of Filipina entertainers in *gijichon*, I had to conceal my actual research topic in my conversations and interviews with these individuals and organizations because the illegal operations and the implications of sex work in the deployment of Filipina entertainers in *gijichon* promised to be controversial. Since I had little knowledge of the networks between government officials, KSTA officials, and club owners, to confront any one of these with the issue might have jeopardized not only my research but, more important, also the safety of the Filipinas with whom I was in touch. Informed consent was thus not possible in this context.

With the exception of the Angel Club owners, who knew briefly about my research interests in Filipinas in *gijichon* as we worked closely for the safe departure of the seven runaway Filipinas, all the other club owners I met with knew me only as a researcher at Seoul National University who by chance became friends with the Filipinas. My acquaintance with them was usually explained as accidental encounters at a fast-food shop nearby. I also pretended to be less fluent in my Korean and communicated in a mixture of English and Korean with the club owners, consolidating my identity as a foreigner who knew little about *gijichon* and thus minimizing any suspicion. While I occasionally posed questions as a curious foreign student, no formal interviews ever took place with club owners.

Dongducheon and Songtan are the only two *gijichon* that have gained the status of Special Tourism Zone—an accreditation system started as part of the globalization initiative during the presidency of Kim Young-sam (1993–97) for areas capable of generating a significant amount of foreign currency and run by the Ministry of Culture and Tourism. Declaring my research interest in "Special Tourism Zones," in particular the development of U.S. military camp towns into "tourist" areas, I managed to meet with government officials on both local and ministerial levels. While my affiliation with SNU was adequate for gaining access to local government officials, a personal connection with a senior bureaucrat in the Ministry of Culture and Tourism was necessary to meet with officials responsible for special tourism in the central government. The ultimate goal in meeting these central government bureaucrats, however, was to make use of their influence to gain an interview with the KSTA, which was responsible for bringing most foreign entertainers into *gijichon*, since our direct request for an interview had been rejected. Though the official's attempt to secure a meeting for us with the Seoul (central) office of the KSTA failed for reasons he could not explain, he helped arrange a meeting with the chairman of the Songtan Special Tourism Committee, who turned out to be the most powerful hotelier in the area. Only after talking to this important man in the area was my request to meet a representative from the KSTA Songtan branch granted. A discussion of business development and management in *gijichon* was used to elicit information on how Filipinas were introduced into the clubs as entertainers. It took not only a camouflaged interest in Special Tourism Zones but also a labored detour up and down the central and local bureaucracies to get the story from a representative of the KSTA.

Working with Organizations and the Media

I volunteered for Saewoomtuh and Hansori, helping people there with English translations and proofreading. In mid-November 1998 Kim Hyun-Sun invited me to join a meeting of different groups concerned with the problems of Filipina women in *gijichon*. Though this meeting was aborted after a few months, it turned out to be an important platform for me to meet all the groups concerned with the issue and to get involved with the different NGO efforts. In March 1999 the YWCA invited Ms. Back and me to conduct week-long research on Filipina entertainers in *gijichon*. The results of this research were presented at the Asian Network of Traffic in Women, YWCA, in May 1999. In May we were commissioned by KCWU to complete a two-month project researching foreign entertainers (both Filipina and Russian) in five different districts. The analysis of the findings was presented in a final report in 1999 (Korea Church Women United, "Fieldwork Report on Trafficked Women in Korea,"). These collaborations with NGOs did not result in a significant change in our research as we had much autonomy in the execution of fieldwork. Furthermore, it was in my capacity as a researcher for KCWU that I met Jean Enriquez of the Coalition against the Trafficking in Women–Asia Pacific (CATW-AP) and subsequently introduced two of the Filipina returnees to CATW-AP.

Decisions in the field were sometimes made not so much for the benefit of research but with consideration of my accountability to the subjects being studied. I agreed to work with NGOs and a Korean broadcasting company with the hope of bettering the women's conditions and protecting their labor and human rights. Neither of these decisions seemed to have worked the way I had hoped. Fortunately, though, my observation in the following months made no suggestion that they had affected the women negatively either.

This ethnography is thus multisited in many senses—in terms of significant fields of relation, South Korea, the United States, and the Philippines are frequent sites of reference; in terms of travel, the ethnography spans South Korea and the Philippines; in terms of tracking the women's movements by global communication networks, the ethnography follows the women to Japan, Malaysia, the United States, and their return to South

Korea. In addition to these places, I also traveled between the distinct social and ideological spaces of entertainers and middle-class activists and along the divide between the global North and South in the larger debate on prostitution and trafficking. The many conflicts I have felt across these spaces and places could be summed up in George Marcus's discussion of the ethnographer as a "circumstantial activist":

> In conducting multi-sited research, one finds oneself with all sorts of cross-cutting and contradictory personal commitments. These conflicts are resolved, perhaps ambivalently, . . . in being a sort of ethnographer-activist, renegotiating identities in different sites as one learns more about a slice of the world system. . . . [T]he identity or persona that gives a certain unity to [an ethnographer's] movement through such disjointed space is the circumstantial activism involved in working in such a variety of sites, where the politics and ethics of working in any one reflects on work in the others.[1]

Appendix II
Employment Contract for a Filipina Entertainer

The poor quality and truncated parts of the employment contract shown here (pp. 240–42) are in the original. The image of this contract is from a faxed copy that I received from an undisclosed source connected with the KSTA.

EMPLOYMENT CONTRACT FOR FILIPINO ENTERTAINER

This CONTRACT is entered into by and between :

KOREA SPECIAL TOURIST ASSOCIATION represented by ....
hereinafter known as employer.

- AND -

_____ Filipino Citizen and holder of Philippine
passport NO. _____ hereinafter known as employee.

THE ABOVE PARTIES in this contract hereby agree to the following terms
and conditions on overseas entertainment / engagement / performance :

1. ENTERTAINER shall perform at the place designated by KOREA SPECIAL
   TOURIST ASSOCIATION.
2. DURATION AND EFFECTIVITY OF THE CONTRACT.
   Duration : less than 12 months
   (Term of contract : According to the performance VISA approval from
                       Ministry of Culture and Sports)
3. EMPLOYEE'S position is ENTERATAINER.
   (Variety Bands, DANCERS, D · J, P · D Manager)
4. COMPENSATION : Minimum monthly compensation of ₩ _____ or
   US $ _____.
   The charge performance shall be adjusted by the day starting performance
   when entertainers arrived in Korea said compensation shall be paid monthly
   by the employer. (Owner)
5. HOURS OF WORK, RESTDAY AND OVERTIME PAY.
   5. 1 Hours of work : Maximum of Eight (8) hours per day.
   5. 2 Restday : Four (4) restdays a month.
       (One day off from Monday through Thursday from every a week)
   5. 3 Overtime Rate : prevailing rate in Korea.
6. FOOD AND ACCOMMODATION : Free living quarters and free food.

Figure 8a. Employment contract for a Filipina entertainer, p. 1

7. ACCIDENT INSURANCE : Accident insurance shall be secured by the Employer in Korea for the ENTERTAINER(S), in the amount of TEN Million Won (₩) with the ENTERTAINERS appointed kin as beneficiary.

8. In the event of death of the ENTERTAINER during the term of this contract his / her remains and personal belongings shall be repatriated to be the Philippines at the expense of employer. In case the repatriation of the remains is not passible, the remains may be disposed of upon prior approval of the entertainer's next of kin or by the Philippine Embassy.

9. TERMINATION BY EMPLOYER : The employer may terminate Entertainer's contract of employment for any of the following just causes.
   Entertainer's serious misconduct or Entertainer's wilful disobedience of the lawful orders of the employer, gross habitual neglect of duties, violation of the laws of the host country. (In cases of pregnant, marry and stay outside from the house etc.) In addition, those who want to return their country, terminating the contract without prior mutual consultation, during the contract period with the association shall compensate for all the expenses, the amount of Three thousand US dollar ($ 3,000) covered for invitating them to Korea. In such case the employee will be repatriated at the employer's expense but wages will cease as from the day of dismissal. The Entertainer shall shoulder the repatriation expenses.

10. If the Entertainer will eacape from the club were they assigned to the factory or another places or else escape for living together with the guys. The Korea Special Tourist Association will reported to the police and immigration by a criminal case. And if the Entertainer will be arrested the association will charge of indemnity and penalty to the Entertainer or a guarantor of Entertainer in the Philippines.
    After the Entertainer will pay to the association, which means shall allowed to depart from the country.

11. The association shall be held 4 months salary (US $ _____) of Entertainers to prevent in case of 'he Entertainer's escape, pregnant, marry ect. Also the association shall be opened the join account with the bank for those salary under the name of the both parties. But Entertainers can get the commission and tips directly from the employer, and when the Entertainers finished their contract, the association will be returned the 4 months salary to the Entertainers.

Figure 8b. Employment contract for a Filipina entertainer, p. 2

12. ABSENCE WITHOUT LEAVE, LATENESS TO WORKINGDAY.

   12. 1 ABSENCE without leave : $ 60 per day.

   12. 2 ABSENCE without leave of 3 times

                       : To the following No. 9 on contract.

  13. 3 LATENESS TO WORKINGDAY

                     : $ 20 per hour. (Also, less than one hour)

                     : lateness of 3 hours is absence of one day.

13. The employer shall assist the employee in remitting a percentage of his salary through the proper banking channel or other means authorized by law;

14. The employee shall observe employer's company rules and abide by the pertinent laws of the host country and respect it's customs and traditions.

15. APPLICABLE LAW : Other terms and conditions of employment which are consistent with the above provisions shall be governed by pertinent laws of the Korean government.

IN WITNESS WHEREOF ..

Figure 8c. Employment contract for a Filipina entertainer, p. 3

Notes

Introduction

1. This is the location of Camp Casey and Camp Hovey, home to the bulk of the fifteen thousand U.S. troops of the Second Infantry Division.

2. Monetary amounts are listed in U.S. dollars unless otherwise noted.

3. Appadurai uses Charles Taylor's concept of "politics of recognition" to argue for the ethical obligation to extend moral cognizance to those who share worldviews deeply different from our own, and to demonstrate how the poor have the cultural capacity to change the terms of recognition. See Appadurai, "The Capacity to Aspire," 80.

4. Scheper-Hughes and Bourgois, "Foreword," xiv.

5. By "existential mobility," I follow Ghassen Hage in referring to an awareness of "going somewhere"—embodying a hope for a better future, preferring the indeterminacy of life away from home to the perceived certainty of "being stuck" at home. See Hage, "A Not So Multi-Sited Ethnography of a Not So Imagined Community."

6. In 1997 the real GDPs (PPPs) of the United States, Korea, and the Philippines were, respectively, $29,010, $13,590, and $3,520. See UNDP, "Human Development Report."

7. Ong, *Flexible Citizenship*.

8. Smith and Guarnizo, *Transnationalism from Below*.

9. Berman, *All That Is Solid Melts into Air*, 16.

Chapter 1. Sexing the Globe

1. Brennan, *What's Love Got to Do with It?*, 16–17. See also Padilla, *Caribbean Pleasure Industry* for the complex dynamics in male sex tourism in the Dominican Republic.

2. Shortly after the Korean War, the United States had about 450 bases in thirty-six countries and was linked by political and military pacts with some twenty countries outside Latin America. See Foot, *A Substitute for Victory*, 5.

3. It is important to note that R & R facilities are not a universal corollary to U.S. military forces stationed abroad but are subject to negotiations between the United States and the host governments. There was no R & R during the Persian

Gulf War, and soldiers were strictly prohibited from approaching local women by the military command. See Moon, *Sex among Allies*, 37.

4. Army general Leon J. LaPorte announced that all of the U.S. Second Infantry Division that was patrolling the region north of Seoul would be moved south of Seoul by 2008. Existing military facilities at Osan Air Base and Camp Humphreys, both located south of Seoul, were being expanded and upgraded to accept the redeployed forces. See Weaver, "97 percent of Yongsan Garrison Will Be Turned Over to South Korea 'as Is.'"

5. "Seoul, Washington Agree to Maintain Current Troop Level Here"

6. Sudworth, "New Dawn for US–S Korea Military Ties."

7. Moon, *Sex among Allies*, 31–32.

8. By 2007 the South Korean economy would boast a gross domestic product of $969.8 billion, with a gross national income of $19,730 (World Bank 2007). (World Bank, *World Development Indicators 2007*).

9. Interview with Mr. Shin (pseudonym), KSTA (Songtan).

10. "Provincial Councillor Mediates Employment of Foreign Hostesses."

11. ADB, *Asian Development Outlook 2008*.

12. Permanent: 4,850; temporary: 33,285; irregular: 9,015. See POEA, "Stock Estimates of Overseas Filipinos in Korea."

13. Mackie, "The Metropolitan Gaze."

14. Enriquez, "Filipinas Prostituted around US Military Bases"; Hughes, Chon, and Ellerman, "Modern-Day Comfort Women."

15. Rubin, "Thinking Sex."

16. The political scientist Cynthia Enloe spearheaded gender analysis in international politics. She cogently analyzed how international diplomacy, war, and militarization affect women's status and conditions, as well as gender relations on the ground. See Enloe, *Does Khaki Become You?*

17. See Enloe, *Bananas, Beaches and Bases*; Enloe, *Maneuvers*; Harrison, "Violence in the Military Community"; Higate, "Revealing the Soldier."

18. Enloe, *The Morning After*, 145.

19. Barry, *Female Sexual Slavery*; MacKinnon, *Are Women Human?*

20. Pateman, *The Sexual Contract*.

21. Hughes, *Wilberforce Can Free Again*. The U.S. Department of State is a key official institution that adopts the language of "modern day slavery" to describe trafficking in persons. See http://www.state.gov/g/tip/.

22. Chapkis, *Live Sex Acts*; Delacoste and Alexander, *Sex Work*; Kempadoo and Doezema, *Global Sex Workers*; Kempadoo, Sanghera, and Pattanaik, eds., *Trafficking and Prostitution Reconsidered*; Nagle, *Whores and Other Feminists*.

23. Bell, ed., *Good Girls, Bad Girls*; Eaves, *Bare*; Pheterson and St. James, *A Vindication of the Rights of Whores*.

24. Doezema, "Loose Women or Lost Women?"; Walkowitz, *City of Dreadful Delight*.

25. Frank, *G-Strings and Sympathy*, 28.

26. Butler, *Bodies That Matter*; Butler, *Gender Trouble*.

27. Altman, *Global Sex*.

28. Bernstein, *Temporarily Yours*.

29. The sociologist Eva Illouz also examined the formation of a "new emotional style" in postindustrial society, arguing that as a result of psychological models of communication promoted by psychology, corporate culture, and feminism, "emotions have become objects to be thought of, expressed, talked about, argued over, negotiated and justified, both in the corporation and in the family." Not only do they shape particular notions of selfhood based on an intense subjective experience of emotions and a set of objective tools to communicate such emotions, Illouz suggests, but these larger social and economic shifts may further generate a remoteness between human beings by turning out "hyperrational fools" (*Cold Intimacies*, 113). While this conclusion, in my view, holds fast to an idealization of an emotional life free from market forces and politics, it speaks to a similar set of dynamics between socioeconomic and political shifts, on the one hand, and an emotional self, on the other.

30. Grewal and Kaplan, *Scattered Hegemonies.*

31. Mohanty, Feminism without Borders, 231–32.

32. O'Connell Davidson, *Children in the Global Sex Trade*, 24.

33. Zatz, "Sex Work/Sex Act."

34. Doezema, "Loose Women or Lost Women?"; Soderlund, "Covering Urban Vice," "Running from the Rescuers"; Vance, "Innocence and Experience"; Walkowitz, *City of Dreadful Delight.*

35. Smith and Guarnizo, *Transnationalism from Below.*

36. Pratt, *Imperial Eyes*, 6–7; Tsing, *Friction*, 3.

37. Tsing, *Friction*, 4.

38. Cheng, "Commentary on Hughes, Chon, and Ellerman"; Hughes, "Response to Cheng."

39. Agustín does point out that migrant men and transgender people are even more neglected in migration studies, as they do not appear in any study at all. See Agustín, "The Disappearing of a Migrant Category," 30.

40. Manalansan, "Queer Intersections."

41. Ibid., 243.

42. Smith and Guarnizo, *Transnationalism from Below*, 21.

43. Brettell, *Anthropology and Migration*, 7.

44. Ortner, *Making Gender.*

45. Recruitment fees ranged between 40,305 pesos (900 USD) for Hong Kong to 311,550 pesos (7,200 USD) for Italy. (ADB, *Country Gender Assessment*, 55)

46. See Parreñas's ("Sex for Sale") detailed discussion of the accruement of debt in the recruitment process of Filipina entertainers working in Japan. For a similar process with domestic workers, see ADB, *Country Gender Assessment: Philippines.*

47. Beattie, "Review Article"; Kondo, *Crafting Selves*; Rosenberger, ed., *Japanese Sense of Self*; Tobin, "Japanese Preschools and the Pedagogy of Selfhood."

48. Kaplan, *Questions of Travel*, 36.

49. Moore, *A Passion for Difference.*

50. See studies of migrant women in different contexts that also express this contradictory set of experiences and sentiments in migration: Anderson, *Doing the Dirty Work?*; Anthias and Lazaridis, *Gender and Migration in Southern Europe*; Bar-

ber, "Transnationalism and the Politics of 'Home' for Philippine Domestic Workers"; Buijs, *Migrant Women*; Constable, "At Home but Not at Home"; Suzuki, "Gendered Surveillance and Sexual Violence at Home."

51. Constable, *Maid to Order in Hong Kong*; Lan, *Global Cinderellas*; Pratt with the Philippine Women Centre (Vancouver), "Inscribing Domestic Work on Filipina Bodies."

52. Barber, "Agency in Philippine Women's Labour Migration and Provisional Diaspora"; Constable, *Maid to Order in Hong Kong*; Gamburd, *The Kitchen Spoon's Handle*; Salih, "Moroccan Migrant Women"; Suzuki, "Between Two Shores"; Suzuki, "Inside the Home"; Yeoh and Huang, "'Home' and 'Away.'"

53. Curran and Saguy, "Migration and Cultural Change"; Piper, "Gendering the Politics of Migration"; Schwenken, "Respect for All."

54. They offer the four analytical dimensions of "geographical scales" (territorial movement between transnational spaces as differentially gendered context), "social location" (social situatedness at the intersection of gender, race, class, sexuality, ethnicity, etc.), "agency" (types and degrees of agency in one social location), and "imagination" (gendered production, interpretation, and appropriation of circulations in the global cultural economy). See Mahler and Pessar, "Gendered Geographies of Power"; Mahler and Pessar, "Gender Matters."

55. For rural-urban migration, see Mills, *Thai Women in the Global Labor Force*; Ong, *Spirits of Resistance and Capitalist Discipline*; Pun, *Made in China*; Yan, "Neoliberal Governmentality and Neohumanism." For transnational migration, see Constable, *Maid to Order in Hong Kong*; Constable, *Romance on a Global Stage*; Lan, *Global Cinderellas*.

56. Mills, *Thai Women in the Global Labor Force*.

57. Moore, *A Passion for Difference*.

58. Appadurai, "Disjuncture and Difference in the Global Cultural Economy."

59. Gamburd, *The Kitchen Spoon's Handle*, 212–13.

60. Pun Ngai examines the intolerance of gender ambivalence by the management of a Chinese factory. Lan Pei-chia finds employers in Taiwan regulating the mobility of domestic workers to prevent them from dating men. Nicole Constable illustrates Hong Kong employers' measures to defeminize (as "sexy" women) and demasculinize (as "lesbian") Filipino domestic workers. See Pun, *Made in China*; Lan, *Global Cinderellas*; Constable, "Sexuality and Discipline among Filipina Domestic Workers in Hong Kong.".

61. Mills, *Thai Women in the Global Labor Force*; Pun, "Becoming *Dagongmei* (Working Girls)."

62. Ehrenreich and Hochschild, eds., *Global Woman*; Hondagneu-Sotelo, *Gendered Transitions*; Mahler and Pessar, "Gendered Geographies of Power"; Phizacklea, "Migration and Globalization"; Piper and Roces, *Wife or Worker?*; Yeoh and Huang, "'Home' and 'Away.'"

63. The historian Theodore Zeldin found romantic love in modern society to be one of the last refuges in which a person can feel able to achieve something noble—one of the few forms of success that can hold its own against self-doubt. See Zeldin, *An Intimate History of Humanity*, 75.

64. Kelsky, *Women on the Verge*.

65. Pieke, "Serendipity."
66. Goodman, "Fieldwork and Reflexivity," 151.
67. Haraway, "Situated Knowledge."
68. Gluckman, *Analysis of a Social Situation in Modern Zululand.* I thank David Parkin and Nancy Abelmann for making suggestions that contributed to this reformulation of the case study method.

Chapter 2. "Foreign" and "Fallen" in South Korea

1. Moon, *Sex among Allies.*
2. Douglas, *Purity and Danger,* 4.
3. Ref. Parkin, *The Cultural Definition of Political Response.*
4. Nelson, *Measured Excess.*
5. Cho, "Living with Conflicting Subjectivities"; Choi, "Nationalism and Construction of Gender in Korea."
6. For example, Kim set up the Presidential Commission on Women's Affairs to handle issues specifically involving women. The commission was elevated and expanded to become the Ministry of Gender Equality in January 2001. Also in 2001 the National Human Rights Commission was founded.
7. The editor's introduction to the new column celebrates: "Looking forward to the new millennium, The Korea Times starts a series of articles *featuring the global citizenship of Koreans, based on the views of social notables including foreign nationals* with a keener interest in Koreans' internationalism, in their ways of thinking and their behaviour patterns. Articles will deal primarily with such topics as Koreans' self-centred nationalism, xenophobia, and Confucianism-based collectivism" (*Korea Times,* November 2, 1999, my emphasis).
8. For discussion of the genealogy of ethnonationalism in Korea, see Shin, *Ethnic Nationalism in Korea.*
9. Republic of Korea, "Fourteenth Periodic Report to the CERD (2007)," my emphasis.
10. Anderson, "New World Disorder," 8.
11. Anderson, *Doing the Dirty Work?*
12. *Migration News* 3, no. 4 (November 1997), http://www.un.org/popin/popls/journals/migratn/mig9704.html (last accessed June 3, 2008).
13. ILO, "When Will It End?"
14. Lim, "Racing from the Bottom in South Korea?"
15. Ahn, "Pressure on to Protect Foreign Workers' Rights."
16. "Detained Migrant Workers Go on Hunger Strike."
17. Amnesty International, *Report on Migrant Workers in Korea,* 32.
18. See Republic of Korea, Fourteenth Periodic Report to the CERD (2007).
19. Lim, "Racing from the Bottom in South Korea?"; Minbyun-Lawyers for a Democratic Society, "NGO Report under ICERD."
20. The regulation of women's sexuality became a key aspect of the neo-Confucian regime during the Choson Dynasty (1392–1910). The control of women became paramount in the preservation of status and power for the patriarchal family. *Kisaeng*—female entertainers skilled in the arts of calligraphy, poetry, painting,

dance, and music for the pleasure of powerful men—came to occupy the lowest caste (*cheonmin*) under the Choson Dynasty because of their accessibility in the public realm. For more discussion, see Deuchler, *The Confucianization of Korea*.

21. These mandatory health examinations were abolished in 1999 after being in force for twenty-one years. Field service providers observed in 2004, however, that the health identification cards system was still in place among local sex workers but that administration had been lax and varied widely between districts.

22. Won, "Hangukssahoe-ui-mae-chunyeoseong-ui-daehan-tongjae-hwa-cha-kchwi-ui-gwanhanyeongu" (A Study on the Control and Exploitation of Prostitutes in Korean Society).

23. Applying the euphemism of tourism to bypass the legal prohibition of prostitution, the state deployed women's sexuality as an instrument in nation-building while reinforcing their outcast status. The Tourism Promotion Law was passed in 1961, the same year as the Anti-Prostitution Law, and the Korea International Tourism Association was founded in 1962. Both were aimed at the U.S. troops and their R & R activities rather than at recreational visitors to Korea, who were still few in those years. These provisions led to the designation of "special districts" and tourist hotels exempted from the Anti-Prostitution Law. Following the normalization of relations with Japan in 1967, the *kisaeng* tourism of the 1970s that provided female company to Japanese tourists was a strictly state-sponsored drive to earn foreign currency. Research has shown that twenty-seven venues of *kisaeng* tourism were opened under government auspices and that fifteen thousand *kisaeng* were employed in the 1970s, during which the annual growth rate in international tourism was 34 percent. In the 1990s, under the auspices of President Kim Young-sam's *Segyehwa* (globalization) drive, tourism promotion gave Dongducheon and Songtan—the two largest *gijichon* remaining—a new lease on life when the Ministry of Culture and Tourism designated them Special Tourism Zones. The designation program sought to identify and help develop areas with high foreign-exchange-earning capacity. See Back, "A Study of Foreign Entertainers in Special Tourism Zones in Gyeonggi-Do."

24. Moon, *Sex among Allies*, 97–98.

25. The Republic of Korea has a low HIV prevalence rate, with a cumulative total of 3,657 HIV/AIDS cases reported, including 527 AIDS cases. The UNAIDS/WHO estimate for the country was, however, between 7,900 and 13,000 out of a total population of 47.8 million. See WHO et al., *Epidemiological Fact Sheets*. Foreigners who reside in South Korea for more than a year and foreign entertainers entering Korea need to prove their HIV status; those found to be HIV-positive are deported. The presumption that foreigners are sources of HIV infection has resulted in increased surveillance of migrant workers. Since 2004 mandatory predeparture testing is required for migrant workers as part of the Employment Permit System, to be followed by tests during their residence.

26. Cheng, "Interrogating the Absence of HIV/AIDS Intervention."

27. Jager, "Women, Resistance and the Divided Nation."

28. Kim, "Anti-Americanism in Korea."

29. That is, the externally generated pollution, however incurred (with or without the woman's collaboration), is a wrong that cannot be undone for the indi-

vidual or society. There is, theoretically, no purification rite that can be performed to cleanse her of foreign pollution.

30. Yuh Ji-yeon made a keen observation of the complexity embedded in the term *yanggongju*: "The use of 'princess' and 'bride' to describe these women can be seen as a rhetorical gesture that acknowledges the material comfort and glamour symbolized by the U.S. while ridiculing the women's efforts to achieve it by selling their bodies to American soldiers" (Yuh, *Beyond the Shadow of Camptown*, 20).

31. Fenkl, *Memories of My Ghost Brother*.

32. Son, "Different Blood . . . It's a Curse."

33. Literary representations, such as *Days and Dreams* by the woman novelist Kang Sok-kyong, speak of the loss of female innocence and the exile of *gijichon* women to the margins in order to contain the sexual violence of U.S. troops. See Kang, "Days and Dreams"; Ahn, *Silver Stallion*.

34. Lee et al., *Camp Arirang*; Korea Church Women United (KCWU), *Great Army, Great Father*; Moon, "South Korean Movements against Militarized Sexual Labor"; Piper, "Transnational Women's Activism in Japan and Korea"; Tagaki and Park, *The Women Outside*.

35. A staff person at the office of the National Campaign for the Eradication of U.S. Military Crimes mentioned that the cruel manner in which Yun was killed was important in getting public support—unlike if she had been killed by, say, strangling. She was found dead with a cola bottle stuck into her vagina, an umbrella penetrating twenty-seven centimeters into her rectum, and two beer bottles in her uterus, and her naked body was covered with multiple injuries and wounds. Since then the National Campaign has organized a commemoration service for Yun every year, as well as a weekly protest in front of the Yongsan U.S. military base in central Seoul. Yun's picture has become ubiquitous in the National Campaign's posters and publication, and the photo of her gruesome death was reproduced for sale for "educational" purposes. (Interview with Lee So-hee, National Campaign office in Seoul, July 26, 1999.)

36. See National Campaign for the Eradication of U.S. Military Crimes, "A History of Endless Pain."

37. Interview with Lee So-hee at National Campaign office in Seoul, July 26, 1999; cf. Kim, "*Yanggongju* as an Allegory of the Nation."

38. For example, "*Go-ri-an De-rim* (Korean Dream)" was the title of a special feature on the TV news program *PD Notebook* (Munhwa Broadcasting Company [MBC], September 16, 1999).

39. For example, Choi's survey of migrant workers in Korea has a section on "Korean Dreams of Respondents." His analysis took up this concept unproblematically: "Among Filipino workers, seven out of ten have a Korean dream that is related to money and economic activities" (Choi, "Foreign Workers' Adjustment in Korea," 173).

40. Oh, "Chu-han gi-ji-chon-e-seo yu-ip-doin pilipin yeo-seong-deul" (Filipinas Imported into American Military Camptowns), 173.

41. Ibid., 167.

42. Back, "A Study of Foreign Entertainers in Special Tourism Zones in Gyeonggi-Do."

43. Oh, "Chuhan Gijichon-Ui-Su-Ip-Doen Piiipin Yeoseongdeul (Filipinas Imported into American Military Camptowns," 168.
44. Yim, *Sisa Maegojin: Kori-an Deu-Rim (Sisa Magazine: Korean Dream).*
45. Ibid.
46. Butler, *Bodies That Matter.*

Chapter 3. Women Who Hope

1. Gimpo Airport was the only airport until the Incheon International Airport opened in 2001.
2. Mills, *Thai Women in the Global Labor Force*; Constable, *Romance on a Global Stage*; Lan, *Global Cinderellas*; Pun, *Made in China*; Yan, "Neoliberal Governmentality and Neohumanism."
3. Rofel, *Desiring China.* In the context of China, Hairong Yan examines the production of human subjectivity that links poverty-relief campaigns, labor migration, and development; Yan examines the discourse of "suzhi"—a sense of the self's value in the market economy and a sense of the lack of selfhood that generates the need to find its development and refinement in migration—as central to a neoliberal governmentality that rearticulates the relationship between the state, the market, and subjectivity in a formation that she calls neohumanism. See Yan, "Neoliberal Governmentality and Neohumanism."
4. Sassen, *Guests and Aliens*, 155.
5. CEDAW, "Consideration of Reports Submitted by States Parties under Article 18 of the Convention on the Elimination of All Forms of Discrimination against Women"; Gonzalez, *Philippine Labour Migration.*
6. Ball, "The Individual and Global Processes."
7. During the 1991 Gulf War, thirty thousand Filipino workers were repatriated from the Middle East. In 1997 there was an increase in deployment of overseas workers by 15 percent to Asia, outnumbering the Middle East for the first time. See Battistella, "Philippine Migration Policy," 20.
8. Asis, "The Overseas Employment Policy."
9. See Tyner, *Made in the Philippines*, 94–100, for a detailed discussion of the various theories of Sioson's death and the political actions that focused on migrant women, who came to embody a dangerous female sexuality.
10. DOLE, "Services for OFWs."
11. Almost half of the long-term public debt is owed to bilateral creditors such as Japan and the United States; a quarter is owed to multilateral creditors, mainly the World Bank and the IMF. The burden of debt is compounded by the depreciation of the peso, the value of which has fallen significantly in relation to the U.S. dollar in the past two decades. The exchange rate changed from 20.5:1 in 1987 to 43:1 in 2000. The government spends more on debt repayments than on health and education combined.
12. Chant and McIlwaine, *Women of a Lesser Cost*, 51.
13. ADB, "Income Poverty and Inequality in the Philippines," 19.
14. National Statistics Office, "2000 Population Census Highlights"; Steinberg, *The Philippines.*

15. ADB, "Enhancing the Efficiency of Overseas Filipino Workers Remittances," 2.

16. BSP, "Overseas Filipinos' Remittances by Country, by Source."

17. POEA, "Stock Estimate of Overseas Filipinos, as of December 2004."

18. Tyner, *Made in the Philippines.*

19. Cohen, *States of Denial*, 107. Cohen's focus is on mass atrocities and suffering, not a comparison I wish to make with entertainers' migration. It is the use of euphemism as a way of denying responsibility that I find provocative in Cohen's work.

20. Ball and Piper, "Globalisation and Regulation of Citizenship," 1022.

21. Law, *Sex Work in Southeast Asia*, 35.

22. Ofreneo and Ofreneo, "Prostitution in the Philippines."

23. See Neumann, "Tourism Promotion and Prostitution," 182–85; Tyner, "Constructions of Filipina Migrant Entertainers," 81–83.

24. As defined by the Bureau of Women and Minors, Ministry of Labor and Employment, in a survey of "hospitality girls" in Manila in 1978, which recorded 1,735 women working in the hospitality industry in Manila. See Heyzer, "The Trade in Female Sexuality," 55.

25. Sixty-six percent of all visitors to the Philippines in 1981 were male. Out of the 20 percent who came from Japan, 80 percent were male. Neumann gives a detailed description of the operation of the "package tour" (Neumann, "Tourism Promotion and Prostitution," 183).

26. Protests confronted Prime Minister Zenko Suzuki of Japan several times on his goodwill visit to the Philippines and Thailand in 1981. Upon his return to Japan, government pressure was exerted on the Japan Association of Travel Agents to stop all promotion of sex tours. Japanese visitors to the Philippines dropped by 26 percent from 1980 to 1981, followed by a further decline of 17 percent in 1982. See Neumann, "Tourism Promotion and Prostitution," 185–86.

27. Heyzer, "The Trade in Female Sexuality"; Ofreneo and Ofreneo, "Prostitution in the Philippines."

28. Law, *Sex Work in Southeast Asia*. For an example that illustrates the proliferation of terms referring to workers whom the government considers in need of STD/HIV monitoring, see a 1998 amendment to ordinance no. 92–048, "The Revised Sanitary Code of the City of Naga": "SECTION 71.—All hostesses/hosts/hospitality girls/boys now known as Guest Relations officers/Space Councilors working in the City of Naga are hereby required to secure HIV-AIDS, RPR, HEPA-B Clearance every January and July from the Naga City Hospital before the issuance of a Working Card/Pink Cards from the Local Health Office" (Ordinance No. 98–109, City of Naga, Republic of the Philippines).

29. Hubbard, "Sexuality, Immorality and the City," 55.

30. Pheterson, "The Whore Stigma."

31. Law, *Sex Work in Southeast Asia.*

32. Tyner, *Made in the Philippines*, 85.

33. See Ateneo de Manila University and WEDPRO, *The Philippine-Belgian Pilot Project against Trafficking in Women*, and http://www.kakammpi.tripod.com.

34. Asis, "The Overseas Employment Policy."

35. This includes the execution of Flor Contemplacion, who worked as a domestic worker in Singapore in 1995, and the trial of fifteen-year-old Sarah Balabagan in the United Arab Emirates in 1995. For more discussion of how these incidents shape debates about national development and labor migration policies in the Philippines, see Rafael, "Your Grief Is Our Gossip"; Tyner, *Made in the Philippines*.

36. Tyner, *Made in the Philippines*, 104.

37. Aguilar, "Ritual Passage and the Reconstruction of Selfhood in International Labour Migration."

38. Interview with labor attaché, Philippine Embassy, March 2, 2000.

39. Quoted in Tyner, "Constructions of Filipina Migrant Entertainers," 87.

40. Tyner, "Constructions of Filipina Migrant Entertainers," 95.

41. *The Flor Contemplacion Story* (1995), directed by Joel Lamangan, written by Boniacio Ilagan and Ricardo Lee, with Nora Aunor as Flor Comtemplacion; *Maricris Sioson—Japayuki* (1993), directed by Joey Romero, written by Lualhati Bautista, with Ruffa Gutierrez as Maricris Sioson.

42. With regard to awareness about the risks of migration, the common remedy proposed is to warn prospective migrants of possible violence, forced prostitution, and other dangers. The United Nations Crimes and Drugs Commission and the International Organization for Migration (IOM) have both released online videos, posters, and other publicity materials for this purpose. However, in spite of well-publicized cases of migrant Filipino domestic workers and entertainers being abused, jailed, and killed overseas, the number of migrant Filipinas going abroad as entertainers and domestic workers has not abated.

43. For a critique of the liberal ideal embedded in wage labor contract, see O'Connell Davidson, *Children in the Global Sex Trade*, 37.

44. Dalagin, *Manila Chronicle*, May 31, 1995; *Star*, November 22, 2007, available at http://www.newsflash.org/hlframe.htm (last accessed June 29, 2008).

45. Tolentino, "National Bodies and Sexualities," 77–78.

46. Monte, "Across Borders."

47. Tadiar, *Fantasy-Production*, 148.

48. Ibid.

49. Ibid., 55.

50. Largoza Maza, 1999, quoted in ibid., 75. Liza Largoza Maza was secretary-general of the GABRIELA National Women's Alliance in 1999. She became congress representative (Gabriela Women's Party) in 2004 and has proposed bills for the advancement of women's rights, including a bill (HB 03461) introducing divorce in the Philippines. Her work as a member of congress is listed on http://www.congress.gov.ph/members/search.php?id=maza. (last accessed March 28, 2008).

51. Laura Agustín has similarly observed feminist scholars who stopped short of recognizing migrant women's agency when the site of labor involves sex work, readily casting them as "victims of trafficking" and erasing their subjectivities in turn. See Agustín, "Migrants in the Mistress's House"; Agustín, "Sex, Gender, and Migrations."

52. Tadiar, *Fantasy-Production*, 148.

53. Chant and McIlwaine found that rural women in the Philippines look for urban employment to escape their disadvantaged position in agriculture, where

men maintain a power base in terms of landownership, employment, and participation in development projects. As in other developing states in Southeast Asia such as Thailand, the bulk of female workers have entered the multinational manufacturing sector and the service sector—in the latter as domestic helpers and sex workers. See Pearson and Theobald, "From Export Processing to Erogenous Zones"; Chant and McIlwaine, *Women of a Lesser Cost.*

54. As percentage ratios of male attendance at educational institutions, female primary, secondary, and tertiary net enrollments between 1996 and 1997 were 100, 102, and 133, respectively (UNDP, *Human Development Report 1999*).

55. According to the 1999 Human Development Report, real GDP per capita for females and males in the Philippines in 1997 was $2,510 and $4,513, respectively.

56. Women, however, are active in the informal sectors and seem "to flourish in the commerce of other households" (Dumont, "Matrons, Maids, and Mistresses," 190).

57. In her study of Filipino migrants in Japan, Nobue Suzuki has found domestic violence and gender surveillance to be important reasons for women to leave home (Suzuki, "Between Two Shores").

58. While poverty may be a reason for migration, utter poverty is not a typical characteristic of women who migrate by illegal means. Scholars of Filipino migration have suggested that those who migrate as entertainers are not those who are despondently poor. Nobuhiko Fuwa, in his study of Filipino entertainers from a village in Pagasinan, found that, while the women were from lower socioeconomic backgrounds, none were from the very bottom of the village hierarchy (Fuwa, "A Note on the Filipino 'Entertainers' in Japan," 337).

59. Ateneo de Manila University and WEDPRO Inc., *The Philippine-Belgian Pilot Project against Trafficking in Women*; Ball, "The Individual and Global Processes"; Catholic Institute for International Relations, *The Labour Trade*; Chant and McIlwaine, *Women of a Lesser Cost*; Dunn, *The Politics of Prostitution in Thailand and the Philippines*; Gonzalez, *Philippine Labour Migration.*

60. Miyazaki, *The Method of Hope*, 163.

61. The United States defeated Spanish colonizers in 1898 and took over the "white man's burden" by declaring sovereignty over the Philippines. Thus began the history of the Philippines as the "little brown brother" of the United States (Rafael, "Your Grief Is Our Gossip"). The first wave of Filipino out-migration took place in the early twentieth century, in the context of this U.S. colonialism, and included laborers and selected children of elites sent to the United States for education on U.S. government education grants—these were the *pensionados* (Asis, "The Overseas Employment Policy"). In the postwar era war veterans and GI brides from the Philippines found their way to the United States. This second wave of migrants also included a "brain drain"—professionals in medical, nursing, accounting, engineering, and other technical fields left in large numbers for the United States. The Immigration Reform Act passed by the U.S. Congress in 1965 later facilitated migration for family reunification.

62. McKay, "Filipinas in Canada," 50.

63. Chu, "To Be 'Emplaced.'"

64. The premises, operations, and effects of brothel raids as part of anti-

trafficking efforts have been questioned by scholars and activists. For example, see Bernstein, "Sexual Politics of the New Abolitionism"; Soderlund, "Running from the Rescuers"; Surtees, "Brothel Raids in Indonesia."

65. Tyner, *Made in the Philippines*, 96.

66. Miller, "Sexuality, Violence against Women, and Human Rights," 39.

Chapter 4. The Club Regime and Club-Girl Power

1. Foucault, *The History of Sexuality*, 86.

2. Lee, "Factory Regimes of Chinese Capitalism"; Pun, "Becoming *Dagongmei* (Working Girls)."

3. Cannell, *Power and Intimacy in the Christian Philippines*.

4. Rodney Clark found that exigencies in the labor market had led to familistic personnel management in Japanese factories by the end of the nineteenth century. Labor shortages in textile factories compelled employers to offer benefits such as food and housing. The metaphor of the family was adapted to justify employment practices in the factory/firm during the Meiji era. See Clark, *The Japanese Company*, 39.

5. Oh, "Marginal Culture of Prostitutes in American Military Camp Towns."

6. Though there might be ulterior motives for such behavior—staff at the Philippine Embassy expressed their suspicions about a GI who brought three Filipinas consecutively, all of them pregnant, to the embassy for repatriation. It was suspected that he was the one who impregnated them and conveniently evaded his responsibility by sending them back. However, there was no confirmation of such suspicion.

7. "Mamasan" is a Japanese term referring to the female owner and/or manager of a hostess bar, as studied by Anne Allison, *Nightwork*. It has been borrowed by similar businesses in other parts of Asia, including South Korea and Hong Kong. "Papasan" is an extension of the term to refer to the male owner or manager.

8. Sally said that she had gone to a motel room with a customer and "only slept" together with him for the night. Unbelievable as it might sound, cases such as these "no sex" bar fines did occur. I think we should read "no sex" as "no penetrative sex."

9. Goffman, *Stigma*, 42.

10. Melhus, "The Troubles of Virtue," 182.

11. Gluckman, "Gossip and Scandal."

12. Abu-Lughod and Lutz, *Language and the Politics of Emotion*.

13. Pile, "Introduction," 1–32.

14. Law, *Sex Work in Southeast Asia*, 48.

15. Foucault, *The History of Sexuality*, 94.

16. Pun, "Opening a Minor Genre of Resistance in Reform China," 551.

17. De Certeau, *The Practice of Everyday Life*, 36–37.

18. Kondo, *Crafting Selves*, 221.

Chapter 5. Love "between My Heart and My Head"

1. This is significantly different from the hostess clubs studied by Anne Allison in *Nightwork,* even though both types of club connect money and women and structure the recreation men pursue. Allison, in her ethnography of a Tokyo hostess club, points out how the packaging of women serves as a currency to flatter and build the male image for corporate executives—as such, a woman functions as a status symbol. However, women and status are not as clearly related in the relatively egalitarian *gijichon* clubs, where there are no significant differences among clubs. In both contexts, however, the man becomes a status symbol. A GI's rank and income have important bearings on his appeal in the clubs. Entertainers are very aware that sergeants make better customers than privates because of their higher incomes. See Chapter 4.

2. Barry, *Female Sexual Slavery*; Hoigard and Finstad, *Backstreets*; Jeffreys, *The Idea of Prostitution*; O'Connell Davidson, *Prostitution, Power and Freedom.*

3. Anzaldúa, *Borderlands/La Frontera.*

4. Tsing, *In the Realm of the Diamond Queen.*

5. Rosaldo, *Culture and Truth.*

6. Scott, *Weapons of the Weak.*

7. Giddens, *The Transformation of Intimacy.*

8. Abu-Lughod and Lutz, *Language and the Politics of Emotion,* 11.

9. In South Korea references to GIs among female activists rarely deviate from the paradigm of criminals and sex maniacs: "Because they frequently commit crimes against Koreans, the U.S. solders [*sic*] are also viewed as beasts who cannot control their sexual urges, as sexual perverts who stagger around from abuse of recreational drugs and alcohol, or men who perceive women only as potential sex partners" (KCWU, *Great Army, Great Father,* 5). See also campaign against U.S. military prostitution in the Philippines on the Web site of PREDA Foundation, http://www .preda.org/navyback.htm.

10. Moon, *Sex among Allies*; Sturdevant and Stoltzfus, *Let the Good Times Roll.*

11. "GI" (for "government issue") was stamped on cartons of supplies sent out by the U.S. government during World War II. During the Korean War, "GI Joe" was Man of the Year in *Time* magazine (January 1, 1951), praised for his valiant defense against communism. Though officially excised by the army as an unfavorable characterization, "GI" has continued to be widely used in American society and the media.

12. The job of an enlistee is generally comparable to a civilian job not requiring college education. We should determine the "social and economic marginality" of GIs on this basis. Defense Manpower Data Center statistics for fiscal year 1996 show that out of 373,473 applications, 179,133 were accepted (48 percent); 89 percent of these enlistees were between the ages of eighteen and twenty-four. The same report also shows that enlisted men actually include a significantly higher proportion of high school graduates or equivalent than do civilians of a similar age range. The declining quality of recruits improved only with major government initiatives to enhance recruiting programs and substantially increase pay and benefits. See Defense Manpower Data Center Data Request Archive, *Active Duty Workforce Profile.*

13. In September 2000 there were only 5,798 command-sponsored dependents in South Korea, where the military strength was 36,565. In Japan there were 40,188 such dependents. See U.S. Department of Defense, *Worldwide Manpower Distribution.*

14. For example, for a Fox News report in March 2002 a reporter went undercover and spoke with off-duty GIs in the club areas, pretending to be someone interested in buying sex. The report portrayed these GIs bragging about their sexual ventures and knowledge in the clubs. See Merriman et al., *Trafficked for the Military.*

15. The appeal of Russian women is less prevalent and seems to lie primarily with young GIs. One thirty-seven-year-old GI explained to me, "We don't like the Russians. We were brought up that way." His words show how cold-war politics shaped individual desires.

16. Allison describes the flirtations between the Japanese corporate patrons of the hostess club she studied and the hostesses as a "romantic exercise" rather than a sexual or emotional one. In the words of a customer whom she interviewed, "If he still wants sex, there are places to go for that, too." See Allison, *Nightwork,*127–28.

17. Yan, *The Flow of Gifts.*

18. Frank, "The Production of Identity and the Negotiation of Intimacy in a 'Gentleman's Club.'"

19. "The figure of 'I love you' refers not to the declaration of love, to the avowal, but to the repeated utterance of the love cry" (Barthes, *A Lover's Discourse,* 67).

20. Scott, *Weapons of the Weak.*

21. Cohen, "Lovelorn Farangs."

22. Roy's return was important to the whole story, whether it was fabricated or not. I have no way to find out the woman's motive for giving the "freebie." Roy was going to leave Korea soon after he met this woman, and his departure prevented any further development in their relationship. I could only guess that, because of his age, Roy looked like a sergeant rather than a mere private or corporal, and thus potentially a good customer. The possibility of "love at first sight" aside, the woman might have provided the "freebie" in the Maussian tradition of the gift in the hope of securing his continual patronage. There is also the possibility that she simply found Roy sexually attractive. If the story or the detail was fabricated, it would still support my argument on the importance of self-affirmation for Roy in the encounter.

23. MacCannell, "Staged Authenticity."

24. Goffman, *The Presentation of Self in Everyday Life.*

25. Frank, "The Production of Identity and the Negotiation of Intimacy in a 'Gentleman's Club.'"

26. When we first met, she told me she had only one child. Six months later she said she had lied and that she actually had three. She was worried that customers might be put off if they knew she had so many children. I interpreted the revelation as a sign of her growing trust in me.

27. Cannell, *Power and Intimacy in the Christian Philippines.*

28. Ibid., 45.

29. Productions such as *Madame Butterfly*, *Miss Saigon*, and *South Pacific* constitute but one of the many forms of representation of this exotica.

30. Such images of Asian women rarely go unchallenged by the "alien lovers" themselves; see Cohen, *Lovelorn Farangs*; Odzer, Patpong Sisters; Tsing, In the Realm of the Diamond Queen; Constable, *Romance on a Global Stage*.

31. Tsing, *In the Realm of the Diamond Queen*.

32. Ibid., 213–29.

33. Clifford, "Diasporas."

34. Bernstein, *Temporarily Yours*; Illouz, *Cold Intimacies*.

Chapter 6. At Home in Exile

1. Tacoli, "Migrating 'for the Sake of the Family'?," 18.

2. Aguilar, "Ritual Passage and the Reconstruction of Selfhood."

3. Constable, "At Home but Not at Home," 213.

4. Ibid., 211. See also Jacka, "Finding a Place"; Mills, *Thai Women in the Global Labor Force*.

5. Gamburd, *The Kitchen Spoon's Handle*.

6. Ibid., 207–8.

7. McKay, "Migration and the Sensuous Geographies of Re-Emplacement in the Philippines," 81.

8. Suzuki, "Gendered Surveillance and Sexual Violence at Home"; Yea, "When Push Comes to Shove."

9. Scheper-Hughes, "Disease or Deception," 168.

10. Pun, "Opening a Minor Genre of Resistance in Reform China."

11. Hondagneu-Sotelo and Avila, "'I'm Here, but I'm There'"; Gamburd, *The Kitchen Spoon's Handle*; Parreñas, *Children of Global Migration*; Lan, *Global Cinderellas*, 143–44. Lan came up with the term "transnational homemaking" to describe how migrant mothers participate in the mundane routines of household reproduction through the transnational flows of goods, information, and messages, reconstituting the boundaries of home and family across borders.

12. In addition to Gamburd's study of "migrant mothering," Diana Martin discusses the parent-centered child-rearing practices of leaving young offspring to nannies in Hong Kong. Carolyn Steedman has shown that the motherhood ideal of constant attention to children is of recent historical development around World War II. See Helterline, "The Emergence of Modern Motherhood"; Martin, "Motherhood in Hong Kong"; Steedman, "The Mother Made Conscious."

13. Building on works on transnationalism, Conradson and Latham focused on the relationship between mobility and friendship in young New Zealanders' projects of self-fashioning—a process of sustained self-experimentation, exploration, and development afforded by the liminality of travel. See Conradson and Latham, "Friendship, Networks and Transnationality in a World City."

14. Ibid.

15. Tyner's informant, a Filipina entertainer who had worked in Japan and then married an American man and moved to the United States, also considered

that her life had been best in Japan, where she had had mobility, financial independence, and a sense of confidence. See Tyner, *Made in the Philippines*.

16. Tsing, *Friction*, 213.

17. King, "Generalisations from the History of Return Migration."

18. "The notion of the diasporic . . . concerns not only tracking the fluid movements of populations and of communities of affect, but also the violence that crystallizes and propels such movements. Equally important, it also inquires into the machineries of disavowal . . . that accompany such movements as well as attempts to combat such disavowals" (Rafael and Abraham, "Introduction," 150–51).

19. Suzuki, "Gendered Surveillance and Sexual Violence at Home." See Lan's study of migrant domestic workers, which found single motherhood to be one of the major forces that push women overseas (Lan, *Global Cinderellas*).

20. The unemployment rate averaged 10.6 percent during the years 1997–2003. While 50 percent of the total employment is estimated to be in the informal sector, women are more likely than men to be own-account workers and subcontract workers and less likely to be owner-operators or paid employees of informal enterprises. See ADB, *Country Gender Assessment*.

21. While an interview with a Korean recruiter suggested that bribes were given to Filipino but not Korean immigration officers (since the former but not the latter were supposed to check the Artist Record Books), circumstantial evidence of women using passports of others ten to twenty years older than them suggests that either corruption or gross negligence was present on the Korean side too.

22. ADB, *Country Gender Assessment*, 31.

23. Appadurai, *Modernity at Large*.

24. Moore, *A Passion for Difference*, 66. See also Mary Beth Mills, *Thai Women in the Global Labor Force*, her study of consumer desires of rural migrants to Bangkok in Thailand, especially chapter 7.

25. Douglas Massey has argued that individual migration would generate a "circular and cumulative causation" of migration through kinship and social networks and turn migration into a household strategy (Massey, "Social Structure, Household Strategies, and the Cumulative Causation of Migration").

26. Gamburd, *The Kitchen Spoon's Handle*, details the struggles between migrants and family members over the use of remittances.

27. Constable, *Romance on a Global Stage*, 74.

28. Tadiar, "Prostituted Filipinas and the Crisis of Philippine Culture."

29. Curran and Saguy, "Migration and Cultural Change."

30. Clifford, *Routes*; Curran and Saguy, "Migration and Cultural Change."

31. Barber, "Agency in Philippine Women's Labour Migration and Provisional Diaspora"; Barber, "Transnationalism and the Politics of 'Home' for Philippine Domestic Workers"; Curran and Saguy, "Migration and Cultural Change"; Gamburd, *The Kitchen Spoon's Handle*.

32. Ong and Peletz, *Bewitching Women, Pious Men*.

33. Golbert, "Transnational Orientations from Home."

34. Appadurai, "The Production of Locality"; Clifford, "Travelling Cultures"; Olwig and Hastrup, *Siting Culture*.

Chapter 7. "Giving Value to the Voices"

1. Merry, *Human Rights and Gender Violence.*
2. Victims of Trafficking and Violence Protection Act of 2000, http://www .state.gov (accessed January 9, 2008).
3. Cheng, "Muckraking and Stories Untold"; Hesford and Kozol, eds., *Just Advocacy?*; Soderlund, "Covering Urban Vice"; Soderlund, "Running from the Rescuers."
4. "By social sector I mean people whose jobs, whether paid or voluntary, are dedicated to improving the condition of society in a wide range of ways. . . . Social agents include social workers, policy makers, individuals in charge of funding, religious personnel, counselors, academics and non-governmental organisation (NGO) employees and volunteers: anyone who, in their work, consciously attempts to better other people's lives" (Agustín, *Sex at the Margins*, 5).
5. Ibid., 96.
6. Ibid.; Bernstein, "Sexual Politics of the New Abolitionism."
7. Agustín, *Sex at the Margins*; Chapkis, "Trafficking, Migration, and the Law"; Cheng, "The 'Success' of Anti-Trafficking Policy"; Kempadoo and Doezema, *Global Sex Workers*; Larson, "Prostitution, Labor and Human Rights."
8. Keck and Sikkink, *Activists beyond Borders.*
9. Miller, "Sexuality, Violence against Women, and Human Rights."
10. Agustín, "Migrants in the Mistress's House"; Agustín, "The Disappearing of a Migrant Category"; Doezema, "Forced to Choose"; Doezema, "Ouch!"; Murray, "Debt-Bondage and Trafficking"; Pickup, "Deconstructing Trafficking in Women."
11. Agustín, *Sex at the Margins*; Chapkis, "Trafficking, Migration, and the Law"; Doezema, "Loose Women or Lost Women?"; Doezema, "Ouch!"
12. Working on a definition of "political opportunity structures" as factors that facilitate or constrain efforts for social change, Nicola Piper seeks to further theorize the concept from a transnational and gender-specific perspective in order to understand social movement and new forms of political protest. She shows that the paradigm shift brought by democratization movements and women's movements in Japan and Korea in the context of a growing global feminist activism allowed the comfort-women issue to be redefined as a crime against women's human rights. See Piper, "Transnational Women's Activism in Japan and Korea."
13. See Jordan, *The Annotated Guide to the Complete UN Trafficking Protocol*; Saunders, "Traffic Violations."
14. Otto, "Disconcerting 'Masculinities,'" 110.
15. Guy, "'White Slavery,' Citizenship and Nationality in Argentina"; Pickup, "Deconstructing Trafficking in Women"; Soderlund, "Covering Urban Vice."
16. This agreement was revised in 1910, 1921, and 1933. For more discussion, see Agustín, *Sex at the Margins*; Guy, "'White Slavery,' Citizenship and Nationality in Argentina"; Walkowitz, *City of Dreadful Delight*; Saunders, "Traffic Violations"; Saunders and Soderlund, "Travelling Threats."
17. CATW defines sex trafficking as "the transport sale and purchase of women and girls for prostitution, bonded labor and sexual enslavement within the country

or abroad" (CATW-AP home page, at www.catw-ap.org [last accessed March 20, 2009]).

18. Before the U.N. Protocol was passed, GAATW defined trafficking as "All acts involved in the recruitment and/or transport of a woman within and across national borders for sale, work or services by means of direct or indirect violence or threat of violence, abuse of authority or dominant position, debt bondage, deception or other forms of coercion" (GAATW, *Practical Guide to Assisting Trafficked Women*, 3).

19. For a historical and critical analysis of these three camps, see Pickup, "Deconstructing Trafficking in Women."

20. Saunders, "Traffic Violations."

21. United Nations, *Protocol to Prevent, Suppress and Punish Trafficking in Persons, Especially Women and Children, Supplementing the United Nations Convention against Transnational Organized Crime*, Article 3(a), (accessed October 22, 2007).

22. Saunders, "Traffic Violations."

23. Previous conventions on trafficking either ignored the issue of consent (for example, the 1904 International Agreement for the Suppression of White Slave Trade) or specified its irrelevance to the definition of trafficking (the 1949 Convention for the Suppression of Traffic in Persons and the Exploitation of the Prostitution of Others).

24. Doezema, "Loose Women or Lost Women?"; Saunders and Soderlund, "Travelling Threats."

25. Researchers have pointed out that effective anti-trafficking interventions cannot be isolated from related initiatives on migration, gender equality, transformation of labor markets, and shifting security concerns. See Anderson and O'Connell Davidson, *Is Trafficking in Human Beings Demand Driven?*; Chapkis, "Trafficking, Migration, and the Law"; Kanics, Reiter, and Uhl, "Trafficking in Human Beings—a Threat under Control?"; Taran and Moreno-Fontes, *Getting at the Roots*.

26. There is a dearth of valid data on both prostitution and trafficking, not to mention on the link between the two. UNESCO, Bangkok office, maintains a Trafficking Statistics Project that traces how numerical estimates circulate between governments, intergovernmental organizations, and nongovernmental organizations. See http://www.unescobkk.org/index.php?id = 1022 (accessed June 2, 2007).

27. Bernstein, "Sexual Politics of the New Abolitionism"; Cheng, "The 'Success' of Anti-Trafficking Policy"; Shah, "South Asian Border Crossings and Sex Work."

28. U.S. Department of State, *Trafficking in Persons Report 2002*; U.S. Department of State, *Trafficking in Persons Report June 2005*.

29. IOM, *A Review of Data on Trafficking in the Republic of Korea*, 5.

30. Ibid., 13.

31. Cf. Agustín, "The Disappearance of a Migrant Category," 29–47.

32. For example, "Sprouting Land" was used as the English translation of Saewoomtuh by the BBC World News ("Crossing Continents") on March 15, 2001, http://news.bbc.co.uk/2/hi/programmes/crossing_continents/asia/1218748.stm (accessed May 6, 2008).

33. I have much respect for the devotion, energies, and drive of its staff, and

particularly of the Saewoomtuh director, Ms. Kim Hyun-sun. Saewoomtuh was an important conduit for my research in *gijichon*. Because of the personal relationships I have built with various members of Saewoomtuh, the casting of a critical perspective on their work has been an emotionally challenging task. The critique is targeted at a more general phenomenon that Saewoomtuh is only a part of, and it is meant to open constructive dialogues.

34. The women were paid at the rate of one hundred won per piece ($1 = 1,200 won in 1999).

35. Kim Hyun-sun, "Filipino Sex Workers in Military Camp Towns—Human Traffic and Sexual Exploitation," presentation at the international conference "Redefining Security for Women and Children" organized by the East Asia–U.S. Women's Network against Militarism," Washington, D.C., October 1998. The term "sex worker" made a premature entry into Korean activist discourse through my translation of the word *maechunyeoseong* (prostitute women) into English for the document distributed at the conference, but no objection was raised against the use of this term at the time.

36. Ibid.

37. The founders of Saewoomtuh were volunteers at the first *gijichon* NGO, Duraebang (My Sister's Place), in Uijeongbu, founded in 1986 by the American wife of a Korean priest. Saewoomtuh's client-members included both ex- and current women workers in the sex industry for the U.S. military.

38. This assertion, ubiquitously found in the comfort-women movement discourses, is complicated by Sarah Soh's nuanced study of the differences in experiences of actual comfort women, "From Imperial Gifts to Sex Slaves."

39. See Moon, "South Korean Movements against Militarized Sexual Labor," 310–27.

40. Paradoxically, in contrast to Saewoomtuh's active pursuits internationally, it made virtually no effort to draw public and government attention to migrant entertainers in Korea during this period.

41. Between 1998 and 2000 Saewoomtuh spoke on the subject of Filipinas at the following international meetings: "Redefining Security for Women and Children," organized by the East Asia–U.S. Women's Network against U.S. Militarism, Washington, D.C., October 1998; "The Hague Appeal for Peace," the Netherlands, 1999; "International Women's Summit: Redefining Security," Okinawa, Japan, 2000; and the ASEM People's Forum Women's Group, Seoul, 2000.

42. Saewoomtuh organizational pamphlet, 1999.

43. An indication of this was the closing down of the nursery and study room run by Saewoomtuh in early 2000 due to the shrinking number of children needing such services.

44. The boomerang pattern refers to local actors seeking to influence their own governments by mobilizing international governmental or nongovernmental forces in their networks. See Keck and Sikkink, *Activism without Borders*, 12–13.

45. Saewoomtuh conducted its first large-scale research study, between August and December 2001, on prostitution in Gyeonggi Province. In the two-hundred-page report, prostitution in *gijichon* is only one of the many areas of investigation (the others include motels, restaurants, massage parlors, and teahouses), and the

"international trafficking" of women is a part of this prostitution. Saewoomtuh also organized the Global Symposium on "Sex Trafficking Eradication Project 2001" in Seoul in October 2001.

46. For a detailed critique of these laws and its effects, see Cheng, "The 'Success' of Anti-Trafficking Policy."

47. Saewoomtuh's proposals include asking home countries to provide more information to women about the risks of working in *gijichon* and establishing cooperation between sending and receiving countries to build a repatriation and rehabilitation program that provides shelter and vocational training for women (Kim J., "The Problem of Filipinas Employed in the Sex Industry in US Military Camp Towns in Korea" [Saewoomtuh, 2001]). In contrast, the Kyungnam Migrant Workers' Counseling Center and Minbyun-Lawyers for a Democratic Society propose looking into labor laws and immigration laws to protect migrant women entertainers' rights and setting up a human-rights counseling center for migrant workers. See Cho, "A Legal Evaluation of the Conditions of Migrant Workers in the Sex Trade in Korea."

48. Enriquez, "Filipinas Prostituted around U.S. Military Bases."

49. The invitation of Enriquez was almost a serendipitous event. The project manager for migrant women at KCWU, who coordinated our research efforts and the press conference, happened to watch an interview with Enriquez on a Korean TV program on migrant Filipino entertainers. Independent of any transnational feminist network, this manager relied on the TV production team's contact to invite Enriquez.

50. Mackie, "The Language of Globalization, Transnationality and Feminism," 183.

51. CATW, http://www.catwinternational.org/about (accessed September 14, 2007).

52. CATW quoted in Korea Church Women United, "Fieldwork Report on Trafficked Women in Korea," 51.

53. All quotes from CATW, http://www.catwinternational.org/about (accessed September 14, 2007).

54. Enriquez, "Filipinas Prostituted around U.S. Military Bases."

55. Murray, "Debt-Bondage and Trafficking," 59.

56. National YWCA of Korea, "Proceedings from Asia-Pacific Regional Workshop on Trafficking in Women." Based on the data we submitted, KCWU staff wrote up the "Fieldwork Report on Trafficked Women in Korea."

57. The conversation took place in English, and this is a verbatim record of the meeting as videotaped.

58. Though Enriquez did mention at one point that CATW was an advocacy organization and thus was not in a position to offer direct assistance, she emphasized that they could refer the two women to relevant organizations.

59. Videotaped recording by author (May 9, 2000); my emphasis.

60. In analyzing cross-cultural encounters between Chinese feminists and their Western counterparts, Shih suggests that there is a politics of selective recognition that "cloaks the lack of desire to know the Other" (Shih, "Towards an Ethics

of Transnational Encounter, or 'When' Does a 'Chinese' Woman Become a 'Feminist'?," 95).

61. The Republic Act No. 9208, "An Act to Institute Policies to Eliminate Trafficking in Persons Especially Women and Children, Establishing the Necessary Institutional Mechanisms for the Protection and Support of Trafficked Persons, Providing Penalties for Its Violations, and for Other Purposes."

62. KASAMA Solidarity Philippines Australia Network, http://cpcabrisbane.org/Kasama/2005/V19n4/NewsFromCATWAP.htm (accessed May 19, 2008).

63. Sunila Abeyesekera quoted in Miller, "Sexuality, Violence against Women, and Human Rights," 18.

64. Otto, "Disconcerting 'Masculinities,'" 128.

65. Ibid., 118.

66. Brown, *States of Injury*.

67. Bunch, "Women's Rights as Human Rights"; Bunting, "Theorizing Women's Cultural Diversity in Feminist International Human Rights Strategies"; Kapur, "The Tragedy of Victimization Rhetoric"; Miller, "Sexuality, Violence against Women, and Human Rights"; Petchesky, *Global Prescriptions*.

68. Kapur, "The Tragedy of Victimization Rhetoric."

Chapter 8. Hop, Leap, and Swerve

1. "A politics of uncertainty, then, is not necessarily a politics of indecision. On the contrary, it can be a politics flexible enough to remain open to new modes of political calculation, and a politics that does not judge events on the basis of a fixed set of pre-existing criteria. This requires nothing less than the admission that there is a politics to our definition of the political. Feminism is perhaps the clearest instances of a force that has retained its political drive precisely through a refusal to be pinned down to certainties" (Elam, *Romancing the Postmodern*, 22).

2. Miyazaki, *The Method of Hope*.

3. Ibid., 26.

4. Hage, "A Not So Multi-Sited Ethnography of a Not So Imagined Community," 474.

5. Spivak, "Can the Subaltern Speak?," 283.

6. The Multifiber Agreement (MFA), which had provided quotas for the textile industry in various developing countries, ended on December 31, 2005, allowing investors to move manufacturing to sites of cheaper labor such as China and India, displacing millions of textile workers, mostly female, who have few alternatives for employment. See McGhie, Kwatra, and Halford, "Rags to Riches to Rags."

7. Berman, *All That Is Solid Melts into Air*.

Appendix I

1. Marcus, "Ethnography of/in the World System," 98.

References

Abu-Lughod, Lila, and Catherine Lutz. *Language and the Politics of Emotion.* Cambridge: Maison des Sciences de l'Homme and University of Cambridge Press, 1990.

ADB (Asian Development Bank). *Asian Development Outlook 2008.* Manila, Philippines: Asian Development Bank, 2008.

———. *Country Gender Assessment: Philippines.* Manila, Philippines: Asian Development Bank, 2004.

———. *Enhancing the Efficiency of Overseas Filipino Workers Remittances.* Manila, Philippines: Asian Development Bank, 2004.

———. Income Poverty and Inequality in the Philippines. In *Poverty in the Philippines: Income, Assets, and Access.* Manila, Philippines: Asian Development Bank, 2005.

Aguilar, Filomeno V., Jr. "The Dialectics of Transnational Shame and National Identity." *Philippine Sociological Review* 44, nos. 1–4 (1996): 101–36.

———. "Ritual Passage and the Reconstruction of Selfhood in International Labour Migration." *Sojourn* 14, no. 1 (1999): 98–139.

———. "The Triumph of Instrumental Citizenship? Migrations, Identities, and the Nation-State in Southeast Asia." *Asian Studies Review* 23 (1999): 307–36.

Agustín, Laura. "The Disappearing of a Migrant Category: Migrants Who Sell Sex." *Journal of Ethnic and Migration Studies* 32, no. 1 (2006): 29–47.

———. "Migrants in the Mistress's House: Other Voices in the 'Trafficking' Debate." *Social Politics: International Studies in Gender, State and Society* 12, no. 1 (2005): 96–117.

———. *Sex at the Margins: Migration, Labour Markets and the Rescue Industry.* London and New York: Zed Books, 2007.

———. "Sex, Gender, and Migrations: Facing up to Ambiguous Realities." *Soundings* 23 (2003): 84–98.

Ahn, Junghyo. *Silver Stallion: A Novel of Korea.* New York: Soho Press, 1993.

Ahn, Mi-Young. "Pressure on to Protect Foreign Workers' Rights." *Asia Times Online,* May 13, 2000, www.atimes.com (accessed January 2, 2008).

Allison, Anne. *Nightwork: Sexuality, Pleasure, and Corporate Masculinity in a Tokyo Hostess Club.* Chicago: University of Chicago Press, 1994.

Altman, Dennis. *Global Sex.* Chicago: University of Chicago Press, 2001.

Amnesty International. *Report on Migrant Workers in Korea.* Seoul: Amnesty International, 2006.

Anderson, Benedict. "New World Disorder." *New Left Review* I/193, no. May-June: 3–13, 2000.

Anderson, Bridget. *Doing the Dirty Work? The Global Politics of Domestic Labour.* London: Zed Books, 2000.

Anderson, Bridget, and Julia O'Connell Davidson. *Is Trafficking in Human Beings Demand Driven? A Multi-Country Pilot Study.* Geneva: International Organisation for Migration, 2003.

Anthias, Floya, and Gabriela Lazaridis. *Gender and Migration in Southern Europe.* Edited by Jackie Waldren. Mediterranea Series. Oxford: Berg, 2000.

Anzaldúa, Gloria. *Borderlands/La Frontera: The New Mestiza.* San Francisco: Spinsters/Aunt Lute, 1987.

Appadurai, Arjun. "The Capacity to Aspire." In *Cultural and Public Action,* edited by Vijayendra Rao and Michael Walton. Stanford: Stanford University Press, 2004.

———. "Disjuncture and Difference in the Global Cultural Economy." *Public Culture* 2, no. 2 (1990): 1–24.

———. *Modernity at Large: Cultural Dimensions of Globalization.* Minneapolis: University of Minnesota Press, 1996.

———. "The Production of Locality." In *Counterworks: Managing the Diversity of Knowledge,* edited by Richard Fardon. London: Routledge, 1995.

Asis, Maruja M. B. "The Overseas Employment Program Policy." In *Philippine Labor Migration: Impact and Policy,* edited by Graziano Battistella and A. Paganoni. Quezon City: Scalabrini Migration Center, 1992.

Ateneo de Manila University, and WEDPRO Inc. The Philippine-Belgian Pilot Project against Trafficking in Women. Manila: Ateneo de Manila University and WEDPRO, Inc., 1999.

Back, Jaehee. "A Study of Foreign Entertainers in Special Tourism Zones in Gyeonggi-Do." Unpublished manuscript, 1999.

———. "A Study of Foreign Women Employed in the Korean Sex Industry—with a Focus on Filipinas in US Military Camp Towns." Master's thesis, Ewha Women's University, 1999.

Ball, Rochelle E. "The Individual and Global Processes: Labor Migration Decision-Making and Filipino Nurses." *Pilipinas: A Journal of Philippine Studies* 34 (Spring 2000): 63–82.

Ball, Rochelle, and Nicola Piper. "Globalisation and Regulation of Citizenship—Filipino Migrant Workers in Japan." *Political Geography* 21 (2002): 1013–34.

Barber, Pauline Gardiner. "Agency in Philippine Women's Labour Migration and Provisional Diaspora." *Women's Studies International Forum* 23, no. 4 (2000): 399–411.

———. "Transnationalism and the Politics of 'Home' for Philippine Domestic Workers." *Anthropologica* 39 (1997): 39–72.

Barry, Kathleen. *Female Sexual Slavery.* Englewood Cliffs, N.J.: Prentice-Hall, 1984.

Barthes, Roland. *A Lover's Discourse: Fragments.* New York: Penguin Books, 1978.

Battistella, Graziano. "Philippine Migration Policy: Dilemmas of a Crisis." *Sojourn* 14, no. 1 (1999): 229–48.

Beattie, J. "Review Article: Representations of the Self in Traditional Africa." *Africa* 50, no. 3 (1980): 313–20.

Bell, Laurie, ed. *Good Girls, Bad Girls: Feminists and Sex Workers Face to Face.* Toronto: Seal Press, 1987.

Berman, Marshall. *All That Is Solid Melts into Air: The Experience of Modernity.* 1982. New York: Penguin Books, 1988.

Bernstein, Elizabeth. "Sexual Politics of the New Abolitionism: Imagery and Activism in Contemporary Anti-Trafficking Campaigns." *differences: Journal of Feminist Cultural Studies* 18, no. 3 (2007): 128–51.

———. *Temporarily Yours: Intimacy, Authenticity, and the Commerce of Sex.* Chicago and London: University of Chicago Press, 2007.

Bernstein, Elizabeth, and Laurie Schaffner. *Regulating Sex: The Politics of Intimacy and Identity.* London and New York: Routledge, 2005.

Bickford, Andrew. "See the World, Meet Interesting People, Have Sex with Them: Tourism, Sex, and Recruitment in the U.S. Military." *American Sexuality Magazine,* 2003, http://nsrc.sfsu.edu/HTMLArticle.cfm?Article = 113&PageID = 8& SID = E4F9C1566920220006B04542679162F4 (accessed January 29, 2004).

Brennan, Denise. *What's Love Got to Do with It? Transnational Desires and Sex Tourism in the Dominican Republic.* Durham and London: Duke University Press, 2004.

Brettell, Caroline. *Anthropology and Migration: Essays on Transnationalism, Ethnicity and Identity.* Walnut Creek, Calif.: Altamira Press, 2003.

Brown, Wendy. *States of Injury: Power and Freedom in Late Modernity.* Princeton, N.J.: Princeton University Press, 1995.

BSP (Bangko Sentral ng Pilipinas). "Overseas Filipinos' Remittances by Country, by Source," 2007. Available at http://www.bsp.gov.ph/statistics/spei/tab11.htm (accessed May 28, 2008).

Buijs, Gina. *Migrant Women: Crossing Boundaries and Changing Identities.* Oxford: Berg, 1993.

Bunch, Charlotte. "Women's Rights as Human Rights: Toward a Re-Vision of Human Rights." *Human Rights Quarterly* 12, no. 4 (1990): 486–98.

Bunting, Annie. "Theorizing Women's Cultural Diversity in Feminist International Human Rights Strategies." *Journal of Law and Society* 20, no. 1 (1993): 6–22.

Butler, Judith. *Bodies That Matter: On the Discursive Limits of Sex.* London: Routledge, 1993.

———. *Gender Trouble: Feminism and the Subversion of Identity.* London: Routledge, Chapman & Hall, 1990.

Caagusan, Flor. *Halfway through the Circle: The Lives of 8 Filipino Survivors of Prostitution & Sex Trafficking.* Quezon City: WEDPRO, 2001.

Cannell, Fenella. "Catholicism, Spirit Mediums and the Ideal of Beauty in a Bicolano Community, Philippines." Ph.D. dissertation, London School of Economics and Political Science, 1991.

———. *Power and Intimacy in the Christian Philippines.* New York: Cambridge University Press, 1998.

Caplan, Patricia. *The Cultural Construction of Sexuality.* London and New York: Tavistock Publications, 1987.

Catholic Institute for International Relations. *The Labour Trade: Filipino Migrant Workers around the World.* London: Catholic Institute for International Relations, 1987.

CEDAW. "Consideration of Reports Submitted by States Parties under Article 18 of the Convention on the Elimination of All Forms of Discrimination against Women: The Philippines." United Nations Committee on the Elimination of Discrimination against Women, 1996.

Chant, Sylvia, and Cathy McIlwaine. *Women of a Lesser Cost: Female Labour, Foreign Exchange, and Philippine Development.* London: Pluto Press, 1995.

Chapkis, Wendy. *Live Sex Acts.* New York: Routledge, 1997.

———. "Trafficking, Migration, and the Law: Protecting Innocents, Punishing Immigrants." *Gender & Society* 17, no. 6 (2003): 923–37.

Cheng, Sealing. "Commentary on Hughes, Chon, and Ellerman." *Violence against Women* 14, no. 3 (2008): 360–63.

———. "Interrogating the Absence of HIV/AIDS Interventions for Migrant Sex Workers in South Korea." *Health and Human Rights* 7, no. 2 (2004): 193–204.

———. "Muckraking and Stories Untold: Ethnography Meets Journalism on Trafficked Women and the U.S. Military." *Sexuality Research & Social Policy* 5, no.4 (2008): 6–18.

———. "The 'Success' of Anti-Trafficking Policy: Women's Human Rights and Women's Sexuality in South Korea." In *Ethnography and Policy: How Much Do We Know about Trafficking?*, edited by Carole Vance. Sante Fe, N.Mex.: School of Advanced Research, forthcoming.

Cho, Haejoang. "Living with Conflicting Subjectivities: Mother, Motherly Wife, and Sexy Women in the Transition from Colonial-Modern to Postmodern Korea." In *Under Construction*, edited by Laurel Kendall. Honolulu: University of Hawai'i Press, 2002.

Cho, Hyeon-chol. *Hanguknae Seongsangop Yijunodongja shiltae-ae daehan popjok gomto* (A Legal Evaluation of the Conditions of Migrant Workers in the Sex Trade in Korea). Seoul: Kyungnam Migrant Workers Center and Minbyun, 2003.

Choi, Byoung Mohk. "Foreign Workers' Adjustment in Korea: Comparing Filipino Workers and Others." Paper presented at the First Japan Economic Policy International Conference, Chuo University, November 29–December 1, 2002.

Choi, Chungmoo. "Nationalism and Construction of Gender in Korea." In *Dangerous Women: Gender and Korean Nationalism*, edited by Chungmoo Choi and Elaine H. Kim. London: Routledge, 1998.

Chu, Julie Y. "To Be 'Emplaced': Fuzhounese Migration and the Politics of Destination." *Identities: Global Studies in Culture and Power* 13 (2006): 395–425.

Chun, Wendy Hui Kyong. "Unbearable Witness: Toward a Politics of Listening." *differences: Journal of Feminist Cultural Studies* 11, no. 1 (1999): 112–49.

Clark, Rodney. *The Japanese Company.* New Haven and London: Yale University Press, 1979.

Clifford, James. "Diasporas." *Cultural Anthropology* 9, no. 3 (1994): 302–38.

———. *Routes: Travel and Translation in the Late Twentieth Century.* Cambridge, Mass.: Harvard University Press, 1997.

————. "Travelling Cultures." In *Cultural Studies*, edited by Lawrence Grossberg, Gary Nelson, and Paula Treichler. London: Routledge, 1992.

Cohen, Erik. "Lovelorn Farangs: The Correspondence between Foreign Men and Thai Girls." *Anthropological Quarterly* 59, no. 3 (1986): 115–27.

Cohen, Stanley. *States of Denial: Knowing about Atrocities and Suffering*. Oxford: Polity Press, 2001.

Conradson, David, and Alan Latham. "Friendship, Networks and Transnationality in a World City: Antipodean Transmigrants in London." *Journal of Ethnic and Migration Studies* 31, no. 2 (2005): 287–305.

Constable, Nicole. "At Home but Not at Home: Filipina Narratives of Ambivalent Return." *Cultural Anthropology* 14, no. 2 (1999): 203–28.

————. *Maid to Order in Hong Kong: Stories of Filipina Workers*. Ithaca, N.Y., and London: Cornell University Press, 1997.

————. *Romance on a Global Stage: Pen Pals, Virtual Ethnography, and "Mail Order" Marriages*. Berkeley: University of California Press, 2003.

————. "Sexuality and Discipline among Filipina Domestic Workers in Hong Kong." *American Ethnologist* 24, no. 3 (1997): 539–58.

Curran, Sara R., and Abigail C. Saguy. "Migration and Cultural Change: A Role for Gender *and* Social Networks?" *Journal of International Women's Studies* 2, no. 3 (2001): 54–77.

de Certeau, Michel. *The Practice of Everyday Life*. Berkeley: University of California Press, 1984.

Defense Manpower Data Center (DMDC) Data Request Archive. *Active Duty Workforce Profile* March 31, 1997. Electronic document, http://cs.itc.dod.mil/files/content/ALLPublic/Workspaces/ (accessed May 4, 2001).

Delacoste, Frederique, and Priscilla Alexander. *Sex Work: Writings by Women in the Sex Industry*. Pittsburgh: Cleis Press, 1987.

Deuchler, Martina. *The Confucianization of Korea: A Study of Society and Ideology*. Cambridge, Mass.: Harvard University Press, 1992.

Doezema, Jo. "Forced to Choose: Beyond the Voluntary v. Forced Prostitution Dichotomy." In *Global Sex Workers: Rights, Resistance, and Redefinition*, edited by Kamala Kempadoo and Jo Doezema, 34–50. London: Routledge, 1998.

————. "Loose Women or Lost Women?: The Re-Emergence of the Myth of 'White Slavery' in Contemporary Discourses of 'Trafficking in Women.'" Paper presented at the International Studies Association Convention, Washington, D.C., February 17–21, 1999.

————. "Ouch!: Western Feminists' 'Wounded Attachment' to the 'Third World Prostitute.'" *Feminist Review* 67 (2001): 16–38.

DOLE (Department of Labor and Employment). "Services for OFWs." Available at http://pinoymigrant.dole.gov.ph/Ofw/op.html (accessed January 3, 2008).

Douglas, Mary. *Purity and Danger: An Analysis of the Concepts of Pollution and Taboo*. London and New York: Routledge, 1966.

Dumont, Jean-Paul. "Matrons, Maids, and Mistresses: Philippine Domestic Encounters." *Philippine Quarterly of Culture & Society* 22 (1994): 174–91.

Dunn, Caroline. *The Politics of Prostitution in Thailand and the Philippines: Policies and Practice.* Clayton, Vic., Australia: Centre of Southeast Asian Studies, Monash University, 1994.

Eaves, Elisabeth. *Bare: On Women, Dancing, Sex and Power.* New York: Knopf Press, 2002.

Ehrenreich, Barbara, and Arlie R. Hochschild, eds. *Global Woman: Nannies, Maids, and Sex Workers in the New Economy.* New York: Metropolitan Books, 2002.

Elam, Diane. *Romancing the Postmodern: Romance, History and the Figure of Woman.* London: Routledge, 1992.

Enloe, Cynthia H. *Bananas, Beaches and Bases: Making Feminist Sense of International Politics.* London: Pandora, 1989.

———. *Does Khaki Become You? The Militarisation of Women's Lives.* London: Pluto Press, 1983.

———. *Maneuvers: The International Politics of Militarizing Women's Lives.* Berkeley, Calif., and London: University of California Press, 2000.

———. *The Morning After: Sexual Politics at the End of the Cold War.* Berkeley: University of California Press, 1993.

Enriquez, Jean. "Filipinas Prostituted around US Military Bases: A Nightmare Recurring, This Time, in Korea." Paper presented at the Press Conference for the Field Report on Trafficked Women in South Korea, Korea Church Women United, Seoul, Republic of Korea, November 19, 1999.

Faier, Lieba. "Filipina Migrants in Rural Japan and Their Professions of Love." *American Ethnologist* 34, no. 1 (2007): 148–62.

Fausto-Sterling, Anne. *Sexing the Body.* New York: Basic Books, 2000.

Felman, Shoshana, and Dori Laub. *Testimony: Crises of Witnessing in Literature, Psychoanalysis, and History.* London: Taylor & Francis, 1992.

Fenkl, Heinz Insu. *Memories of My Ghost Brother.* New York: Dutton, 1996.

Fog Olwig, Karen, and Kirsten Hastrup. *Siting Culture: The Shifting Anthropological Object.* London: Routledge, 1997.

Foot, Rosemary. *A Substitute for Victory: The Politics of Peacekeeping at the Korean Armistice Talks.* Ithaca, N.Y.: Cornell University Press, 1990.

Foucault, Michel. *The History of Sexuality.* 1st American ed. New York: Random House, 1978.

Frank, Katherine. *G-Strings and Sympathy: Strip Club Regulars and Male Desire.* Durham, N.C.: Duke University Press, 2002.

———. "The Production of Identity and the Negotiation of Intimacy in a 'Gentleman's Club.'" *Sexualities* 1, no. 2 (1998): 175–201.

Fuwa, Nobuhiko. "A Note on the Filipino 'Entertainers' in Japan: A View from a Sending Village." *Philippine Studies* 47 (1999): 319–50.

GAATW (Global Alliance Against Traffic in Women). *Practical Guide to Assisting Trafficked Women.* Bangkok: GAATW, 1997.

Gamburd, Michele Ruth. *The Kitchen Spoon's Handle: Transnationalism and Sri Lanka's Migrant Housemaids.* Ithaca, N.Y., and London: Cornell University Press, 2000.

Giddens, Anthony. *The Transformation of Intimacy: Sexuality, Love and Eroticism in Modern Societies.* Cambridge: Polity Press, 1992.

Gluckman, Max. *Analysis of a Social Situation in Modern Zululand*. Vol. 28, Rhodes-Livingstone Papers. 1940. Manchester: Manchester University Press, 1958.

―――. "Gossip and Scandal." *Current Anthropology* 4, no. 3 (1963): 307–16.

Goffman, Erving. *The Presentation of Self in Everyday Life*. New York and London: Anchor Books, 1959.

―――. *Stigma: Notes on the Management of Spoiled Identity*. New York: Simon & Schuster, 1963.

Golbert, Rebecca. "Transnational Orientations from Home: Constructions of Israel and Transnational Space among Ukrainian Jewish Youth." *Journal of Ethnic and Migration Studies* 27, no. 4 (2001): 713–31.

Gonzalez, Joaquin L. *Philippine Labour Migration: Critical Dimensions of Public Policy*. Singapore: Institute of Southeast Asian Studies, 1998.

Goodman, Roger. "Fieldwork and Reflexivity: Thoughts from the Anthropology of Japan." In *Anthropologists in a Wider World: Essays on Field Research*, edited by Paul Dresch, Wendy James, and David Parkin. New York: Berghahn Books, 2000.

Grewal, Inderpal, and Caren Kaplan. *Scattered Hegemonies: Postmodernity and Transnational Feminist Practices*. Minneapolis: University of Minnesota Press, 1994.

Guy, Donna. "'White Slavery,' Citizenship and Nationality in Argentina." In *Nationalisms and Sexualities*, edited by Andrew Parker. London: Routledge, 1992.

Hage, Ghassan. "A Not So Multi-Sited Ethnography of a Not So Imagined Community." *Anthropological Theory* 5, no. 4 (2005): 463–75.

Haraway, Donna. "Situated Knowledge: The Science Question in Feminism as a Site of Discourse on the Privilege of Partial Perspective." *Feminist Studies* 14, no. 3 (1988): 575–99.

Harrison, Deborah. "Violence in the Military Community." In *Military Masculinities*, edited by Paul Higate. Westport, Conn.: Praeger, 2003.

Helterline, Marilyn. "The Emergence of Modern Motherhood: Motherhood in England, 1899–1959." *International Journal of Women's Studies* 3, no. 6 (1980): 590–615.

Hesford, Wendy S., and Wendy Kozol, eds. *Just Advocacy? Women's Human Rights, Transnational Feminism, and the Politics of Representation*. New Brunswick, N.J.: Rutgers University Press, 2005.

Heyzer, Noeleen. "The Trade in Female Sexuality." In *Working Women in South-East Asia: Development, Subordination and Emancipation*, by Noeleen Heyzer. Philadelphia: Open University Press, 1986.

Higate, Paul. "Revealing the Soldier: Peacekeeping and Prostitution." *American Sexuality Magazine* 1, no. 5 (2003). Available at http://nsrc.sfsu.edu/HTMLArticle.cfm?Article = 111&PageID = 8&SID = 61735F7D6C 566894E5598052FCABBC85 (accessed May 24, 2004).

Hoigard, Cecilie, and Liv Finstad. *Backstreets: Prostitution, Money and Love*. University Park: Pennsylvania State University Press, 1986.

Hondagneu-Sotelo, Pierrette. *Gendered Transitions: Mexican Experiences of Immigration*. Berkeley and Los Angeles: University of California Press, 1994.

Hondagneu-Sotelo, Pierrette, and Ernestine Avila. "'I'm Here, but I'm There': The

Meanings of Latina Transnational Motherhood." *Gender & Society* 11, no. 5 (1997): 548–71.

Hubbard, Phil. "Sexuality, Immorality and the City: Red-Light Districts and the Marginalisation of Street Prostitution." *Gender, Place, and Culture* 5, no. 1 (1998): 55–72.

Hughes, Donna. "Response to Cheng." *Violence against Women* 14, no. 3 (2008): 364–65.

———. Wilberforce Can Free Again. *National Review Online*, 2008. Available at http://article.nationalreview.com/?q = M2UyZWJjN2E2MTQ3ZDQ3MGFmNT kymWMyNDEwOGQzMWY = (accessed June 12, 2008).

Hughes, Donna, Katherine Y. Chon, and Derek P. Ellerman. "Modern-Day Comfort Women: The U.S. Military, Transnational Crime, and the Trafficking of Women." *Violence against Women* 13, no. 9 (2007): 901–22.

Illouz, Eva. *Cold Intimacies: The Making of Emotional Capitalism.* Cambridge: Polity Press, 2007.

———. "Constructing the Romantic Utopia." In *Consuming the Romantic Utopia: Love and Cultural Contradictions of Capitalism*, edited by Eva Illouz. Berkeley: University of California Press, 1997.

ILO (International Labor Organization). "When Will It End? Report: Asian Financial Crisis Is Far from Over, Poverty, Unemployment Seen Rising." *World of Work* 25 (1998).

IOM (International Organisation for Migration). *A Review of Data on Trafficking in the Republic of Korea.* Geneva: International Organisation for Migration, 2002.

Jacka, Tamara. "Finding a Place: Negotiations of Modernization and Globalization among Rural Women in Beijing." *Critical Asian Studies* 37, no. 1 (2005): 51–74.

Jager, Sheila. "Women, Resistance and the Divided Nation: The Romantic Rhetoric of Korean Unification." *Journal of Asian Studies* 55, no. 1 (1996): 3–21.

Jager, Sheila Miyoshi. *Narratives of Nation Building in Korea: A Genealogy of Patriotism.* Armonk, N.Y., and London: M. E. Sharpe, 2003.

Jeffreys, Sheila. *The Idea of Prostitution.* North Melbourne, Vic., Australia: Spinifex, 1997.

Jordan, Ann. *The Annotated Guide to the Complete UN Trafficking Protocol.* Washington, D.C.: International Human Rights Law Group, 2002.

Kang, Sokkyung. "Days and Dreams." In *Words of Farewell: Stories by Korean Women Writers*, edited by Sok-Kyong Chi-Won and Chong-Hui. Washington, D.C.: Seal Press, 1989.

Kanics, Jyothi, Gabriele Reiter, and Barbel Heide Uhl. "Trafficking in Human Beings—a Threat under Control? Taking Stock Four Years after Major International Efforts Started." *Helsinki Monitor* 16, no. 1 (2005): 53–67.

Kaplan, Caren. *Questions of Travel: Postmodern Discourses of Displacement, Theory and Cultural Studies.* Durham, N.C.: Duke University Press, 1996.

Kapur, Ratna. "The Tragedy of Victimization Rhetoric: Resurrecting the 'Native' Subject in International/Post-Colonial Feminist Legal Politics." *Harvard Human Rights Journal* 15, no. 1 (2002): 1–37.

Keck, Margaret, and Kathryn Sikkink. *Activists beyond Borders: Advocacy Networks in International Politics.* Ithaca, N.Y., and London: Cornell University Press, 1998.

———. "Transnational Networks on Violence against Women." In *Activists beyond Borders,* edited by Keck and Sikkink. Ithaca, N.Y.: Cornell University Press, 1998.

Kelsky, Karen. *Women on the Verge: Japanese Women, Western Dreams.* Edited by Rey Chow and H. D. Harootunian. Asia-Pacific: Culture, Politics, and Society Series. Durham, N.C., and London: Duke University Press, 2001.

Kempadoo, Kamala, and Jo Doezema. *Global Sex Workers: Rights, Resistance, and Redefinition.* New York and London: Routledge, 1998.

Kempadoo, Kamala, Jyoti Sanghera, and Bandana Pattanaik, eds. *Trafficking and Prostitution Reconsidered: New Perspectives on Migration, Sex Work, and Human Rights.* Boulder, Colo., and London: Paradigm, 2005.

Kim, H. S. "Yanggongju as an Allegory of the Nation: Images of Working-Class Women in Popular and Radical Texts." In *Dangerous Women,* edited by Elaine H. Kim and Chungmoo Choi. London: Routledge, 1998.

Kim, Hyun-sun. "Filipino Sex Workers in US Military Camp Towns—Human Traffic and Sexual Exploitation." Paper presented at Redefining Security for Women and Children, Washington D.C, 1998.

Kim, Seung-Hwan. "Anti-Americanism in Korea." *Washington Quarterly* 26, no. 1 (2002–3): 109–22.

King, Russell. "Generalisations from the History of Return Migration." In *Return Migration,* edited by Bimal Ghosh. Geneva: IOM and UN, 2000.

Kondo, Dorinne K. *Crafting Selves: Power, Gender, and Discourses of Identity in a Japanese Workplace.* Chicago: University of Chicago Press, 1990.

Korea Church Women United (KCWU). *Fieldwork Report on Trafficked Women in Korea.* Seoul: Counselling Center for Migrant Women Workers, Korea Church Women United, 1999.

———. *Great Army, Great Father: The USFK and Prostitution in Korea.* Seoul: Korea Church Women United, 1996.

Kulick, Don. "Fe/Male Trouble: The Unsettling Place of Lesbians in the Self-Images of Brazilian Travesti Prostitutes." *Sexualities* 1, no. 3 (1998): 301–14.

Kulick, Don, and Margaret Willson. *Taboo: Sex, Identity and Erotic Subjectivity in Anthropological Fieldwork.* London: Routledge, 1995.

Lan, Pei-Chia. *Global Cinderellas: Migrant Domestics and Newly Rich Employers in Taiwan.* Durham, N.C., and London: Duke University Press, 2006.

Laqueur, Thomas. "Orgasm, Generation, and the Politics of Reproductive Biology." In *The Gender/Sexuality Reader: Culture, History, Political Economy,* edited by Roger Lancaster and Micaela Di Leonardo. London: Routledge, 1997.

Larson, Jane E. "Prostitution, Labor and Human Rights." *University of California Davis Law Review* 37 (February 2004): 673–700.

Law, Lisa. *Sex Work in Southeast Asia: The Place of Desire in a Time of AIDS.* London: Routledge, 2000.

Lee, Ching Kwan. "Factory Regimes of Chinese Capitalism: Different Cultural Logics in Labour Control." In *Ungrounded Empires: The Cultural Politics of Mod-*

ern Chinese Transnationalism, edited by Aihwa Ong and Donald Macon Non-ini. New York: Routledge, 1997.

Lee, Diana S., Grace Yoonkung Lee, Mary Beth Bresolin, Amy Hill, and Camp Arirang Productions. *Camp Arirang.* San Francisco, Calif.: Camp Arirang Productions, National Asian American Telecommunications Association, 1995. Documentary film.

Lim, Timothy C. "Racing from the Bottom in South Korea? The Nexus between Civil Society and Transnational Migrants." *Asian Survey* 43, no. 3 (2003): 423–42.

MacCannell, Dean. "Staged Authenticity: Arrangements of Social Space in Tourist Settings." *American Journal of Sociology* 79, no. 3 (1973): 589–603.

Mackie, Vera. "The Language of Globalization, Transnationality and Feminism." *International Feminist Journal of Politics* 3, no. 2 (2001): 180–206.

———. "The Metropolitan Gaze: Travellers, Bodies and Spaces." *Intersections: Gender, History and Culture in the Asian Context* 4 (September 2000). Available at http://wwwsshe.murdoch.educ.au/intersections/issue4/vera.html (accessed September 2, 2005).

MacKinnon, Catherine A. *Are Women Human? And Other International Dialogues.* Cambridge, Mass.: Belknap Press of Harvard University Press, 2006.

Mahler, Sarah J., and P. Pessar. "Gendered Geographies of Power: Analyzing Gender across Transnational Spaces." *Identities: Global Studies in Culture and Power* 7, no. 4 (2001): 441–59.

Mahler, Sarah J., and Patricia Pessar. "Gender Matters: Ethnographers Bring Gender from the Periphery toward the Core of Migration Studies." *International Migration Review* 40, no. 1 (2006): 27–63.

Manalansan, Martin F., IV. "Queer Intersections: Sexuality and Gender in Migration Studies." *International Migration Review* 40, no. 1 (2006): 224–49.

Marcus, George. "Ethnography of/in the World System: The Emergence of Multi-Sited Ethnography." *Annual Review of Anthropology* 24 (1995): 95–117.

Martin, Diana. "Motherhood in Hong Kong: The Working Mother and Child-Care in the Parent-Centered Hong Kong Family." In *Hong Kong: The Anthropology of a Chinese Metropolis,* edited by Grant Evans and Maria Tam. London: Curzon Press, 1997.

Massey, Douglas. "Social Structure, Household Strategies, and the Cumulative Causation of Migration." *Population Index* 56, no. 1 (1990): 3–26.

McGhie, John, Anjali Kwatra, and John Davison. *Rags to Riches to Rags.* London: Christian Aid, 2004.

McKay, Deirdre. "Filipinas in Canada: Deskilling as a Push toward Marriage." In *Wife or Worker? Asian Women and Migration,* edited by Nicola Piper and Mina Roces. Oxford: Rowman & Littlefield, 2003.

———. "Migration and the Sensuous Geographies of Re-Emplacement in the Philippines." *Journal of Intercultural Studies* 26, nos. 1–2 (2005): 75–91.

Melhuus, Marit. "The Troubles of Virtue: Values of Violence and Suffering in a Mexican Context." In *The Ethnography of Moralities,* edited by Signe Howell. London: Routledge, 1997.

Merriman, Tom, Greg Easterly, Ron Mounts, Mark DeMarino, Dave Hollis, and Tim Roskey. *Trafficked for the Military.* WJW-TV (Cleveland), 2002.

Merry, Sally. *Human Rights and Gender Violence: Translating International Law into Local Justice.* Chicago: University of Chicago Press, 2006.

Miller, Alice. "Sexuality, Violence against Women, and Human Rights: Women Make Demands and Ladies Get Protection." *Health and Human Rights* 7, no. 2 (2004): 17–47.

Mills, Mary Beth. *Thai Women in the Global Labor Force.* New Brunswick, N.J., and London: Rutgers University Press, 2001.

Minbyun-Lawyers for a Democratic Society. "NGO Report under ICERD." Seventy-first session of the Committee on the Elimination of Racial Discrimination on the Fourteenth Periodic Report submitted by the Republic of Korea under Article 9 of the International Convention on the Elimination of All Forms of Racial Discrimination, Geneva, 30 July–18 August 2007.

Miyazaki, Hirokazu. *The Method of Hope: Anthropology, Philosophy, and Fijian Knowledge.* Stanford, Calif.: Stanford University Press, 2003.

Monte, Janice Lee. "Across Borders: Sex Trafficking of Women." GABRIELA News and Features, February 25, 1999. Available at http://www.hartford-hwp.com/archives/54a/235.html (accessed March 23, 2008).

Montgomery, Heather. "Public Vice and Private Virtue: Child Prostitution in Pattaya, Thailand." D.Phil. thesis, University of Cambridge, 1996.

Moon, Katharine H. S. "Resurrecting Prostitutes and Overturning Treaties: Gender Politics in the South Korean 'Anti-American' Movement." *Journal of Asian Studies* 66, no. 1 (2007): 129–57.

———. *Sex among Allies: Military Prostitution in U.S.-Korea Relations.* New York and Chichester: Columbia University Press, 1997.

———. "South Korean Movements against Militarized Sexual Labor." *Asian Survey* 39, no. 2 (1999): 310–27.

———. "Strangers in the Midst of Globalization." In *Korea's Globalization*, edited by Samuel S. Kim. Cambridge: Cambridge University Press, 2000.

Moon, Seungsook. *Militarized Modernity and Gendered Citizenship in South Korea.* Durham, N.C., and London: Duke University Press, 2005.

Moore, Henrietta. *A Passion for Difference: Essays in Anthropology and Gender.* Cambridge: Polity Press, 1994.

Murray, Alison. "Debt-Bondage and Trafficking: Don't Believe the Hype." In *Global Sex Workers*, edited by Kamala Kempadoo and Jo Doezema. London: Routledge, 1998.

Nagle, Jill. *Whores and Other Feminists.* New York: Routledge, 1997.

National Campaign for the Eradication of U.S. Military Crimes. *Kkeut-na-ji anh-eun a-peum-eui yeog-sa* (A History of Endless Pain: U.S. Military Crimes). Seoul: Gaemasowon, 2000.

National Statistics Office, Republic of the Philippines. "2000 Population Census Highlights." 2001. Available at http://www.census.gov.ph (accessed June 2, 2008).

Nelson, Laura C. *Measured Excess: Status, Gender, and Consumer Nationalism in South Korea.* New York: Columbia University Press, 2000.

Neumann, A. Lin. "Tourism Promotion and Prostitution." In *The Philippines Reader: A History of Colonialism, Neocolonialism, Dictatorship and Resistance*, edited by D. B. Schirmer and S. R. Shalom. Boston: South End Press, 1987.

O'Connell Davidson, Julia. *Children in the Global Sex Trade*. London: Routledge, 2005.

———. *Prostitution, Power and Freedom*. Ann Arbor: University of Michigan Press, 1998.

———. "The Sex Tourist, the Expatriate, His Ex-Wife and Her 'Other': The Politics of Loss, Difference and Desire." *Sexualities* 4, no. 1 (2001): 5–24.

Ofreneo, Rene E., and Rosalinda Pineda Ofreneo. "Prostitution in the Philippines." In *The Sex Sector: The Economic and Social Bases of Prostitution in Southeast Asia*, edited by Lin Lean Lim. Geneva: International Labour Office, 1998.

Oh, Ji-yeon. "Migun-gijichon Maechun-yeoseong-dul-Ui Jubyeonjog Munhwa" (Marginal Culture of Prostitutes in American Military Camp Towns). Master's thesis, Seoul National University, 1997.

Oh, Yeon-ho. "Chu-han Gi-ji-chon-e-seo Yu-ip-doin Pilipin Yeo-seong-deul" (Filipinas Imported into American Military Camptowns). *Mal* (August 1998): 162–73.

Ong, Aihwa. *Flexible Citizenship: The Cultural Logics of Transnationality*. Durham, N.C. and London: Duke University Press, 1999.

———. *Spirits of Resistance and Capitalist Discipline: Factory Women in Malaysia*. SUNY Series in the Anthropology of Work. Albany: State University of New York Press, 1987.

Ong, Aihwa, and Michael G. Peletz. *Bewitching Women, Pious Men: Gender and Body Politics in Southeast Asia*. Berkeley: University of California Press, 1995.

Ortner, Sherry B. *Making Gender: The Politics and Erotics of Gender*. Boston: Beacon Press, 1996.

Otto, Diane. "Disconcerting 'Masculinities': Reinventing the Subject of International Human Rights Law." In *International Law: Modern Feminist Approaches*, edited by Doris Buss and Ambreena Manji. Oxford: Hart, 2005.

Padilla, Mark. *Caribbean Pleasure Industry: Tourism, Sexuality, and AIDS in the Dominican Republic*. Chicago: University of Chicago Press, 2007.

Padilla, Mark, Jennifer S. Hirsch, Miguel Muñoz-Laboy, Robert Sembert, and Richard Parker, eds. *Love and Globalization: Transformations of Intimacy in the Contemporary World*. Nashville, Tenn.: Vanderbilt University Press, 2007.

Parkin, David J. *The Cultural Definition of Political Response: Lineal Destiny among the Luo of Kenya*. London: Academic Press, 1978.

Parreñas, Rhacel Salazer. "Sex for Sale: Trafficked? Filipino Hostesses in Tokyo's Nightlife Industry." *Yale Journal of Law and Feminism* 18 (2006): 145–51.

Parreñas, Rhacel Salazer. *Children of Global Migration: Transnational Families and Gendered Woes*. Stanford, Calif.: Stanford University Press, 2005.

Pateman, Carole. *The Sexual Contract*. Cambridge: Polity Press, 1988.

Pearson, Ruth, and Sally Theobald. "From Export Processing to Erogenous Zones: International Discourses on Women's Work in Thailand." *Millennium: Journal of International Studies* 27, no. 4 (1998): 983–93.

Petchesky, Rosalind Pollack. *Global Prescriptions: Gendering Health and Human Rights*. London: Zed, 2003.

Pheterson, Gail. "The Whore Stigma: Female Dishonor and Male Unworthiness." *Social Text* 37 (Winter 1993): 39–64.

Pheterson, Gail, and Margo St. James. *A Vindication of the Rights of Whores*. Seattle: Seal Press, 1989.

Phizacklea, A. "Migration and Globalization: A Feminist Perspective." In *The New Migration in Europe*, edited by K. Koser and H. Lutz. London: Macmillan, 1998.

Pickel, Andreas. "Explaining, and Explaining with, Economic Nationalism." *Nations and Nationalism* 9, no. 1 (2003): 105–27.

Pickup, Francine. "Deconstructing Trafficking in Women: The Example of Russia." *Millennium: Journal of International Studies* 27, no. 4 (1998): 995–1021.

Pieke, Frank. "Serendipity: Reflections on Fieldwork in China." In *Anthropologists in a Wider World*, edited by Dresch, James, and Parkin. New York: Berghahn Books, 2000.

Pile, Steve. "Introduction: Opposition, Political Identities and Spaces of Resistance." In *Geographies of Resistance*, edited by Steve Pile and Michael Keith. London: Routledge, 1997.

Piper, Nicola. "Foreign Migrant Workers and Protective Mechanisms: Transnational NGOs in East and Southeast Asia." Unpublished manuscript, 2000.

———. "Gendering the Politics of Migration." *International Migration Review* 40, no. 1 (2006): 133–64.

———. "Transnational Women's Activism in Japan and Korea: The Unresolved Issue of Military Sexual Slavery." *Global Networks* 1, no. 2 (2001): 155–70.

Piper, Nicola, and Mina Roces. *Wife or Worker? Asian Women and Migration*. Lanham, Md.: Rowman & Littlefield, 2003.

POEA (Philippine Overseas Employment Agency). "Stock Estimate of Overseas Filipinos, as of December 2004." Available at www.poea.gov.ph/docs/STOCK%2-0ESTIMATE%202004.xls (accessed June 29, 2008).

Pratt, Geraldine, with the Philippine Women Centre (Vancouver). "Inscribing Domestic Work on Filipina Bodies." In *Places through the Body*, edited by Heidi J. Nast and Steve Pile. London: Routledge, 1998.

Pratt, Mary Louise. *Imperial Eyes: Travel Writing and Transculturation*. London: Routledge, 1992

"Protocol to Prevent, Suppress and Punish Trafficking in Persons, especially Women and Children, Supplementing the United Nations Convention Against Transnational Organized Crime." Geneva: United Nations.

Pun, Ngai. "Becoming Dagongmei (Working Girls): The Politics of Identity and Difference in Reform China." *China Journal* 42 (July 2000): 1–18.

———. *Made in China: Women Factory Workers in a Global Workplace*. Durham, N.C.: Duke University Press; Hong Kong: Hong Kong University Press, 2005.

———. "Opening a Minor Genre of Resistance in Reform China: Scream, Dream, and Transgression in a Workplace." *Positions* 8, no. 2 (2002): 531–55.

Rafael, Vincente. "Your Grief Is Our Gossip." In *White Love and Other Events in Filipino History: Overseas Filipinos and Other Spectral Presences*, edited by Vincente Rafael. Durham, N.C.: Duke University Press, 2000.

Rafael, Vincente and Itty Abraham. "Introduction." *Sojourn: A Journal of Social Issues in Southeast Asia* (Institute of Southeast Asian Studies, Singapore) 12, no. 2 (1997): 145–52.

Rebhun, L.A. *The Heart Is Unknown Country: Love in the Changing Economy of Northeast Brazil.* California: Stanford University Press, 1999.

Republic of Korea. "Fourteenth Periodic Report to the Committee on Elimination of Racial Discrimination [CERD) at the United Nations." Geneva, August 10, 2007. Available at http://www.unog.ch/unog/website/news_media.nsf/ (httpNewsByYear_en)/383FB64 FCAAAA5EAC12573330045B8E4?OpenDocument (accessed March 8, 2008).

Rofel, Lisa. *Desiring China.* Durham, N.C.: Duke University Press, 2007.

Rosaldo, Renato. *Culture and Truth: The Remaking of Social Analysis.* Boston: Beacon Press, 1989.

Rosenberger, Nancy, ed. *Japanese Sense of Self.* Cambridge: Cambridge University Press, 1992.

Rosenblum, Peter. "Teaching Human Rights: Ambivalent Activism, Multiple Discourses, and Lingering Dilemmas." *Harvard Human Rights Journal* 15, no. 1 (2002): 301–15.

Rubin, Gayle S. "Thinking Sex: Notes for a Radical Theory of the Politics of Sexuality." In *Pleasure and Danger: Exploring Female Sexuality,* edited by Carole S. Vance. 1984. Repr., London: Pandora, 1992.

Salih, Ruba. "Moroccan Migrant Women: Transnationalism, Nation-States and Gender." *Journal of Ethnic and Migration Studies* 27, no. 4 (2001): 655–71.

Sassen, Saskia. *Guests and Aliens.* New York: New Press, 1999.

Saunders, Penelope. "Traffic Violations: Determining the Meaning of Violence in Sexual Trafficking versus Sex Work." *Journal of Interpersonal Violence* 20, no. 3 (2005): 343–60.

Saunders, Penelope, and Gretchen Soderlund. "Travelling Threats: Trafficking as Discourse." *Canadian Woman Studies* 22 (2003): 35–46.

Scheper-Hughes, Nancy. "Disease or Deception: Munchausen by Proxy as a Weapon of the Weak." *Anthropology and Medicine* 9, no. 2 (2002): 153–73.

Scheper-Hughes, Nancy, and Philippe Bourgois. Foreword. In *Laughter Out of Place: Race, Class, Violence, and Sexuality in a Rio Shantytown,* edited by Donna M. Goldstein. Berkeley: University of California Press. 2003.

Schwenken, Helen. "Respect for All: The Political Self-Organization of Female Migrant Domestic Workers in the European Union." *Refuge* 21, no. 3 (2003): 45–52.

Scott, James C. *Weapons of the Weak: Everyday Forms of Peasant Resistance.* New Haven, Conn.: Yale University Press, 1987.

Shah, Svati. "South Asian Border Crossings and Sex Work: Question of Migration in Anti-Trafficking Interventions." *Sexuality Research & Social Policy* 5, no. 4 (2008): 19–30.

Shih, Shu-Mei. "Towards an Ethics of Transnational Encounter, or 'When' Does a 'Chinese' Woman Become a 'Feminist'?." *differences: A Journal of Feminist Cultural Studies* 13, no. 2 (2002): 90–126.

Shin, Gi-Wook. *Ethnic Nationalism in Korea*. Stanford, Calif.: Stanford University Press, 2006.

Smith, Michael Peter, and Luis Eduardo Guarnizo. *Transnationalism from Below*. Edited by Michael Peter Smith. Comparative Urban Community Research Series. New Brunswick, N.J.: Transaction Publishers, 1998.

Soderlund, Gretchen. "Covering Urban Vice: The New York Times, 'White Slavery,' and the Construction of Journalistic Knowledge." *Critical Studies in Media Communication* 19, no. 4 (2002): 438–60.

———. "Running from the Rescuers: New U.S. Crusades against Sex Trafficking and the Rhetoric of Abolition." *National Women's Studies Association (NWSA) Journal* 17, no. 3 (2005): 64–87.

Soh, Sarah Chunghee. "From Imperial Gifts to Sex Slaves: Theorizing Symbolic Representations of the 'Comfort Women.'" *Social Science Japan Journal* 3, no. 1 (2000): 59–76.

Son, Wonjae. "Different Blood . . . It's a Curse." *Hankyorae 21*, May 22, 2001. Available at http://www.hani.co.kr/section-021065000/2001/05/021065000200105220 (accessed June 2, 2002).

Spivak, Gayatri Charavorty. "Can the Subaltern Speak?" In *Marxism and the Interpretation of Culture*, edited by Cary Nelson and Lawrence Grossberg. Urbana-Champaign: University of Illinois Press, 1988.

Steedman, Carolyn. "'The Mother Made Conscious': The Historical Development of a Primary School Pedagogy." *History Workshop Journal* 20, no. 1 (1985): 149–63.

Steinberg, David J. *The Philippines: A Singular and Plural Place*. 4th ed. Boulder, Colo.: Westview Press, 2000.

Sturdevant, Saundra Pollock, and Brenda Stoltzfus. *Let the Good Times Roll: Prostitution and the U.S. Military in Asia*. New York: New Press, 1993.

Sudworth, John. "New Dawn for US–S Korea Military Ties." BBC Online News, March 8, 2008. Available at http://news.bbc.co.uk/2/hi/asia-pacific/7285650.stm (accessed March 20, 2008).

Surtees, Rebecca. "Brothel Raids in Indonesia: Ideal Solution or Further Violation." *Research for Sex Work* 6 (2003): 5–7.

Sutton, Constance R. "Some Thoughts on Gendering and Internationalizing Our Thinking about Transnational Migrations." In *Towards a Transnational Perspective of Migration: Race, Class, Ethnicity, and Nationalism Reconsidered*, edited by Nina Glick Schiller, Linda Basch, and Cristina Blanc-Szanton. New York: New York Academy of Sciences, 1992.

Suzuki, Nobue. "Between Two Shores: Transnational Projects and Filipina Wives in/from Japan." *Women's Studies International Forum* 23, no. 4 (2000): 431–44.

———. "Gendered Surveillance and Sexual Violence at Home: Pre-Departure Experiences and Their Consequences for Filipina Migration to Japan." In *Gender Politics in the Asia Pacific Region*, edited by Brenda Yeoh, Peggy Teo, and Shirlena Huang. London: Routledge, 2002.

———. "Inside the Home: Power and Negotiation in Filipina-Japanese Marriages." *Women's Studies* 33 (2004): 481–506.

Tacoli, Cecilia. "Migrating 'for the Sake of the Family'? Gender, Life Course and

Intra-Household Relations among Filipino Migrants in Rome." *Philippine Sociological Review* 44, nos. 1–4 (1996): 12–32.

Tadiar, Nerferti Xina M. *Fantasy-Production: Sexual Economies and Other Philippine Consequences for the New World Order.* Hong Kong: Hong Kong University Press, 2004.

———. "Prostituted Filipinas and the Crisis of Philippine Culture." *Millennium: Journal of International Studies* 27, no. 4 (1998): 927–54.

Tagaki, J. T., and Hye Jung Park. *The Women Outside* (Documentary Film). New York:Third World Newsreel, 1996.

Taran, Patrick A., and Gloria Moreno-Fontes. *Getting at the Roots: Stopping Exploitation of Migrant Workers by Organized Crime.* Geneva: International Labor Organisation, 2003.

Tobin, Joseph. "Japanese Preschools and the Pedagogy of Selfhood." In *Japanese Sense of Self*, edited by Nancy Rosenberger. Cambridge: Cambridge University Press, 1992.

Tolentino, Rolando B. "National Bodies and Sexualities." *Philippine Studies* 48 (2000): 53–79.

Tsing, Anna L. *Friction: An Ethnography of Global Connection.* Princeton, N.J.: Princeton University Press, 2005.

Tsing, Anna Lowenhaupt. *In the Realm of the Diamond Queen: Marginality in an Out-of-the-Way Place.* Princeton, N.J.: Princeton University Press, 1993.

Tyner, James. "Constructions of Filipina Migrant Entertainers." *Gender, Place and Culture* 3, no. 1 (1996): 77–93.

———. *Made in the Philippines: Gendered Discourses and the Making of Migrants.* London and New York: Routledge, 2004.

UNDP (United Nations Development Program). *Human Development Report 1997.* Geneva: United Nations Development Program, 1997.

———. *Human Development Report 1999.* Geneva: United Nations Development Program, 1999.

U.S. Department of Defense. "Inspector General Report on Force Structure Changes in the U.S. Pacific Command: Roles and Responsibilities of Headquarters and Support Functions." Washington, D.C.: U.S. Department of Defense, 2007.

———. *Worldwide Manpower Distribution by Geographical Area.* Washington, D.C.: U.S. Department of Defense, 2000.

U.S. Department of State. *Trafficking in Persons Report 2002.* Washington, D.C.: U.S. Department of State, 2002.

———. *Trafficking in Persons Report 2005.* Washington, D.C.: U.S. Department of State, Office of the Undersecretary for Global Affairs, 2005.

Vance, Carole. "Innocence and Experience: Melodramatic Narratives of Sex Trafficking and Their Consequences for Health and Human Rights." Paper presented at "Sex Slaves in the Media" panel, Columbia University, April 15, 2004.

Vance, Carole S. "Pleasure and Danger: Toward a Politics of Sexuality." In *Pleasure and Danger: Exploring Female Sexuality*, edited by Vance. London: Pandora, 1982.

"Victims of Trafficking and Violence Protection Act of 2000." H.R. 3244. 2000. Available at http://www.state.gov (accessed January 9, 2008).

Walkowitz, Judith R. *City of Dreadful Delight: Narratives of Sexual Danger in Late-Victorian London*. Chicago: University of Chicago Press, 1992.

Weaver, Teri. "97 Percent of Yongsan Garrison Will Be Turned Over to South Korea 'as Is.'" *Stars and Stripes*, Pacific ed., December 21, 2004. Available at http://www.stripes.com/article.asp?section = 104&article = 25240&archive = true (accessed January 29, 2008).

Weeks, Jeffrey. *Sexuality and Its Discontents: Meanings, Myths, and Modern Sexualities*. London and Boston: Routledge & Kegan Paul, 1985.

WHO, UNICEF, UNAIDS, and EU. *Epidemiological Fact Sheets: Republic of Korea*. 2006.

Won, Mihye. "Han-gug-sa-hoi-eui mae-chun-yeo-seong-eui dae-han tong-jae-hwa chang-chui-e gwan-han-yeon-gu" (A Study on the Control and Exploitation of Prostitutes in Korean Society). Master's thesis, Ewha Women's University, 1997.

World Bank. *World Development Indicators 2007*. Washington, D.C.: World Bank, 2007. http://web.worldbank.org/WBSITE/EXTERNAL/DATASTATISTICS/0,, contentMDK:20535285~menuPK:1192694~pagePK:64133150~piPK:64133175~ theSitePK:239419,00.html (last accessed August 3, 2009).

Yan, Hairong. "Neoliberal Governmentality and Neohumanism: Organizing Suzhi/ Value Flow through Labor Recruitment Networks." *Cultural Anthropology* 18, no. 4 (2003): 493–523.

Yan, Yunxiang. *The Flow of Gifts: Reciprocity and Social Networks in a Chinese Village*. Stanford, Calif.: Stanford University Press, 1996.

Yea, Sallie. "When Push Comes to Shove: Sites of Vulnerability, Personal Transformation, and Trafficked Women's Migration Decisions." *Sojourn* 20, no. 1 (2005): 67–95.

Yim, Yongso. *Sisa Maegojin: Kori-an Deu-rim* (Sisa Magazine: Korean Dream), Munhwa Broadcasting Company (MBC), September 19, 1999.

Yeoh, Brenda S. A., and Shirlena Huang. "'Home' and 'Away': Foreign Domestic Workers and Negotiations of Diasporic Identity in Singapore." *Women's Studies International Forum* 23, no. 4 (2000): 413–29.

Yuh, Ji Yeon. *Beyond the Shadow of Camptown: Korean Military Brides in America*. New York and London: New York University Press, 2003.

YWCA (Young Women Christians Association). *Proceedings from Asia-Pacific Regional Workshop on Trafficking in Women*. Seoul, South Korea, May 6–8, 1999.

Zatz, N. D. "Sex Work/Sex Act: Law, Labor, and Desire in Constructions of Prostitution." *Signs: Journal of Women in Culture and Society* 22, no. 2 (1997): 277–308.

Zeldin, Theodore. *An Intimate History of Humanity*. London: Minerva, 1995.

Newspaper Articles

"Detained Migrant Workers Go on Hunger Strike." *Korea Times*, October 11, 2002.

"Do-ui-won-i oe-gug-in jeop-dae-bu-chwi-eop al-seon" (Provincial Councillor

Mediates Employment of Foreign Hostesses). *Hankyorae Shinmun*, August 23, 1999.

"Roundup of Migrant Workers Suffocate Small Businesses." *Korea Times*, March 4, 2004.

"Seoul, Washington Agree to Discuss Defense Cost, Troop Reduction." *Korea Times*, April 8, 2008.

Index

Acknowledgments

First and foremost, I am grateful to the Filipinas who have
shared with me their stories, introduced me to their families, and given me
the opportunity to learn from their lives. In particular, I want to thank Ira
for her friendship over the last ten years.

Roger Goodman and David Parkin at the Institute of Social and Cultural Anthropology, Oxford University; Grant Evans, who retired from the
Department of Sociology at the University of Hong Kong in 2007; as well
as Professor Katharine Moon at the Department of Political Science at
Wellesley College have been important sources of intellectual support in
formulating this project over the years.

In South Korea my field research was made possible with the generous
help of countless people and organizations. I am able to express my gratitude to only a few here. Professor Kim Kwang-ok at Seoul National University and Professor Moon Ok-pyo at the Academy for Korean Studies have
patiently guided me since 1997, when I first arrived in South Korea as a
language student. Professor Chun Kyung-su hosted me at the Institute for
Cross-Cultural Studies at Seoul National University. The following organizations gave me various support during my fieldwork: Hansori, Saewoomtuh, Korea Church Women United, YWCA, and Magdalena House. I thank
Father Glenn at the Filipino Center for his trust and my admiration for his
tireless commitment to his work. My heartfelt gratitude goes to Sister Te-
resa O'Connell, Kim Hyun-Sun, Lee Ok-Jung, Won Mi-hye, Om Sang-Mi,
Yu Tae-Hee, Hong Chun-Hee, Sheila Miyoshi Jager, Rebecca Ruhlen, and
Park Sang-un for the benefit of their knowledge and friendship during and
after my fieldwork. My endless thanks to Back Jaehee, godmother to this
book and my guardian angel in South Korea.

My eighteen months on the Rockefeller Postdoctoral Fellowship in the
Program on Sexuality, Gender, Health, and Human Rights at the Mailman
School of Public Health, Columbia University, in 2003–4 gave me the in-
valuable opportunity to learn from a community of academics and advo-

cates. I am indebted to Carole Vance, director of the program, for her intellectual guidance and support over the years. In addition, Ali Miller, Penny Saunders, Elizabeth Bernstein, Kerwin Kaye, Mark Padilla, Svati Shah, Shohini Ghosh, Denise Brennan, Gretchen Soderlund, Katharine Frank, Ann Jordan, Melanie Orhant, Juhu Thukral, David Feingold, Mindy Roseman, Susana Fried, Darby Hickey, and Cynthia Rothschild have been important sources of inspiration as colleagues and friends, as well as models of professionalism.

I thank Nancy Abelmann and Nicole Constable for introducing me to Peter Agree and Erica Ginsburg, my editors at the University of Pennsylvania Press, who have been incredibly patient and supportive. Kathy Moon, Nancy Abelmann, Nicole Constable, Sheila Miyoshi Jager, Kim Hyun-Mee, Kim Eunshil, Nobue Suzuki, and Grant Evans have read and commented on the many proposals, drafts, articles, and various incarnations of writing that cumulated in this book, and they generously helped me think critically about this project. My uncle Dominic P. K. Cheng, Sikying Ho, Rosanna Hertz, Kerwin Kaye, Julie Chu, Stephanie Kuttner, and Thomas Barker read various parts of this book and gave many constructive suggestions.

I could not have asked for a more supportive group of colleagues in the Women's Studies Department at Wellesley College. My students and community at Wellesley have given me the energy to deal with the stress of (not) writing. Suzanne Rizzo at Wellesley College and Alice Lui in Hong Kong were dedicated research assistants. John Thorne plodded through the entire manuscript with editorial rigor, and Kate Broad and Leila Walker provided final editing and formatting assistance. At the risk of claiming more credit than is due, I shall follow the convention of stating that all faults in this book are mine alone.

This project was made possible by the following funding sources: the Korea Foundation Language Fellowship; the Swire/Cathay Pacific Scholarship at St. Antony's College, Oxford University; the Emslie Horniman Scholarship Fund of the Royal Anthropological Institute; the Peter Fitzpatrick Travel Scholarship, St. Antony's College; and the Faculty Award of Wellesley College. A different version of Chapter 5 appeared as "Romancing the Clubs: Filipina Entertainers in US Military Camp Towns in South Korea," in *Love and Globalization: Transformations of Intimacy in the Contemporary World*, edited by Mark Padilla, Jennifer S. Hirsch, Miguel Muñoz-Laboy, Robert Sembert, and Richard Parker (Nashville, Tenn.: Vanderbilt University Press, 2007); and an earlier version of Chapter 7 appeared as "The Traffic in 'Trafficked Filipinas': Sexual Harm, Violence, and Victims' Voices," in *Violence and Gender in the Globalized World: The Intimate and the Extimate*, edited by Sanja Bahun-Radunovic and V. G. Julie Rajan (Farnham: Ashgate Publishing Company, 2008).

Thanks are also due to my many other friends who have simply been there for me over the years: Sikying Ho, Stephanie Kuttner, Katrin Hansing, Fuyubi Nakamura, Red Chan, Luis Mah Silva, Darius Edler, Pieter Serneels, Kim Aeryung, Jeffrey Kim, Helena Chung, Fenny Wong, and Janice Tsang. Finally, my gratitude goes to my mother, Nancy Loo, and Tse Tsz Wah, whose loving support and unquestioning faith in me have made this project, among many other things in life, possible.